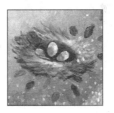

CELEBRATING MOTHERHOOD

A COMFORTING COMPANION FOR EVERY EXPECTING MOTHER

CREATED BY

ANDREA ALBAN GOSLINE
& LISA BURNETT BOSSI
with AME MAHLER BEANLAND

Foreword by Judy Ford,
author of *Expecting Baby*

········· CONARI PRESS ·········

BERKELEY, CALIFORNIA

Conari Press books are distributed by Publishers Group West.

We gratefully acknowledge permission to reprint the following:
Excerpts from *The Life Within* ©1991 by Jean Hegland. Reprinted by permission of Humana Press. Reprinted by permission of the author. From *Living Buddha, Living Christ* ©1995 Thich Nhat Hanh. Used by permission of Putnam Berkeley, a division of Penguin Putnam Inc. Ann Fuller piece reprinted by permission of the author. "Magnificat" ©1981 by Chana Bloch. Reprinted by permission of the author. *Editorial and art permissions and credits are continued on page 298 which constitutes an extension of this copyright page.*

COVER PHOTOGRAPHY: ©Chris Briscoe/Index Stock Imagery/Picture Quest
COVER DESIGN: Lisa Buckley
INTERIOR DESIGN: *AmbleDance Studios*, Lisa Burnett Bossi and Andrea Alban Gosline

This has been previously catalogued by the Library of Congress under this title:
Alban Gosline, Andrea. 1959–

   Mother's Nature: timeless wisdom for the journey into motherhood / created by Andrea Alban Gosline and Lisa Burnett Bossi, with Ame Mahler Beanland; foreword by Judy Ford.

      p.   cm.
Includes bibliographical references
ISBN: 1-57324-152-0
1. Pregnancy—Literary collections. 2. Childbirth—Literary collections. 3. Motherhood—Literary collections. 4. American literature—20th century 5. American literature—Women authors. 6. Women—Literary collections. I. Burnett Bossi, Lisa. II. Mahler Beanland, Ame. III. Title
PS509.p67 A4 1999   98-54823
808.8'0354—dc21   CIP

Printed in the United States of America.
02 03 04 RRD NW 10 09 08 07 06 05 04 03 02 01

dedication

To my mother, who filled my shelves with books of wonder and nurtured the poet in me. And to both of my parents: thank you for giving me life. —A.A.G.

To Mum, for the custom birthday cakes, your famous yard sale wisdom, and for reminding me that we live in a world of possibility. —L.B.B.

For my Mama, who still thinks I can do anything and whose wisdom, love, strength, and compassion awe and inspire me. —A.M.B.

foreword

When I decided over twenty years ago that I wanted to have a child, I had only a vague notion of what it meant to be a mother. In fact, I never really thought about mothering at all except in some general way. When I was pregnant I felt a responsibility to my unborn child to eat a good diet and have prenatal checkups. When my daughter was a baby, I knew that mothering included such things as diapering and getting up in the middle of the night. I started collecting children's books because I wanted to read her bedtime stories; I bought her a sand box and a swing. Beyond that I wasn't sure what being a mother was all about. I knew that having a child would give me a meaningful connection to another person, and I imagined that it would be wonderful, and it is, but I never imagined that being someone's mother would consume me so completely.

My daughter has called me Mom for over twenty years, and while certain mothering tasks and challenges have been difficult, I adore my daughter. From the day she was born, I was fascinated: she's amazing. She's the spring in my step; she makes life worth living. Seeing the world through her eyes, watching her take the best of me and make it better has renewed my faith in myself, my family, my friends, and fellow travelers. Watching her take her first steps, seeing her smile, teaching her how to jump rope, dropping what I'm doing to comfort her, helping her choose her prom dress, and waiting for her to come home so that we can have a midnight powwow are deeply satisfying moments. And more astounding is that although she is embarking on her adult life, there continue to be thousands of mother/daughter moments that captivate me. I am transformed again and again because I'm enthralled with her. Being a mother has wrapped me in love and opened my heart and soul to a dimension of grace that I hadn't known before.

Celebrating Motherhood is about the love that pours through your child and blesses you forever. From fertility fashions and conscious conception to Jesse Barnard's powerful letter to her unborn child; from the family bed to the Iroquois Thanksgiving Speech; from Sister Carol Ann Nawracaj's description of trust to Thich Nhat Hanh's reminder that we are all "sons and daughters of God and the children of our parents," Andrea Gosline, Lisa Bossi, and Ame Beanland have given us an expansive collection of wisdom. Within these pages is a treasure trove of prayers, blessings, reflections, rituals, facts, meditations, lore, and folk tales that exquisitely honor the richness of mothering.

If you are already a mother, about to become a mother, or hope to be one some-day, then you are embarking on a journey that will change the nature of who you are forever. You won't be the same person that you were before you thought about having a child. Once you feel the first wiggle of life within your womb or feel your baby's tiny hand grasp your finger, the focus of your attention is altered forever. When your longing to be a mother becomes a reality, the alchemy has begun. This book is the perfect guide for your journey.

—Judy Ford, author of *Wonderful Ways to Love a Child*, *Wonderful Ways to Be a Family*, and *Wonderful Ways to Be a Stepparent*

safe passage

Create each day anew
by clothing yourself with heaven
and earth, bathing yourself
with wisdom and love,
and placing yourself in the
heart of Mother Nature.

—Morihei Ueshibe

The morning I discovered I was pregnant with my first child, I walked through my neighborhood with new eyes, smiling at women sporting ripe bellies, at mothers strolling their babies, and at the children, in perpetual motion everywhere I looked. I longed to invite them to walk with me, to share the wonder of bringing forth life. I wanted to belong to their circle and talk about the myriad emotions filling my heart, as I grappled with what it meant to become a mother. One moment I happily anticipated the years ahead. The next I worried about how unprepared I felt, hurtling into the unknown, my body and mind undergoing dramatic change. I had urgent questions to ask—lots of them.

When my mother raised her family in the 1960s, companionship and advice from women friends and relatives were an inspiring part of her daily life. While the children romped in the backyard, their mothers sat in the kitchen, drinking coffee, chatting about their hopes and concerns, comforting each other, telling stories, passing on the timeless wisdom of women who had mothered before them.

Now, in the '90s, my friends either work full time outside the home or live too far away for spontaneous, leisurely conversation. Backyards are smaller, children go to day care, and our mothers (and grandmothers) have their own jobs keeping them busy. Somehow the hectic pace of our long-distance, complex world has silenced the reassuring voices of the kitchen table.

So I turned to my local bookseller and searched the shelves for writings about women's experiences carrying, birthing, and nurturing their children. What I found were books that focused primarily on the practical, physical, and medical aspects of pregnancy, childbirth, and parenting; on all that could go wrong with my body and my baby; and the interventions and solutions available. According to these authors, pregnancy was a condition, childbirth a potential crisis, and parenthood simply a set of learned skills.

I valued knowing what to expect during pregnancy and early motherhood, but I also wanted a deeper, more soulful connection. Where was the one book I could keep on my bedside table, to curl up with morning and night, that would enrich this adventure and help me develop trust in myself as a mother? The elusiveness of this book was the first seed for *Celebrating Motherhood*.

I survived my pregnancy without the wisdom of the ages! Carl and I welcomed a son, Jacob, into our family on May 17, 1990, and in his sleepy first weeks I wondered why I had worried so. Our home was a warm cocoon. Our son nursed contentedly and slept eighteen hours each day.

We bonded and cuddled. We reveled in the magic of this new being and were suspended in idyllic baby time.

But then Jacob "awakened" and began a crying jag that lasted three months. Everyone we consulted had a different opinion about what to do and considered themselves to be an expert. Feed him on a strict schedule every three hours; you don't want to spoil him. Feed him "on demand;" you can't spoil a baby. Don't nurse him more than thirty minutes; you're not a human pacifier. Nurse him as long as he wants; babies thrive on closeness and comfort. Let him cry; it builds character. Pick him up before he starts crying; it builds self-esteem.

We were just beginning to wonder if there was an "exchange policy" for babies when, to our great relief, he started "singing" along with our lullabies and rewarding us with great big, crooked smiles. But this peaceful time was fleeting and we soon realized that "colic" was only the first in a long line of confusing developmental milestones we would contend with as parents. Of course, there were plenty of wonderful times, too, but the tribulations overwhelmed me.

I devoured volumes of books on parenting, discovering helpful solutions to my caretaking problems, but it quickly became apparent that the confidence I desperately searched for was not to be found in the pages of a how-to book. I was frustrated and emotionally fatigued. My voice grew shrill. My muscles strained. I cried when I was alone. I feared that I was not the kind of mother my son could be proud of as he grew up. I knew I had so much to improve in myself if I was going to teach him the ways of the world.

One day, after a particularly long, sleepless night, Jacob refused to eat his favorite breakfast which I had so lovingly prepared. I asked Carl to watch him and fled outdoors, sobbing. There was a narrow wooden deck off my kitchen that is shaded by a large, leafy plum tree. I sank down under its protective branches and had a good cry. Eventually my tears dried and I listened to the sound of the wind and the birdsongs. I was soothed. Silently, earnestly, I prayed: Please teach me grace. Show me what to do. Help me be strong and patient and wise. When I opened my eyes, I noticed the long row of golden sunflowers peeking over my neighbor's tall fence. They seemed to be smiling at me. I breathed deeply over and over again as I watched a hummingbird flit among the flowers, and I smiled. The more deep breaths I took, the quieter my mind and body became. My doubts fell away and I relaxed. When I went back inside to my son, my presence was loving and appreciative.

As the years passed, I discovered that by regularly making time to sit quietly, I achieved a sense of balance and peacefulness I had never experienced before. My emotions settled and my wise mother's nature, which until now had been a mere whisper, spoke clearly. Even in the midst of turmoil, I discovered that I possessed the inner resources I needed to handle whatever challenges I faced as a parent. By residing in a place of hope and appreciation, envisioning the best for my life, I became more resilient. I flourished as a mother.

I was moved to compile a book celebrating motherhood because I knew I was not alone in my quest for heightened spiritual awareness as a woman, more peace and knowingness as a parent. I began to collect the reflections of diverse women, past and present, for an inspirational reader and was amazed by the discovery of a common thread and spiritual link among the voices. Whether the writings were by African women or European, Aboriginal or Native American, Balinese or Japanese, no matter what culture or historical time period, how famous or ordinary, these women expressed the same message in unison: creating life is sacred and mothering is a journey of discovery.

I was six months' pregnant with my second child when Conari Press agreed to publish *Celebrating Motherhood*. During my last trimester, I completed the first draft of the book and wrote the nine Mother Poems, just in time for the birth of my daughter, Lily Camille, on July 9, 1998. I collaborated with Lisa Burnett Bossi, an extraordinary artist who was also pregnant. Her evocative paintings and book design gave life to the reflections, birth stories, poetry, and mother lore we gathered together. Ame Mahler Beanland assisted in both the editorial and production phases of the book. As a woman contemplating motherhood, she brought a fresh perspective to the writing selections and informational sidebars to create a timeless, wide-angle view of motherhood.

Celebrating Motherhood is organized into nine sections: Anticipate, Flourish, Nurture, Wonder, Voice, Stand, Listen, Envision, and Embrace, representing the spiritual touchstones that guide our transformation during pregnancy. Each section encompasses thirty readings, titled with powerful affirmations and layered with multicultural lore, facts, rituals, activities, and contemplations. We suggest you read one page daily, allowing its uplifting message to imprint your best intentions on your soul. Whether you are considering conception, are already pregnant, or are a new—or seasoned—mother, we believe this book will help you connect more deeply with your mother essence.

- To *anticipate* the joy and love of tomorrow.
- To *flourish* as a woman and mother.
- To *nurture* yourself as you nurture your loved ones.
- To *wonder* at the natural world.
- To *voice* your thoughts more clearly.
- To *stand* for your children.
- To *listen* more thoughtfully.
- To *envision* a happier, more peaceful life.
- To *embrace* your circle of friends and family and find that you've always belonged.

We wish you safe passage on your journey into motherhood.

Andrea Alban Gosline
San Francisco, Summer 1998

anticipate

Looking for tomorrow

across the blue jewel sea,

I heard your soul whisper,   When?

And you hovered in the canopied mist

counting life lines crossing my salty, blushed palms,

expecting someday

I would be your gate.

When he kissed forever on my lips

your heart, a mere purr, drummed.

Tonight I rise

in the full sacred night

and catch the moon glimpse in your eyes.

You roll with me

down the grass back of mountains

and stroll the old bridge

where life begins.

I see our tomorrow:

the ancient moment

you slip into welcoming hands

joy spills from my eyes

your fingers graze mother's cheek, me.

Tracing lines on your barely etched palms,

I see your family waiting there.

ANDREA ALBAN GOSLINE

I anticipate

The time has been full of a deep breath of content and waiting. All good things lie in the future.

—REBECCA HARDING DAVIS

Spring is in the air. The breeze is gentle with the smell of birthing, the earth radiates freshness, the birds sing with more abandon than they have for months. The first wildflowers are in bloom in the deep forest: the hardy toothwort, the delicate purple shooting star. The tender green of new growth is everywhere.

My attention is drawn to a small oak tree, not far from where I lie. Outlined against the clear blue sky, little bits of newborn green are barely visible on the tips of the gray moss-covered branches. Strings of Spanish moss drip toward the earth, dancing now and then in the breeze.

And then I am the tree. [A] jay alights and I feel its touch as on a distant extremity. I am still here, still flat on the hillside hidden from the wind, but somehow I extend above and beyond and around myself to include the tree, the earth, the rocks, the breeze.

The earth, the rocks, the sky, and I interpenetrate. We are one. I feel a deep, beatific relaxation. The boundaries that I think of as "me" are suddenly no more than illusion.

—Barbara Dean, from *The Many and The One*

WHY I WANT TO BE A MOTHER

*To participate in
the mysteries of mother nature.
To celebrate the love between
my partner and myself.
To be immortal.
To have an adventure.
To grow a family.
To be creative.
To prove that I am healthy.
To carry on the family
traditions.
To journey back in time
to the world of my childhood.
To laugh out loud.
To give my children
a sister or brother.
To enlarge my capacity
to bond and love.
To learn the art of surrender.
To open my heart.*

—ANDREA ALBAN GOSLINE

❖ Mbuti see their life as beginning the moment they were wanted, for that is when they were conceived, and from these stories told to them throughout childhood all Mbuti have a detailed, though not necessarily exact or verifiable, knowledge of their earliest beginnings. —Colin Turnbull

I am the source

My huge mother body… monthly sends a white-stone egg down from my natural mind, with the moon, each month, a possible life. —KATE GREEN

The mother
grows first one child, then the other.
She plants teeth like seed corn
in their velvet mouths.
They will come up in the spring
and gnaw on the bones of their ancestors.
She makes feet which will grasp the
bark of trees,
cartwheel the heavens, a star between
each toe,
dance in the rain beside the railroad
tracks.
They will leave bloody prints in the snow
but wear their boots in the house.
She plows into their bones
a furrow of longing.
A wind of desolation which howls
through the ruins of January.
They will summon God on a cliff
above the bay of Espiritu Santos
watching whales breach.
The boy reels her in from her place in
the sky
ten times a day
by telling her he loves her.
Sometimes he hates her.
The girl only tugs, tugs,
but grows a rose at her center.
The mother

gives them the best berries,
the last of the butter.
She circles their sleep with webs of light:
She doesn't sleep.
She will give them all that is left of
her grace.
It is never enough.
Yet in spite of her
they will fill with glory,
as they build the rose window
into her soul.

—Elisabeth Curry, "The Mother"

❖ The navel was accorded much spiritual significance in ancient times since it was the prenatal point of contact between mother and child, and the link through which every child's life was initially received. Many center-of-the-earth shrines were viewed as the cosmic navel, a source of life force for the world.

I am the sea

A pregnant woman aboard a ship contemplates the pregnant whale swimming alongside:

"I wonder what a whale thinks of its calf? So large a creature, so proven peaceful a beast, must be motherly, protective, shielding benevolence against all wildness. It would be a sweet and milky love, magnified and sustained by the encompassing purity of water."

… A swarm of insectlike creatures, sparkling like a galaxy, each a pulsing lightform in blue and silver and gold. The whale sang for them, a ripple of delicate notes, spaced in a timeless curve. It stole through the lightswarm, and the luminescence increased brilliantly.

Deep within her, the other spark of light also grew. It was the third calf she had borne; it delighted her still, that the swift airy copulation should spring so opportunely to this new life. She feeds it love and music, and her body's bounty. Already it responds to her crooning tenderness, and the dark pictures she sends it. It absorbs both, as part of the life to come, as it nests securely in the waters within.

—Keri Hulme, from *The Windeater/Te Kaihau*

Float on the water,
In my arms, my arms,
On the little sea,
On the big sea,
The channel sea,
The rough sea,
The calm sea,
On this sea.

— SUNG BY A MOTHER WHILE BATHING HER CHILD (CAROLINES, ULITHI ATOLL)

ACTIVITY

Fill a shoebox with symbols of the qualities you hope your child will possess. These might include objects found on a nature walk, pictures and verses cut from magazines or greeting cards, and relics from your childhood. Label each with a blessing or wish. When your child is old enough to discuss her spiritual self, the two of you will delight in "discovering" the treasures found in this box.

I smile

Suppose you are expecting a child. You need to breathe and smile for him or her. Please don't wait until your baby is born before beginning to take care of him or her. You can take care of your baby right now, or even sooner. If you cannot smile, that is very serious. You might think, "I am too sad. Smiling is just not the correct thing to do." Maybe crying or shouting would be correct, but your baby will get it — anything you are, anything you do, is for your baby. Even if you do not have a baby in your womb, the seed is already there. Even if you are not married, even if you are a man, you should be aware that a baby is already there, the seeds of future generations are already there. Please don't wait until the doctors tell you that you are going to have a baby to begin to take care of it. It is already there.  Whatever you are, whatever you do, your baby will get it. Anything you eat, any worries that are on your mind will be for him or her. Can you tell me that you cannot smile? Think of the baby, and smile for him, for her, for the future generations.

—Thich Nhat Hanh, from *Being Peace*

PRAYER FOR
CONCEPTION NIGHT

This prayer, part of the Yiddish prayer tradition known as the tekhines, *celebrates the many miracles that God has worked through water.*

O Great God!
Through water you have made
great miracles many times:
The righteous Noah was saved
from the floodwater.
Our teacher Moses was drawn
forth out of the water.
The well of Miriam went with
Israel through the desert
bringing water.
Show today also your miracle
that I who would be helped
through this water
to have a child,
one who will be completely
righteous,
who will study Torah day and
night,
who will light my path—after
many days—straight to Heaven.
May I, through his merit, be
worthy
To sit with the matriarchs in
the women's section of the
world-to-come.
Amen.

I am magic

Above all, watch with glittering eyes the whole world around you, because the greatest secrets are always hidden in the most unlikely places. Those who don't believe in magic will never find it. —ROALD DAHL

✤ **Some Hawaiian midwives, called** *kahunas,* **are believed to possess the power to take childbirth pain on themselves or transfer it to another person: "The last painless birth was when my older sister was born. In the next room was a lazy relative…While others helped with the birth, he just lay in bed. My uncle, the** *kahuna pale keike,* **prayed to Haumea, the goddess of birth. Then he directed the pain to that lazy brother-in-law of his. The poor fellow began to moan and groan. He moaned until my sister arrived. My mother felt no pain at all! —described by Mary Kawena Pukui**

There was a star danced, and under that I was born.

—WILLIAM SHAKESPEARE

It was my mother who taught me the southern way of the spirit in its most delicate and intimate forms. My mother believed in the dreams of flowers and animals. Before we went to bed at night as small children, she would reveal to us in her storytelling voice that…bees dreamed of roses, that roses dreamed of the pale hands of florists, and that spiders dreamed of luna moths adhered to silver webs. As her children, we were the trustees of her dazzling evensongs of the imagination, but we did not know that mothers dreamed.

Each day she would take us into the forest or garden and invent a name for any animal or flower we passed. A monarch butterfly became an "orchid-kissing blacklegs"; a field of daffodils in April turned into a "dance of the butter ladies bonneted." With her attentiveness my mother could turn a walk around the island into a voyage of the purest discovery. Her eyes were our keys to the palace of wildness.

—Pat Conroy, from *The Prince of Tides*

I transcend

Heaven is my father and earth my mother and even such a small creature as I finds an intimate place in its midst. That which extends throughout the universe I regard as my body, and that which directs the universe I regard as my nature. All people are my brothers and sisters, and all things are my companion. —CHANG TSAI (11TH CENTURY)

✦ A bride from a wealthy American colonial family entered into marriage with a trousseau consisting of her own clothes and household items as well as a set of fine linens intended for pregnancy: maternity petticoats and chemises, silk pillowcases for postpartum, embroidered baby clothing, and knitted blankets. It was not uncommon for the bride's mother to borrow the items back from her daughter upon discovering herself pregnant again.

LIFE OF THE MARRIAGE

Childbirth is part of marriage, and however dramatic and thrilling having a baby is for the couple, there is a large part of their lives together which continues, for better or for worse, side by side with the pregnancy and early days and months of parenthood. So perhaps talking about training the couple for childbirth poses only half the problem. What they really need to learn is how to adapt themselves to changing roles vis á vis each other, and how to acquire the capacity of enjoying each transitional phase of their lives together. For the whole of marriage is really a series of transitions, in which the identity of each partner is transmuted by processes involving birth and development of children, the new stresses involved in changing relationships in the family, and the daily battles and satisfactions and pleasures of living together. Each marriage has a life of its own and is as alive and growing as a tree.

—Sheila Kitzinger, from *Giving Birth*

I persevere

I can imagine the pain and the strength of my great-great-grandmothers who were slaves and my great-great-grandmothers who were Cherokee Indians trapped on reservations. I remember my great-grandmother who walked everywhere rather than sit in the back of the bus. I think about North Carolina and my hometown and I remember the women of my grandmother's generation: strong, fierce women who could stop you with a look out of the corners of their eyes. Women who walked with majesty; who could wring a chicken's neck and scale a fish. Who could pick cotton, plant a garden, and sew without pattern. Women who boiled clothes white in big black cauldrons and who hummed work songs and lullabies. Women who visited the elderly, made soup for the sick and shortnin bread for the babies.

Women who delivered babies, searched for healing roots and brewed medicines. Women who darned sox and chopped wood and layed bricks. Women who could swim rivers and shoot the head off a snake. Women who took passionate responsibility for their children and for their neighbors' children too.

—Assata Shakur, from "Women in Prison: How We Are," *Black Scholar*

However young,
The seeker who sets out upon the way
Shines bright over the world.
But day and night the person who is awake
Shines in the radiance of the spirit.

Meditate.
Live purely.
Be quiet.
Do your work, with
mastery.
Like the moon,
Come out from behind
the clouds!
Shine. —THE BUDDHA

AMERICAN FOLKLORE

Swing a silver needle over the mother
to tell if it's a boy or a girl.
Swing a golden ring over the mother
to tell if it's a boy or a girl.
If it spins, it'll be a girl.
If it swings, it'll be a boy.

If you carry the baby low, it'll be a boy.
If you carry the baby high, it'll be a girl.
If you're pointed, it's a girl.
If you're round or broad, it's a boy.

I am soulful

When I take a walk on a crisp autumn day and see scarlet leaves against a brilliant azure sky, my soul is nurtured as I see God incarnate in the vivid colors of nature.

…The soul, for me, is in everything in life. It is in all the beauty as well as in all the agony. Some of the most profound "soul moments" I have experienced during my lifetime have been the most agonizing. I have sat by the bedside of a dying loved one. I have helped "midwife" a soul into the next world. I have died to this world for the days of transition. I have experienced rebirth on a new spiral in my own life.

What lies behind us and what lies before us are tiny matters compared to what lies within us. —RALPH WALDO EMERSON

We all experience "soul moments" in life—when we see a magnificent sunrise, hear the call of a loon, see the wrinkles in our mother's hands, or smell the sweetness of a baby. During these moments, our body, as well as our brain, resonates as we experience the glory of being a human being.

—Marion Woodman, from *Handbook for the Soul*

DAUGHTER OR SON?

Previous to the birth of a [Zuni] child, if a daughter is desired, the husband and wife, sometimes accompanied by a doctress or a female relative, visit the Mother rock, on the west side of *To'wa yal'lanne* (Corn Mountain). The pregnant woman scrapes a small quantity of the rock into a tiny vase made for the purpose and deposits it in one of the cavities in the rock, and they all pray

that the daughter may grow to be good and beautiful and possess all virtues, and that she may weave beautifully and be skilled in the art of making pottery. If a son is desired, the couple visit a shrine higher up the side of the mountain, in a fissure in the same rock, and sprinkle meal and deposit *te'likinawe*, with prayers that a son may be born to them and that he may be distinguished in war and after death become great among ancestral gods.

—Matilda Stevenson, from "The Zuni"

I expect

I am honored to be in the presence of the Expecting Mother…Your eyes are those of a Young Spirit looking outward. I thank the Creator for this Gift of Birth that we as a People may continue tomorrow. — LEONARD MARTIN

I paint and I think. And most often I think about my future child, of course. I am having it in the middle of my career, and I think: Almost none of the major ballerinas of this century had children.…Will the ballet take second place to my child? Will the responsibility for its life break my

attachment to the stage? And how will I be able to coordinate my endless travelling from city to city and from country to country with my child's daily need of me and my need for it? Or can I possibly live completely without the ballet?

…I can imagine myself not being on stage—but I cannot imagine existing outside art. Yet it is difficult to believe that there will be no more rehearsals, no more feverish agitation before performances; that there will be something else instead. I have done much, but strangely, no feeling of peace follows from that. And it seems to me at this moment that I have simply sat down for a rest, in expectation of something new.

—Natalia Makarova, prima ballerina, from *A Dance Autobiography.*

On February 1, 1978, André Michel was born. By the middle of May, Natalia Makarova was dancing Jerome Robbins' "Other Dances" at the Met, partnered with Mikhail Baryshnikov.

✥ In ancient Babylon, the potter's craft was analogous to the shaping of life, and the phrase for rebirth was: "We are as fresh-baked pots." The ancient Egyptians believed that the ram-headed god Khnum molded human beings on a potter's wheel. Believing that God fashions children in the womb, women of Rwanda leave water ready, before retiring to sleep, so that God may use it to form the clay of which humans are made.

CONTEMPLATION

Consider whether your expectations of your unborn baby are truly in his best interest. Imagine what he expects of life in his early years. Be mindful of how you communicate your expectations to one another.

In ancient Egypt, the first act of creation was said to have been the rising of a mound of land out of the primordial watery abyss called Nun.

The primal watery landscape of the Cheyenne of North America was transformed when a watercoot brought up from the depths a beakful of mud, which was then transformed into the first dry land by All-Spirit, the great deity.

In Chinese myth, the divine ancestor Pan Gu grew for 18,000 years inside an egg until it split into two parts which became the heavens and the earth.

The world, according to Saharan Africans, is believed to have been made from the segments of the sacrificed serpent Minia.

Hindus believe that the great god Vishnu, resting on the coils of the cosmic serpent Ananta in the waters of chaos, sprouted a lotus from his navel which opened to reveal the creator god Brahma. He meditated to create the universe.

I create

4 May 1941

My dearest,

Eleven weeks from today you will be ready for this outside world. And what a world it is this year! It has been the most beautiful spring I have ever seen. Miss Morris (a faculty colleague) says it is because I have you to look forward to. She says she has noticed a creative look on my face in my appreciation of this spring. And she is right. But also the world itself has been so particularly sweet, aglow with color. The forsythia were yellower and fuller than any I have ever seen. The lilacs were fragrant and feathery.... Nature is outdoing herself to prepare this earth for you. But also I want to let all this beauty get into my body. I cannot help but think of that other world. The world of Europe where babies are born to hunger, stunted growth, breasts dried up with anxiety and fatigue. That is part of the picture too. And I sometimes think that while my body in this idyllic spring creates a miracle, forces are at work which within twenty or twenty-five years may be preparing to destroy the creation of my body. My own sweet, the war takes on a terrible new significance when I think of that.... Your father thinks parents ought to get down on their knees and beg forgiveness of children for bringing them into such a world. And there is much truth in that. But I hope you will never feel like that. I hope you will never regret the life we have created for you out of our seed. To me the only answer a woman can make to the destructive forces of the world is creation. And the most ecstatic form of creation is the creation of new life.

—Jessie Barnard, from a letter to her unborn child

I begin

The Mother of Songs, the mother of our whole seed, bore us in the beginning. She is the mother of all races and the mother of all tribes. She is the mother of the thunder, the mother of the rivers, the mother of the trees and all kinds of things. She is the mother of songs and dances. She is the mother of the stones. She is the mother of the dance paraphernalia and of all temples and the only mother we have. She is mother of animals, the only one, and the mother of the Milky Way. She is the mother of the rain, the only one we have. She alone is the mother of things, she alone.

—from the Kagaba (South American Indian)

✤ **The practice of using "the infant" as a symbol of the start of a new cycle began in ancient Greece about 600 B.C.E. It was customary at the festival of Dionysus, god of wine and general revelry, to parade a baby cradled in a winnowing basket. This represented the annual rebirth of the god as the spirit of fertility.**

When you begin,
begin at the beginning.
Begin with magic,
begin with the sun,
begin with the grass.
—HELEN WOLFERT

PREGNANT PARENTS' RIGHTS

You and your partner are transforming from simply "a couple" into "pregnant parents." Examining your beliefs now about your rights in your relationship will help you immeasurably when you bring your baby home and become new parents. Here is a list of parents' rights adapted from Jack Heinowitz's book Pregnant Fathers:

I HAVE THE RIGHT: To my expectations, feelings, hopes, and preferences / To ask for what I need and want / To cry, laugh, shout, or whisper / To make mistakes / To say "no" / To say "yes" / To not know the answer / To change my mind / To not always be responsible / To put myself first / To be alone / To lead / To follow.

I am blessed

Your life—and the lives of your children—is filled with many blessings—blessings you know and blessings that are still to be revealed to you. You can help your children appreciate and celebrate their life and their many blessings—and the source of their blessings—when you literally count your blessings. When you take a piece of paper and make a list, you and your children can see how very many blessings of goodness you have, and how richly and strongly you are supported. When you show your children how much good they have, you can teach them how to give thanks to the source of their blessings, and you can help give them the inner fortitude to face adversity when they must. When you count your blessings, you say to yourself and your children, "Blessed am I. Blessed are you."

—Wayne Dosick, from *Golden Rules: The Ten Ethical Values Parents Need to Teach Their Children*

IRISH CHARM

Ulster midwives marked every corner on the outside of a house with a cross, then recited the following prayer before crossing the threshold:

There are four corners to her bed,
Four angels at her head:
Mathew, Mark, Luke, and John;
God bless the bed she lies on,
New moon, new moon, God bless me,
God bless the house and family.

I move through my day-to-day life with a sense of appreciation and gratitude that comes from knowing how fortunate I truly am and how unearned all that I am thankful for really is. To have this perspective in my everyday consciousness is in itself a gift, for it leads to feeling "graced," or blessed, each time.

—JEAN SHINODA BOLEN

I dream

*There was a child went
forth every day,
And the first object he
looked upon, that object
he became,
And that object became
part of him for the day
or a certain part of the/day,
Or for many years or
stretching cycles of years.
The early lilacs became
part of this child,
And grass and white
and red morning glories,
and white and red
clover, and
the song of the phoebe-bird,
And the third-month
lambs and sow's
pink-faint litter, and
the/mare's
foal, and the cow's calf.*

—WALT WHITMAN

DREAMS: WAITING

First Trimester
Fruits and fish all spilling out filling out
spilling in profusion all stages, shapes of endless vigorous
alarming disarming unstoppable snakes and birds
and kittens snails and foals and dancing starfish,
stone smooth sand dollars, small blue lizards
this endless streaming life arising from the secret place
within a waiting time…are you really in there?
Second Trimester
Sleeping warm this winter night and then
the treepainted borders fall away
and sunlight's filling up with green spring rites
and jeweltone women
singing, shining
all for you; and you
can hear them deep inside
I know it makes you grow more smoothly
Third Trimester
Desert born you stand
and talk and walk
the earth is speaking
through your babysilk hair
new eyes wavering in invisible heat but clear
a wind, a sandstorm flings us down
let's go! you cry and tug my hand
my waxing golden breasts
and veils of skin releasing say:
"The moon is three times three, the time is done" and here,
through oceans and aeons of form and time, are you
my arms are warm…you're born

—Stephanie Keenan Moon

I pray

The warming waters poured over my head and body. Lifting my face, I closed my eyes. Raising my arms straight upwards, I opened my hands and prayed: "Dear God, please send me a little being who needs my love. I beg this of you. I will be a good mother." It was March of 1984, and there I was praying in the manner of the ancients—arms extended. Never before had I prayed that way, yet for the first time it seemed the natural thing to do and I did so without thinking. I was in the shower, my favorite praying place. I imagined, as always, that the water was the white light of God, surrounding me with radiance....

On December 2, 1984, our little Anna Rose joined us in this world. She has been beauty and joy—and health—since the first day of her life.... More than ever before, I am amazed at the miracle of life. I was full of wonder when my sons were born, but it seems that now I am even more humbled by all the gifts I've received. Maybe it's because I'm older and take things less for granted. Every day I marvel at the fact that Anna Rose is here, that she's healthy, and that she can take nourishment from my body.

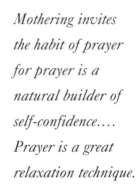

Once I heard the story of an old Buddhist who was asked what the best prayer was. The old man said, "There is only one proper prayer. And it is this: THANK YOU." Thank you, dear God.

—Gail Grenier Sweet, from *Conscious Conception*

OMAHA
BIRTH PRAYER

Ho! All ye of the heavens,
all ye of the air,
all ye of the earth:
I bid you all hear me!
Into your midst has come a
new life,
Consent ye, consent ye all,
I implore!
Make its path smooth.

Mothering invites
the habit of prayer
for prayer is a
natural builder of
self-confidence....
Prayer is a great
relaxation technique.

—MURSHIDA VERA
JUSTIN ÇORDA

I unfurl

One man tells me the only miracle he had ever experienced were the births of his children. But it seems to me that childbirth is only the first of the miracles. Each growth spurt, each burst of consciousness in my sons, is also a miracle. Even my older son's early adolescence, his tentative pulling away, is a miracle of one more birth. Something more fully formed is emerging from the cocoon, with unfolding antennae and wet and crumpled wings, reaching back to me but emerging, emerging.... Is this any less a miracle than one, so many short years ago, when I first saw the slick crown of his head?

—Richard Louv, from *The Web of Life*

Our baby Anastasia was beautiful at birth, but became more so as the day broke. It was truly fabulous to watch her face unfold like a flower during those first few hours.

—RUTH HARPER

ACTIVITY

Begin photo documentation of your ripening, pregnant body as soon as you receive confirmation of your pregnancy. Shoot in black and white film against a dark background which will enhance the contrast of the photos and lend a soft, mysterious effect. Choose the same date every month and pose smiling with the knowledge of the unfurling new life inside of you.

THE MONTH IS LEFT BEHIND

To women in tribal cultures, being pregnant does not mark any significant change in their day-to-day lives. Consequently, they are not as concerned about when their pregnancies began or how far along they are. They first learn they are pregnant by interpreting subtle physical changes in their bodies. These "pregnancy tests" are more challenging to read but are no less immediate and definitive than the tests we buy at the pharmacy.

❖ The most obvious sign of pregnancy is the cessation of menstruation—or as the Swazi say, "the month" is left behind.

❖ In the Philippines, the Negritos look for darkening of the armpits, inner arms and areas near the stomach, thighs, and groin to verify pregnancy.

❖ Moroccan midwives can positively confirm pregnancy by the fortieth day after a woman first misses her cycle by ascertaining raised temperatures, pronounced glands around the nipples, changes in the color of the face, and an obvious enlargement of the abdomen.

❖ In West Africa, a woman appears to have "seized a belly" when she begins to show. The time of birth is considered imminent when her nipples darken or veins protrude in her breasts, her belly button gains a pronounced outward appearance after eating, or she exudes a recognizable smell from her skin.

I am sacred

I think it is always rare that we are able to witness the events that change our lives. The phone call at night, the tidal wave, the telegram, all announce things that began as we were lifting a fork to our mouths, sweeping a floor, setting a bowl of apples on the table. Even the sun's light is old by the time it reaches us. Still, I mull back over the days when this conception must have occurred, sifting through the details that compose my life, trying to reconstruct among my doings that moment of beginning. In that lost second something happened that seems more momentous than even my own breath and blood and digestion, and I long to know exactly when that instant was.

—Jean Hegland, from *The Life Within*

With visible breath
I am walking.
A voice I am sending
as I walk.
In a sacred manner
I am walking.
With visible tracks
I am walking.
In a sacred manner
I walk.
—Oglala Sioux Sacred Woman

I am the ark

For forty weeks, day and night,
Noah and Namah's children floated
in the waters of her womb. When her
waters finally broke, all the creatures
of the earth burst forth and fed from
her breasts until she became dry.

—DEBORAH KRUGER

1
Now the fingers and toes are formed,
the doctor says.
Nothing to worry about. Nothing
to worry about

2
I will carry my belly to the mountain!
I will bare it to the moon, let the wolves howl,
I will wear it forever.
I will hold it up every morning in my ten fingers,
crowing
to wake the world.

3
This flutter that comes with me everywhere
is it my fear

or is it your jointed fingers
is it your feet

4
You are growing yourself
out   of   nothing:
there's   nothing
at last I can
do: I stop
doing: you
are

5
Miles off in the dark,
my dark,
you head for dry land,

naked, safe
in salt waters.

Tides lap you.

Your breathing
makes me an ark.

—Chana Bloch, "Magnificat"
author of *The Past Keeps Changing*
and *Mrs. Dumpty*

THE CHILDREN ARE THE FUTURE

All cultures are concerned with children, not only because children are vulnerable but also because they are a society's investment in the future. It is our children who will eventually grow up to be in charge of the future. Because humans are social creatures living in complex social groups, we must all take some interest in our culture's youngest members. But underlying these societal concerns is the biology of the individual. In a biological sense, children are bits of ourselves, an individual's way to pass on genes from one generation to the next.... As a result, we are motivated to love them, care for them, nurture them, and favor them; natural selection has hard-wired this attentiveness toward children and our natural attraction to babies into our very souls. Like eating and breathing, the desire to conceive, give birth, and care for infants is one of the most elemental urges on earth. In this we are no different from a kangaroo mother who holds a joey in her pouch, or a male marmoset monkey who hauls an infant around on his back. In one of the most elegant dances that nature has ever devised, we are good parents because we must be.

—Meredith F. Small, from *Our Babies, Ourselves: How Biology and Culture Shape the Way We Parent*

I am the future

We can know the future only in the laughter of healthy children.

—ANN WILSON SCHAEF

You know, no matter what we say about men and women and their individual part in producing a child, I am constantly awed by the wonder of it. Whatever you say about different social attitudes towards birth over the centuries, giving birth is a power and a privilege. Something men  are dwarfed by....I never consider that it's convenient for my wife to carry and bear our child, that it's wonderful and that I don't have that burden. I don't feel it's a burden at all. It's a mysterious process...maybe that's why I unconsciously step back from it because it's awesome and fearsome...primordial. Maybe that's why I stare so much...as if you are the goddess, the Divine Mother.

—A new father in a pregnancy support group, from *Bonding Before Birth*

I cross

Mothers are the essence of tomorrow. A mother's interaction with her child shapes the way her child will treat others in the future. She instills self-esteem in her child, offering an enduring love that enables her child to love himself. A mother teaches the earliest and deepest lessons, those of lasting emotional value…

Throughout pregnancy and childbirth a woman is driven to dig deep into herself for an inner strength she had not known existed. After birth, the smell of her baby opens a mother's soul to a new intimacy. She has crossed the threshold into motherhood.…I have had the privilege of living with indigenous mothers around the world and of seeing first hand their age-old ways of loving and teaching their children. I learned from these mothers that the natural world has eternity in it, and a mother's instincts during pregnancy, birth, and child rearing links her to this eternal chain of life.

While living with mothers from the Himalaya, the Sahara, Finmark, the Aboriginal Outback, the Amazon territory, above the Arctic Circle, and Mongolia, I saw their guiding hands and basic lives gave so much to their children. They taught their children through example to grow confident, caring, and connected with their natural environment. The indigenous women that I met as I traveled taught me and influenced my life, even before I myself became a mother.

—Jan Reynolds, from *Mother & Child: Visions of Parenting from Indigenous Cultures*

ZUNI PRAYER

*Now this is the day.
Our child,
Into the daylight
You will go out standing.
Preparing for your day,
We have passed our days.*

You are entirely engrossed in your own body and the life it holds. It is as if you were in the grip of a powerful force; as if a wave had lifted you above and beyond everyone else. In this way there is always a part of a pregnant woman that is unreachable and is reserved for the future. —SOPHIA LOREN

All Life Comes from an Egg

*Mother Earth lies in the world's midst
rounded like an egg and all Blessings are there
inside her as in a honeycomb.*

—Petronious (First-century A.D. Roman)

Stretching skyward, bulbs, shoots, and buds burst forth from the earth, exploding open, exposing their tender green growth. The sweet sap rises. The birth waters break. The skies open. It rains, it pours, it mists…. It is as if the great egg of the whole world has hatched. And so it has in the collective imagination and symbolism of many cultures. [Their] myths…all describe an original cosmic egg from which the universe is born. The latin proverb *Omne vivum ex ovo* proclaims, "All life comes from an egg." It is only natural and not so subtle to assign the birth of the world to a Great Mother Goddess who laid the egg of life. All of nature, after all, is a constant cyclical reminder of a fertile female force.

—Donna Henes, from *Celestially Auspicious Occasions: Seasons, Cycles & Celebrations*

RITUAL

The time of birthing in thirteenth-century Europe was called "In her waiting." During this passage, the women of the village shared a special bond as they gave advice and helped with the delivery. Choose three people to wait with you during early labor. Assign each of them a "comfort" task: playing your favorite music, massaging your back and neck, reading inspirational passages.

I wait

I am a doorway
Through which you came.

You are the doorway
Through which you go.

Once together, now always apart,
The severed cord stretched
Like a spider's thread
Suspended in space.

We traveled on a journey
Which we chose
Ourselves—you and I;
We passed, and said hello;
We lingered here, we hastened there;
We met again, and passed;
We held each other close,
And then moved on.

You, whom I have born,
But not created,
Live in the world
You have helped to make,
You are your own father and your own child,
You are your own self.

—Rhoda Curtis, "Mother's Day"

I shed

I was tying the boat, when I saw what looked like a very large spider, crawling up from the water and out on a board. It moved with such effort and seemed so weak that I was tempted to put it out of its pain. But if I have learned nothing else in all these months, in the woods, I have thoroughly learned to keep hands off the processes of nature…So I gave the creature another glance and prepared to go about my business, when I noticed a slit in its humped back, and a head with great, dull beads of eyes pushing out through the opening. Then I sat down to watch, for I realized that this was birth and not death.

No force of mind or body can drive a woman in labor, by patience only can the smooth force of nature be followed.

— GRANTLY DICK-READ

Very slowly the head emerged and the eyes began to glow like lamps of emerald light. A shapeless, pulpy body came working out and two feeble legs pushed forth and began groping for a firm hold. They fastened on the board and then, little by little and ever so slowly, the whole insect struggled out, and lay weak, almost inanimate, beside the empty case that had held it prisoner so long.

Two crumpled lumps on either side began to unfurl and show as wings. The long abdomen, curled round and under, like a snail shell, began to uncurl and change to brilliant green…The transparent membrane of the wings, now held stiffly erect, began to show rainbow colors, as they fanned slowly in the warm air, and, at last, nearly three hours after the creature had crept out of the water, the great dragonfly stood free, beside its cast-off body lying on the dock.

—Laura Lee Davidson, from *The Miracle of Renewal*

❖ An old Hawaiian custom suggests that pregnant women gently move their abdomens back and forth while bathing to ensure that the baby does not stick.

I am faithful

Do not think that love, in order to be genuine, has to be extraordinary. What we need is to love without getting tired.

How does a lamp burn? Through the continuous input of small drops of oil. If the drops of oil run out, the light of the lamp will cease, and the bridegroom will say, I do not know you (Matthew 25:12).

My daughters, what are these drops of oil in our lamps? They are the small things of daily life: faithfulness, punctuality, small words of kindness, a thought for others, our way of being silent, of looking, of speaking, and of acting. These are the true drops of love…

Be faithful in small things because it is in them that your strength lies.

—Mother Teresa

INVOCATION

May this woman give birth happily!
May she give birth,
May she stay alive,
May she walk in health before
thy divinity!
May she give birth happily
and worship thee!

—MESOPOTAMIAN INVOCATION TO ISHTAR,
THE GODDESS OF MORNING

HILDEGARD VON BINGEN: ON CREATION

Hildegard von Bingen, who lived in Germany during the twelfth century, was a nun and a writer whose prose reflects a profound sensitivity to nature and expresses compassion for the feminine experience. Below are a sampling of her viewpoints on creation (excerpted from *Scivias and Hildegard of Bingen 1098-1179: A Visionary Life* by Sabrina Flanagan):

❖ Eve, symbolized by "a white cloud, which had come forth from a beautiful human form and contained within itself many and many stars," is described as "bearing in her body the whole multitude of the human race, shining with God's preordination."

❖ Hildegard describes men and women alike as bearing in their bodies human seed for procre- ation. Her descrip- tion of pregnancy and childbirth chal- lenged the view of her time that wo- men were impotent males: "After a wo-  man has conceived by human semen, an infant . . . is formed in the secret chamber of her womb! . . . and shows by the move- ments of its body that it lives, just as the earth opens and brings forth the flowers of its use when the dew falls on it."

I am rich

She is a fair lady,
gentle, soft,
with years of hardship resting on the hands,
that gently touched a babe, that washed bruises,
that sliced wild meat, that held rosaries,
the voice soft and yet tainted with years of poverty,
as she tells the tales, in the late eve,
as the children listen, with huge eyes,
the ugly broken doors of the cupboards draw the
attention, as little hands break a piece of bannock,
and you smile, the warmth, present, always
your door has no locks, just a rope,
the richness is not in the doors of the home,
but in your eyes, and in your heart,
mother.

—Molly Chisaakay, "Mother," from *Writing the Circle*

CRADLESONG

Sleep, little one, your father is bringing
a spotted deer to be your pet,
a rabbit's ear to be your necklace,
spotted bramble fruits to be your toys.

—FROM THE MBYA, TRANSLATED BY
LEON CADOGAN, FROM *AYOU RAPYTA:*
TEXTOS MITICOS DE LOS MBYA-GUARANI DEL GUAIR

TOUCH THE SACRED EARTH

The Lakota was a true naturist—a lover of nature. He loved the earth and all things of the earth, the attachment growing with age. The old people came literally to love the soil and they sat or reclined on the ground with a feeling of being close to a mothering power. It was good for the skin to touch the earth and the old people liked to remove their moccasins and walk with bare feet on the sacred earth. The birds that flew in the air came to rest upon the earth and it was the final abiding place of all things that lived and grew. The soil was soothing, strengthening, cleansing and healing.

That is why the old Indian still sits upon the earth instead of propping himself up and away from its life-giving forces. For him, to sit or lie upon the ground is to be able to think more deeply and to feel more keenly; he can see more clearly into the mysteries of life and come closer in kinship to other lives about him…

—Chief Luther Standing Bear

I am close

I knew I was pregnant before it was confirmed medically; you appeared to me in a dream, just as your brother, Nicolas, did later. [You] were two years old and your name was Paula. You were a slender child, with dark hair, large black eyes, and a limpid gaze like that of martyrs in the stained glass windows of some medieval churches. You were wearing a checked coat and hat, something like the classic costume of Sherlock Holmes. In the next months I gained so much weight that one morning when I stooped down to put on my shoes, the watermelon in my belly rolled up to my throat, toppling me head over heels and so definitively displaced my center of gravity that it was never restored: I still stumble my way through the world. Those months you were inside me were a time of perfect happiness; I have never felt so closely accompanied. We learned to communicate in code.

—Isabel Allende, from *Paula*

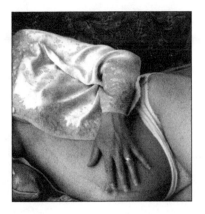

CONTEMPLATION

Your body encloses a developing child. You are a vessel, an essential participant in the creation of your baby. As she grows and shows herself to the world, enjoy the sensations of your body. Relish the fullness of being "with child."

There is nothing in human nature more resonant with charges than the flow of energy between two biologically alike bodies, one of which has lain in amniotic bliss inside the other, one of which has labored to give birth to the other. —ADRIENNE RICH

I perceive

When I stopped seeing my mother with the eyes of a child, I saw the woman who helped me give birth to myself. —Nancy Friday

A Zen poem says, "After the wind stops I see a flower falling. Because of the singing bird I find the mountain calmness." Before something happens in the realm of calmness, we do not feel the calmness; only when something happens within it do we find the calmness. There is a Japanese saying, "For the moon, there is the cloud. For the flower, there is the wind." When we see a part of the moon covered by a cloud, or a tree, or a weed, we feel how round the moon is. But when we see the clear moon without anything covering it, we do not feel that roundness the same way we do when we see it through something else.

—Shunryu Suzuki, f rom *Zen Mind, Beginner's Mind*

*The god to whom little boys
say their prayers has a face very
much like their mother's.*

—Sir James M. Barrie

❖ Traditional Chinese medical texts suggest that the best time for fertilization to take place is after midnight, around the time of the first cock crow between three and five a.m. The energy at this time of day is balanced Yin to Yang with Yang ascendancy.

MOONLIGHT BLESSING

*The moon scoops up light
and pours it over the city.
Each silver ray falls over me
like cream.
I hum and sway in the garden,
white flowers nod in the moonlight.*

—Robin Heerens Lysne,
from *Dancing Up the Moon*

I am honored

My friend Claudia often shares the story of how I coached her through the birth of her son Colin with a hysterical rendition of the events delivered in a southern accent that makes me sound like a cross between Minnie Pearl and Prissy from *Gone With the Wind*. I always wholeheartedly join in on the laughter, for it was an incredibly joyful event. But in my heart I hold that experience as one of the most profound moments of my life. Words like "miracle," "life-changing," "amazing," they don't even come close to capturing the essence of seeing that baby enter my world. Hair-matted, red-faced and bellowing—he was a living, breathing marvel. This tiny creature suddenly within our presence with a voice, a soul, and a purpose, immediately unfolding and unfurling, hopefully ahead of him. I am so grateful to Claudia for allowing me to be present with her, to share the blessing and witness the power of a life just beginning.

—Ame Mahler Beanland

FERTILITY FASHIONS

Throughout history, women's clothes have made more than just a fashion statement—they invoked fertility, communicated marital status, and even proffered divine protection. In many ancient European cultures, women wore skirts made of twisted strings suspended from hip bands. Such skirts, evident in the prehistoric wardrobe for twenty thousand years, appear to have been associated with the ultimate power of creating new life. Many were woven with patterns of lozenges, graphically depicting a woman's vulva, which were generally thought of as strong fertility symbols.

In areas of Romania, a young unmarried woman would string a chain with rings and keys and hang it from her apron to attract a mate. If she reached the age of thirty without having born children—a woman's most valued work in ancient society—she moved the chain to the bottom of her costume, to symbolize the wasting of her childbearing years.

In Greece, a red woolen girdle, called a zostra, was used as a talisman for conceiving and bearing children, and was known to work wonders when placed over the abdomen of a woman in difficult labor. Some contemporary Greek women still possess string skirts for this purpose.

I am a pilgrim

It was only when I had children of my own to appreciate and to study that I finally realized the full extent of the distance I had traveled. — PETER USTINOV

Saturday the 4th of August [1849] we reached the South Pass of the Rocky Mountains…the highest point in our road, where we passed from the Atlantic to the Pacific Slope…I had looked forward for weeks to the step that should take me past the point. In the morning of that day I had taken my last look at the waters that flowed eastward, to mingle with the streams and wash the shores where childhood and early youth had been spent; where all I loved, save, O, so small a number, lived; and now I stood on the almost imperceptible elevation that, when passed, would separate me from all these, perhaps forever. Through what toils and dangers we had come to reach that point; and, as I stood looking my farewell, a strong desire seized me to mark the spot in some way…Yes, I would make a little heap of stones, and mark on one of them, or on a stick, the word "Ebenezer."

Nobody would notice or understand it; but my Heavenly Father would see the little monument in the mountain wilderness, and accept the humble thanks it recorded. So I turned to gather stones. But no stone could I find, not even pebbles enough to make a heap—and no stick either…So I stood still upon the spot til the two wagons and the little company had passed out of hearing; and when I left not a visible sign marked the place.

—Sarah Royce, from *A Frontier Lady*

❖ There were three pregnant women on the Mayflower—Elizabeth Hopkins, Susanna White, and Mary Norris Allerton. Only one of the women, Elizabeth Hopkins, gave birth on the ship to a little boy christened Oceanus. She was probably helped by a young midwife on board, Bridget Lee Fuller, who went on to continue her practice in Plymouth.

I intend

…The woman and the swan sailed across an ocean many thousands of *li* wide, stretching their necks toward America. On her journey she cooed to the swan: "In America I will have a daughter just like me. But over there nobody will say her worth is measured by the loudness of her husband's belch. Over there nobody will look down on her, because I will make her speak only perfect American English. And over there she will always be too full to swallow any sorrow! She will know my meaning, because I will give her this swan, a creature that became more than what was hoped for."

But when she arrived in the new country, the immigration officials pulled her swan away from her, leaving the woman fluttering her arms and with only one swan feather for a memory. And then she had to fill out so many forms there, she forgot why she had come and what she had left behind.

Now the woman was old. And she had a daughter who grew up speaking only English and swallowing more Coca-Cola than sorrow. For a long time now the woman had wanted to give her daughter the single swan feather and tell her, "This feather may look worthless, but it comes from afar and carries with it all my good intentions." And she waited, year after year, for the day she could tell her daughter this in perfect American English.

—Amy Tan, from *The Joy Luck Club*

BALINESE GIRLS REVERE PREGNANCY

"I Wajan is pregnant, someday you will be pregnant. My! what a fat little tummy you have. Are you perhaps pregnant now?" In Bali, little girls between two and three walk much of the time with purposely thrust-out little bellies, and the older women tap them playfully as they pass. "Pregnant," they tease. So the little girl learns that although the signs of her membership in her own sex are slight, her breasts mere tiny buttons no bigger than her brothers', her genitals a simple inconspicuous fold, someday she will be pregnant, someday she will have a baby. And having a baby is, on the whole, one of the most exciting and conspicuous achievements that can be presented to the eyes of small children: The little girl learns that she will have a baby not because she is strong or energetic or initiating, not because she works and struggles and tries, and in the end succeeds, but simply because she is a girl.

—Margaret Mead, from *Male and Female*

❖ 29 ❖

I am the wings

*My mother wanted me
to be her wings, to fly
as she never quite had the
courage to do. I love her for
that. I love the fact that she
wanted to give birth to her
own wings.* —ERICA JONG

And a woman who held a babe against her
bosom said, Speak to us of Children.
And he said:
Your children are not your children.
They are the sons and daughters of Life's
longing for itself.
They come through you but not from you,
And though they are with you, yet they belong not to you.
You may give them your love but not your thoughts.
For they have their own thoughts.
You may house their bodies but not their souls,
For their souls dwell in the house of tomorrow,
which you cannot visit, not even in your dreams.
You may strive to be like them, but seek not
to make them like you.
For life goes not backward nor tarries with yesterday.
You are the bows from which your children
as living arrows are sent forth.
The archer sees the mark upon the path of
the infinite, and He bends you with His might
that His arrows may go swift and far.
Let your bending in the archer's hand be for gladness;
For even as he loves the arrow that flies, so
He loves also the bow that is stable.

—Kahlil Gibran, from *The Prophet*

RITUAL

*The couples I have known who have chosen conscious conception have worked with a number of elements
to create a sacred vessel in which they make love. For most couples this takes place in the comfort of
their own bedroom, but I have known couples who have chosen to travel to traditional pilgrimage sites
in the world, such as Jerusalem, Egypt or Glastonbury to conceive. Others have gone to special places
in nature. Everyone I have encountered who has successfully conceived has set the tone with prayers
and verbally called in the spirit of the child.* —ADELE GETTY, FROM *A SENSE OF THE SACRED*

I am romantic

For me, motherhood has been the one true, great, and wholly successful romance. It is the only love I have known that is expansive and that could have stretched to contain with equal passion more than one object…

—Irma Kurtz

It still seems…inconceivable. While Rob and I basked in lazy afterglow, those long-dormant pipes of mine chugged into action. My body only knew sperm when it saw them, but went out of its way to make the little swimmers feel right at home.

"Gentlemen callers!" my eggs must have cried. "Catch them!"

In retrospect, I suppose I could say that our lovemaking that night felt extra special. That Rob's joyful contribution made me think somehow of shooting stars. That in some profound and, indeed, rather flaky way, I could almost trace the distance that one particular star was traveling, its long night's journey into day.

—Carol Weston, from *From Here to Maternity*

ASIAN ZODIAC

Unlike the Western zodiac, which names each month for a different star formation, the Asian zodiac names a cycle of twelve years after twelve animals, each with its own traits and characteristics. Find your child's birth year (your own too!) on this chart, for a prediction of what basic traits she will possess.

Rat: thrifty, quick-tempered, charming 1960, 1972, 1984, 1996 **Ox:** stubborn, patient, trusting, dependable 1961, 1973, 1985, 1997 **Tiger:** sensitive, passionate, daring 1962, 1974, 1986, 1998 **Rabbit:** affectionate, cautious, good head for business 1963, 1975, 1987, 1999 **Dragon:** full of vitality and strength, sets high standards 1964, 1976, 1988, 2000 **Snake:** deep thinker, soft-spoken 1965, 1977, 1989, 2001 **Horse:** cheerful, perceptive, quick-witted, loves to be where action is 1966, 1978, 1990, 2002 **Ram:** strong beliefs, compassionate, artistic 1967, 1979, 1991, 2003 **Monkey:** inventor and improviser 1968, 1980, 1992, 2004 **Rooster:** sharp and neat, extravagant in dress, prefers working alone 1969, 1981, 1993, 2005 **Dog:** loyal, trustworthy and faithful, makes a good but reluctant leader 1970, 1982, 1994, 2006 **Pig:** studious, well informed, reliable 1971, 1983, 1995, 2007

flourish

Child's call, fresh as sunrise,
deep as velvet dusk,

rings wild on wind's chime.

Ten toes dig down

roots in red earth.

Bloom inside, fragile one.

I will not sleep

in this time of ten moons.

Touch me, I am native drum,

rhapsody in hollow cave

To child's pace I slow
and build the feathered nest.
Skin pulls taut over soft, flat plains.

Steady trumpet vine,

I pose for the sun.

My dance is ripe,

your mystery fills the passage.

Exploring corners in my home,

I hear ancestral hum.

Between the wooden walls,

the web of life is spun. Welcome to my feast.

I hold my family's heart in mine

and toast the weaving of our souls.

ANDREA ALBAN GOSLINE

I flourish

The seeds of the plants are blown about by wind until they reach the place where they will grow best.

—OKUTE, TETON SIOUX

ACTIVITY

Plant a patch of flower seeds in a sunny spot in your garden or neighborhood. Observe the flowers' growth every day. Weed this cultivated patch of earth. When the flowers have grown and blossomed, cut them and make a gift of them to the world.

In the beginning…there was love. And it could not be seen, and it could not be felt. But it was, and the air was filled with it. And it was good to breathe. And the mountain spring cascaded with it. And it was good to drink.

And the sun rose over the mountain and looked, and smiled. And love sprouted seeds, and grass grew out of the earth. And bushes blossomed, and flowers bloomed, and the trees were laden with love. And its fruit was good to eat.

And a sweet-smelling rain came whispering down and watered the seeds with love. And a drop of creation fell into a brook and another in the hollow of a tree. And fish splashed in the pond in shimmering colors, with scales and gills. And the deer leapt over the brook and into the forest, and the bird and the frog exchanged a love song. And it was good to hear. And it was good to see. And it was good to feel.

And a wind blew through the canyon, and an echo came out of the deep. And the earth shook for a moment…then all was still.

Then from the womb came we and saw. From the womb came we and heard. From the womb came we and were. And we shook our heads and we knew. And we knew we had eyes to see with. And we knew we had ears to hear with. And we knew we had a life to live.

—Jay Frankston, from *The Offering*

I am beautiful

What is beautiful is good,
And who is good will soon be beautiful.

—SAPPHO

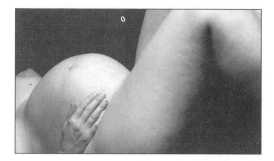

The beauty of my body is not measured by the size of the clothes it can fit into, but by the stories that it tells. I have a belly and hips that say, "We grew a child in here," and breasts that say, "We nourished life." My hands, with bitten nails and a writer's callus, say, "We create amazing things."

—Sarah, from *I Am Beautiful: A Celebration of Women in Their Own Words*

I love every curve of my silky flesh. Shoulder, breast, belly, thigh—this roundness is surely the shape that I was meant to be. At forty years old, carrying my fourth child, I feel strong and sensuous, my juices flowing freely. I cherish this last chance of glowing in the round. I am a full moon, the Goddess incarnate.

—Susan, from *I Am Beautiful: A Celebration of Women in Their Own Words*

TREES OF LIFE

A mysterious, treelike symbol appears in numerous alchemical texts, always as a crowned, naked woman with branches sprouting from her head. Fruits and a phoenix bird adorn the branches of the tree, and the sun appears to her right, the moon to her left, while objects that possibly represent roots or wands of power extend from her hands. This powerful icon seems to be an ancient version of the primal mother-tree.

Cultures throughout the world identify certain trees as life-giving symbols or sources. In China the graceful ailanthus tree was chosen for its tenacious ability to flourish almost anywhere. Iranians revered the *Haoma*, the sacred vine, while in Syria and Babylon, the meandering vine was considered to be a sacred tree of life. Japanese mythology features the sacred *sakaki* trees which grew on the Mountains of Heaven. The *peepul* or *bo* tree is the sacred tree of Buddha and known as the "Tree of Knowledge."

❖ **Young girls of many non-industrial societies learn from an early age that pregnancy is fruition and that they will become more, not less, beautiful when pregnant.**

I am spring

April 1920
Is it not possible that the rage for confession [and] autobiography, especially for memories of earliest childhood, is explained by our persistent yet mysterious belief in a self which is continuous and permanent; which, untouched by all we acquire and all we shed, pushes a green spear through dead leaves and through the mould, thrusts a scaled bud through years of darkness until, one day, the light discovers it and shakes the flower free and—we are alive—we are flowering for our moment upon the earth? This is the moment which after all, we live for—the moment of direct feeling when we are most ourselves and least personal.

—Katherine Mansfield, from *The Letters and Journals of Katherine Mansfield*

❖ The female "cup" or Christian chalice, holding the divine essence of life, was derived from the calyx (cup) of the lily flower of Europe and the lotus flower of the Orient.

May there always be sunshine!
May there always be blue skies!
May there always be Momma!
May there always be me!

—LEV OSHANIN, FROM THE SONG
"MAY THERE ALWAYS BE SUNSHINE"

The songwriter was six years old when his song became a hit in the U.S.S.R. He originally hand-lettered the lyrics at the bottom of one of his paintings: a blue sky with a big yellow sun and a mother and child standing underneath.

ACTIVITY *Mandalas symbolize the human need for balance and wholeness. Tibetan Buddhists believe mandalas help one focus energy and maintain perspective. Draw your own mandala. Start with a circle. Color it and draw anything you wish inside. Be spontaneous. Focus on the task, not the form. Enjoy the energy and strength of your circular creation.*

I am wild

Wild Woman. When women hear those words, an old, old memory is stirred and brought back to life. The memory is our absolute, undeniable, and irrevocable kinship with the wild feminine, a relationship which may become ghosty from neglect, buried by over domestication, outlawed by the surrounding culture, or no longer understood anymore. We may have forgotten her names, we may not answer when she calls ours, but in our bones we know her, we yearn toward her; we know she belongs to us and we to her.

There are times when we experience her, even if only fleetingly, and it makes us mad with wanting to continue. For some women, this vitalizing "taste of the wild" comes during pregnancy, during nursing their young, during the miracle of change in oneself as one raises a child, during attending to a love relationship as one would attend to a beloved garden.

A sense of her also comes through the vision; through sights of great beauty. I have felt her when I see what we call in the woodlands a Jesus-God sunset. I have felt her move in me from seeing the fishermen come up from the lake at dusk with lanterns lit, and also from seeing my newborn baby's toes all lined up like a row of sweet corn. We see her where we see her, which is everywhere.

—Clarissa Pinkola Estes, from *Women Who Run with the Wolves*

I hope you will glisten with the glisten of ancient life, the same beauty that is in a leaf or a wild rabbit, wild sweet beauty of limb and eye.

— MERIDEL LE SUEUR

✤ In a total of twenty-seven pregnancies, Mrs. Feodor Vassilyev of Shuya, Russia, gave birth to sixty-nine children, comprising sixteen pairs of twins, seven sets of triplets, and four sets of quadruplets.
— FROM *THE GUINNESS BOOK OF WORLD RECORDS*

I am fruitful

Children of Mother Corn
Perhaps if we are lucky
Our earth mother
Will wrap herself in a fourfold robe
Of white meal,
Full of frost flowers;
A floor of ice will spread over the world,
The forests,
Because of the cold, will lean to one side,
Their arms will break beneath the weight of snow.
When the days are thus,
The flesh of our earth mother
Will crack with cold.
Then in the spring when she is replete with living waters,
Our mothers,
All different kinds of corn,
In their earth mother
We shall lay to rest.
With their earth mother's living waters
They will be made into new beings:
Into their sun father's daylight
They will come out standing;
Yonder to all directions
They will stretch out their hands calling for rain.
Then with their fresh waters
[The rain makers] will pass us on our roads.
Clasping their young ones in their arms,
They will rear their children.
Gathering them into our houses,
Following these toward whom our thoughts bend,
With our thoughts following them,
Thus we shall always live.

—Zuni poem, translated by Ruth Bunzel, from "Zuni Ritual Poetry"

Every mother contains her daughter in herself and every daughter her mother. Every woman extends backwards into her mother and forward into her daughter.

—CARL JUNG

❖ In Latin America women who wish for fertility buy a pomegranate in the name of Yemaya, the beautiful Yoruba moon goddess and patroness of motherhood. After cutting the fruit in half and covering it in honey, the woman writes her name on a piece of paper and places it between the two halves. A prayer is said to Yemaya for health and fertility as the pomegranate is fruitful and filled with seeds.

I am the flower

May your life be like a wildflower, growing freely in the beauty and joy of each day.
—NATIVE AMERICAN PROVERB

Riddle, now that you have a name, I find myself addressing you as though you could already understand my words, as though you, who reside in my womb and share the products of my blood, could also live in my mind and share my thoughts. I find myself thinking of you, who are privy to my life in a way that no one had ever been, as I used to think of God when I was a child, as an unseen, constant presence in my life…who knew my thoughts when I thought them….Little Riddle, I think of you as being as wise as God used to be….

I want to know you. I feel the gardener's urge to brush back the earth and inspect her crop. I try to imagine you, Riddle, floating within me, weightless, implacable, silently growing toes, making a liver for yourself, sprouting wisps of ribs…changing shape like a tadpole, a caterpillar, a cloud, unfolding like a Chinese paper pellet that blossoms into a flower when it is placed in a bowl of water.

—Jean Hegland, from *The Life Within*

ZEN TEACHING STORY

A university professor approached a master hoping to learn about the nature of Zen. "I know a great deal about the workings of the physical world," the scholar explained, "but perhaps you could add to my knowledge by offering some thoughts about the nature of the spiritual world."

"Let us have a cup of tea," said the master, "and then we shall talk." The professor held out his cup as the master poured, filling the cup to the brim and then continuing to pour while the tea spilled onto the floor.

"It is overflowing!" protested the professor. "No more will go in!"

"Yes, it is so," said the master. "Just as this cup is full to overflowing, so is your mind filled with opinions and speculations, leaving no room to receive the teachings. Only when you empty your cup, can we begin."

—from *Zen Flesh*, *Zen Bones*, compiled by Paul Reps

I am grateful

With one gloved hand on my abdomen, the other inside, my doctor said not to me, but to the nurse, "A well-established pregnancy. Very well established." She patted me on the stomach as she grasped a wand which would detect the heartbeat, if everything was right—please, please…. After a heart-stopping interval, I heard it, like a motor, an engine, fast and loud…. In her office she used words like excellent, perfect, fine—superlatives we drank into our skin….

I walked home alone through the park—a sunny, nearly flawless day—on the gravel path along the reservoir, with the words "well established" running through my head like a mantra. A line of gulls had settled on the jetty which looked like the minute hand of a giant clock. One day, I thought, I'll retrace these steps with my child and say, "This is where I first believed in you." I cried, too, for the first time, conjuring the presence next to me, a tiny hand in mine, a head at my waist, my hem at my baby's shoulders. "Thank you, thank you," I cried silently to my doctor, interpreter of sounds and vials of blood, possessor of magic wands who interprets my body to me.

—Roberta Israeloff, from *Coming to Terms*

Let us give thanks
for this beautiful day.
Let us give thanks for this life.
Let us give thanks
for the water without which life
would not be possible.
Let us give thanks for
Grandmother Earth who protects
and nourishes us.

—DAILY PRAYER OF THE LAKOTA
AMERICAN INDIAN

I am enthusiastic

We act as though comfort and luxury were the chief requirements in life, when all we need to make us really happy is something to be enthusiastic about. —CHARLES KINGSLEY

The kitchen gave a special character to our lives; my mother's character. All my memories of that kitchen are dominated by the nearness of my mother sitting all day long at her sewing machine, by the clacking of the treadle against the linoleum floor, by the patient twist of her right shoulder as she automatically pushed at the wheel with one hand or lifted the foot to free the needle where it had got stuck in a thick piece of material. The kitchen was her life. Year by year, as I began to take in her fantastic capacity for labor and her anxious zeal, I realized it was ourselves she kept stitched together.

The kitchen was the great machine that set our lives running, it whirred down a little only on Saturdays and holy days. From my mother's kitchen I gained my first picture of life as a white, overheated, starkly lit workshop redolent with Jewish cooking, crowded with women in housedresses, strewn with fashion magazines, patterns, dress material, spools of thread—and at whose center, so lashed to her machine that bolts of energy seemed to dance out of her hands and feet as she worked, my mother stamped the treadle hard against the floor, hard, hard, and silently, grimly at war, beat out the first rhythm of the world for me.

—Alfred Kazin, from *A Walker in the City*

❖ Colorful theories abound about the identity of "Mother Goose," from the notion that the Queen of Sheba was Mother Goose to the belief that an eighteenth-century Bostonian, Mrs. Elizabeth Foster Goose, mother and stepmother to sixteen children and scores of grandchildren, was the prolific storyteller. Nursery-rhyme scholars trace the origin of Mother Goose to France, where peasants believed in a bird-mother who entertained children with stories. This benevolent bird-mother myth is also found in Celtic culture. Others believe that Queen Berthe, who was Pepin's wife and Charlemagne's mother (mid-eighth century), was the original Mother Goose.

I am ripe

Love is a fruit in season at all times.

—MOTHER TERESA

ANCIENT HEBREW
FAMILY LINE

Pregnancy is a numinous and magical state. It is a time when the barrier between the conscious and unconscious realms thins. It is a time to feel the presence of another soul developing alongside your own. It is a time when inner voices offer wise counsel louder and more clearly than usual, when we become aware that life is a contiuum, when a woman may experience a bodily sense that everything around her is alive. Our connection to the cellular mystery of life is vibrantly stark and immediate. When you are pregnant, the polite and restrictive masks of everyday life that we have each created to survive can be stripped away, and you are immersed in the very juice of existence. No matter how many pictures of fetuses you look at or how many scientific facts you ingest, pregnancy remains a stunning, not-quite-possible-to-grasp marvel, a naked connection to the enigma of life. You can't escape the awe—and why would you want to?

—Jennifer Louden, from *The Pregnant Woman's Comfort Book*

"Lo, children are a heritage of Jehovah; and the fruit of the womb is his reward. As arrows in the hand of a mighty man, so are the children of youth. Happy is the man that hath his quiver full of them." (Psalm 127:33-5). Here is a poetical expression of desire for children and delight in their coming (of the ancient Hebrews). Sons in particular were wanted, to carry on the family line, to inherit and preserve estates when these existed, and to become workers and warriors. Daughters too had an economic value. But over and above these materialistic considerations it seems clear that children were desired for their own sake. Hence there was often, if not generally, rejoicing at the birth of a child.

I transform

In the eyes of its mother every beetle is a gazelle.

—Moroccan proverb

Each painting I make still begins from some deep source where my mother, grandmother, and all my foremothers live. For me it is as if the line moving from my pen or brush coils back to the original matrix, back to the creative womb, a cauldron of transformation. What gestates in that cauldron are memories waiting for transformation into pictures. Like any artist, I animate what I remember, what has been given to me I draw and paint from my own myth of personal origin, from my own remembering....

Images are like children. Children come out of our bodies as distinct creatures with their own life form.... They have come out of us, but they have their own energy separate from us.

Women create—we all create—out of our bodies.... The creativity in women's bodies, the potential in our bodies for making children from our many eggs is, I think, no different from the potential for making imagery from our many eggs....It is very important for we women to understand that whether we are creating biologically or metaphysically from those eggs, it is all the fruit of our body, the fruit of our creativity.

—Meinrad Craighead, from *Sacred Stories*

When Changing Woman
gets to be a certain age,
she goes walking toward the east.
After a while she sees herself
 in the distance looking
 like a young girl
walking toward her.
They both walk until they
 come together and
after that there is only one.
She is like a young girl again.

—Apache

I bloom

31 October 1976
Dear Naomi,
How strange that my sense of mothering comes to me so strongly on Halloween of all days. I'm reliving my own childhood watching you. I've at last overcome my fear of goblins, my fear of both differentness and conformity, my fear that this ultimate female role would destroy my goals I've so desperately clung to.

But I've allowed you to nourish me as I've nourished you. I've allowed that bond between mother and daughter to gradually grow, to reach beyond the limits I've always held. Not that I didn't love your brother and sisters—how they overwhelmed me—but with your birth, the child whom I didn't want but at last proved my worth so that I could say, Enough, I myself began to bloom. Is this my tie with you? That I've finally learned becoming a mother will not change my love of learning, my desire to write?…

You came on a cool rainy June evening. Not until the last minute did I believe you were here. With your birth some primitive joy was released. Like tonight on Halloween when witches come forth. But it was spring then, not fall like today; it was Shavuot, the holiday of First Fruits. We gave you an old name, Naomi, that all your friends mispronounce. At the sight of your long legs and dark hair, all my fears died, and I wrote a poem to you, and I write this now and know why.
Love, Your Ema

—Elaine Marcus Starkman, from *Between Ourselves: Letters Between Mothers & Daughters* edited by Karen Payne

It is the best thing,
I should always like
to be pregnant,
Tummy thickening
like a yogurt,
Unbelievable flower.

—SANDRA MCPHERSON

A [pregnant] woman has not necessarily gone blank when she falls silent or lets herself float along in a foggy mood. She is, so to speak, sitting next to the flow of life, close to its source. If one induces her to talk, she is likely to be able to describe the experience in detail. Even her language is enriched. Commonplace words have become fuller and more significant—carrying new life, like the woman herself.

—ARTHUR AND LIBBY COLEMAN, FROM *PREGNANCY: THE PSYCHOLOGICAL EXPERIENCE*

I am boundless

Just as a mother would protect her only child, even at the risk of her own life, even so let one cultivate a boundless heart toward all human beings.

—THE BUDDHA

In the womb the child's life unfolded like a play in two acts; two seasons as different as summer from winter. In the beginning, the "golden age." The embryo, a tiny plant, budding, growing and one day becoming a fetus. From vegetable to animal; movement appears, spreading from the little trunk outward, to the extremities. The little plant has learned to move its branches, the fetus is now enjoying his limbs. Heavenly freedom! Yes, this is the golden age! This little being is weightless: free of all shackles, all worries.

Carried weightless by the waters, he plays, he frolics, he gambols, light as a bird, flashing as quickly, as brilliantly as a fish.

In his limitless kingdom, in his boundless freedom, as if, passing through the immensity of time, he tries on all the robes, he tastes and enjoys all the forms which Life has dreamed up for Itself.

—Frederick Leboyer, from *Birth Without Violence*

From the moment of the Indian mother's recognition that she has conceived to the end of the child's second year of life…it was supposed by us that the mother's spiritual influence was supremely important.

Her attitude and secret meditations must be such as to instill into the receptive soul of the unborn child the love of the Great Mystery and a sense of connectedness with all creation…

She wanders prayerful in the stillness of great woods, or on the bosom of the untrodden prairie, and to her poetic mind the imminent birth of her child prefigures the advent of a hero—a thought conceived in the virgin breast of primeval nature, and dreamed out in a hush that is broken only by the sighing of the pine trees or the thrilling orchestra of a distant waterfall.

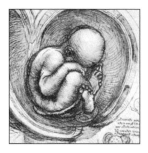

And when the day of days in her life dawns— the day in which there is to be a new life…she seeks no human aid…. Childbirth is best met alone…where all nature says to her spirit: "It's love! It's love! The fulfilling of life!" When a sacred voice comes to her out of the silence, and a pair of eyes open upon her in the wilderness, she knows with joy that she has borne well her part in the great song of creation!

—Charles Alexander Eastman, from *Native American Wisdom*

I am life

What is life? It is the flash of a firefly in the night. It is the breath of a buffalo in the wintertime. It is the little shadow which runs across the grass and loses itself in the sunset.

—Crowfoot, Blackfoot Elder

Birth story

Perhaps the most vivid account of childbirth that I have heard was given me by Jai Gopal, a little Pardhan boy of about five, who was present at the birth of his younger brother. "What happened?" I asked him. He thought for some time and said, "Fire." He referred to the lighting of a fire to warm the mother, and perhaps to banish evil spirits. "And then?" Another long pause. "Blood!" Another pause. "Water!" Another pause. "Pain. Much pain." Yet another pause. "Life!"

—Judith Goldsmith, from *Childbirth Wisdom*

Shining light

What are the values you wish to embrace and uphold for your child? What type of role models will you and your partner be? Who do you want your children to see when they raise their eyes to yours for the first time?

Opportunities for spiritual change arise each day, but most often one waits for markers—the last week of summer, a New Year's resolution, the silent remembering of vows with your partner at a wedding ceremony.

Awaiting the birth of a child can be just such a spiritual touchstone. The many months of pregnancy allow for deep examination of the heart and a slow unfolding and renewal of your inner life.

Your urge to "nest," to create order and harmony in the home, may be an outward manifestation of your spirit's desire for the same. Pregnancy is a time to revisit your beliefs and habits and contemplate your spiritual path, always aware that your children will look to you for wisdom and guidance throughout their lives. Envision they are following you, walking with small steps toward your shining light.

I become

one hesitates to bring a child into this world with-out fixing it up a little. paint a special room. stop sexism. learn how to love. vow to do it better than it was done when you were a baby. vow to make, if necessary, new mistakes. vow to be awake for the birth. to believe in joy even in the midst of unbearable pain.

to bear a child. to bare oneself to that experience. to touch a being with love that hasnt done a damn thing to earn your love. to learn how to love. to care for when it cant take care of you when you're sick. to step out of yourself & learn to step back into yourself. this is the second step, the one we, as women, are just learning. to love without giving oneself away. to stand up without being sat back down.

to watch how the children do it, & let them love us. to realize ourselves in a reciprocal world.

—Alta, "I would be a fool to want more children," from *Shameless Hussy*

These are her endless years,
woman and child, in dream
molded and wet, a bowl
growing on a wheel,
not mud, not bowl, not clay,
but this becoming,
winter and split of darkness,
years of wish.

—MURIEL RUKEYSER

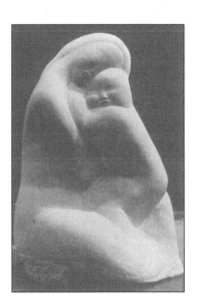

····· **A C T I V I T Y** ·····

You have chosen to become a mother. This is a profound decision which will create new meaning in your life. Write a letter to your baby, outlining your reasons for choosing motherhood. Give the letter to your child when he learns to read.

I am a miracle

I am thinking now of the women,
the heroines of the Bible...
Sarah, who laughed out loud
when the angels came to tell her
she would, at ninety, bear a son.
She was baking when they
arrived, and probably offered
them a roll or sweetcake. I can
see her rocking, her bones had
already dried and shriveled,
laughter splitting her sides,
laughter breaking her in two.
Sarah is patience, piety. The rock
of mother into which the moss
digs and grows, opening tiny
thistles and flowers.

—JUDITH HARRIS,
FROM "WHEREVER IN THE LANGUAGE OF
JEWISH WOMEN A GARDEN GROWS"

Knowing [the Mother], we will know that we are her divine children in a relationship of complete, unconditionally loving intimacy; we will know that nature is holy in all its sacred particulars because it is everywhere vibrant with her light and her love…What knowing the Mother means above all is daring to put love into action. The Mother herself is love-in-action, love acting everywhere and in everything to make creation possible. Coming into contact with the Mother is coming into contact with a force of passionate and active compassion in every area and dimension of life, a force that longs to be invoked by us to help transform all the existing conditions of life on earth so that they can mirror ever more clearly and accurately her law, her justice, her love.

—Andrew Harvey, from *Mystics: The Soul's Journey into Truth*

A baby is God's opinion that the world should go on. Never will a time come when the most marvelous recent invention is as marvelous as a newborn child.

—CARL SANDBURG

I am the essence

Wildness has no conditions, no sure routes, no peaks or goals, no source that is not instantly becoming something more than itself, then letting go of that, always becoming. It cannot be stripped to its complexity by CAT scan or telescope. Rather, it is a many-pointed

truth, almost a bluntness, a sudden essence like the wild strawberries strung along the ground on scarlet runners under my feet. Wildness is source and fruition at once, as if every river circled round, the mouth eating the tail—and the tail, the source.

To trace the history of a river, or a raindrop, as John Muir would have done, is also to trace the history of the soul, the history of the mind descending and arising in the body. In both, we constantly seek and stumble on divinity, which, like the cornice feeding the lake and the spring becoming a waterfall, feeds, spills, falls, and feeds itself over and over again.

—Gretel Ehrlich, from "River History," from *Montana Spaces*

LULLABY

Baby swimming
down the river:
Little driftwood legs,
Little rabbit legs.

—KIOWA, TRANSLATED
BY NATALIE CURTIS,
THE INDIANS' BOOK

"BEING PREGNANT" AKA

living in seduced circumstances
rehearsing lullabies
to be in the pudding club
bow-windowed
wearing the bustle wrong
up the pole
infanticipating
baby-bound
belly up
heir-conditioned
full of heir
in the family way
declaring a dividend
storked
a bun in the oven

I am proud

*I meet my work with strong limbs,
open hands, proud heart.*

—SHEA DARIAN

I thought the happiest day of my life was the day my husband and I got married, and it was, until the day came that we found out we were expecting our first child, then that became the happiest day of my life, and it was, until the day came that we gave birth to James, then that became the happiest day of my life, and it was, until the days came that he began rolling over, cut his first tooth, took his first step, and they all were, until the day came that he said "mama" for the first time, then that became the happiest day of my life, and it was, until the day came when he saw me coming up the walk to his school and he came running full sprint into my arms and said "I love you, Mommy, you're my best friend," then this became the happiest day of my life, except I'm sure the best is yet to come.

—Renée Turcott

❖ Woodrow Wilson, the twenty-eighth president of the United States, was proud to be a "mama's boy." Christened Thomas Woodrow, he replaced "Thomas" with his mother's maiden name, "Woodrow." Wilson's admiration of his mother, Jessie Woodrow, is evident in many of his quotes: "[I] clung to her till I was a great big fellow," and "love of the best womanhood came to me and entered my heart through her apron-string." It is no surprise that in 1914 he signed the resolution that established the second Sunday in May as Mother's Day. It directed government facilities and private citizens alike to raise the flag "as a public expression of our love and reverence for the mothers of our country."

I am virtuous

There were no other [Quakers] in the town where Henry's father had taken his young bride, so she had no Meetings to go to. But sometimes she and little Henry had Meeting by themselves....

Henry liked Meeting pretty well, although there wasn't much to it. All you did was just to sit quiet. Sometimes when he was still very small, he sat on his mother's lap. Sometimes he sat beside her and held her hand. She let him do whatever he felt like doing, so long as he was quiet. Sometimes, when they had Meeting out-of-doors, he slid down and lay on his back on the ground, looking up into the strong, crooked, rough branches of the old oak tree, and through them at the blue, blue sky. Once or twice he dozed off into a nap. Once or twice his mother prayed. Always the same prayer, "God please make my little boy strong and good." ..."What is 'God'?" he asked her curiously, but shyly, for a string inside him had been softly plucked by the sound of her voice when she said the word. She answered him, "When a little boy wants to do what's right, that's God in his heart." But mostly there was no talk at all. Just a stillness, and Mother's face so quiet and calm that it made Henry feel quiet and calm to look at it.

—Dorothy Canfield Fisher, "The Forgotten Mother," from *A Harvest of Stories*

To be a mother means you are asking to be entrusted with the soul of an innocent child. It means that you are enthusiastic and ready to share all that you are and all that you have. It means that you will watch over the body, heart, and soul of your baby. Patience, compassion, truthfulness, generosity, steadfastness, gratitude, playfulness: These are the virtues of motherhood.

The true virtues have nothing to do with morality, but rather with wisdom. A moth-

er is expected to be wiser than her child; she has to be. To be a wise mother you need the wisdom of knowing yourself well enough that you have room in your heart to love a baby who has colic, a dirty diaper, and projectile vomiting. It's being aware of yourself so that you are able to respond—to behave responsibly—rather than merely reacting out of an old pattern or fear.

To ready yourself, you must be willing and eager to cultivate the virtues of motherhood. To do so requires that you let go of self-centeredness and greed so you can fill your heart with gratitude and your mind with positive thoughts.

—Judy Ford, from *Blessed Expectations*

I provide

✤ In ancient Persia, a new baby was welcomed as a dear friend returning from a long journey. The baby and mother rested together for six days and on the seventh day arrangements were made to move the infant to a nearby cradle. A small piece of cake or bread was wrapped up in a piece of cloth and placed inside the baby's blanket as food for the journey to the cradle.

Let us put our minds together
and see what we will make for our children.

—SITTING BULL

My mother believes that a baby comes with a loaf of bread under her arm and all you need to do is add a cup of water to the soup and open your heart. When I think about having a family of my own, I always remember my mother's words. They are simple and naïve by many standards, but they have a way of cutting through the intellect and speaking to my heart. They remind me that my healthy body and soul alone are enough to sustain and nurture a baby for the nine months until she is ready to bless my life. Her wisdom comforts me when I worry about being a good provider and quiets the cynic that allows the material concerns to override the meaning and the miracle of having a family. I am not just a woman, or a lover, or a mother—I hold within my body a piece of the Divine. The promise of hope and renewal—a family and a heritage.

—Ame Mahler Beanland

AFRICAN PRAYER

Let us take care of the children,
for they have a long way to go.

Let us take care of the elders,
for they have come a long way.

Let us take care of those in between,
for they are doing the work.

Expecting parents have to be very careful because they carry within them a baby, one who might become a Buddha or Lord Jesus.... Our mothers and fathers helped us come to be and even now, they continue to give us life. Whenever I have difficulties, I ask for their support, and they always respond.

Our spiritual ancestors have also given birth to us, and they too, continue to give birth to us. In my country, we say that an authentic teacher has the power to give birth to a disciple. If you have enough spiritual strength, you will give birth to a spiritual child, and through your life and practice, you continue giving birth, even after you die. We say the sons and daughters of the Buddha came forth from the mouth of the Buddha, because

the Buddha offered them the Dharma, his teachings. There are many ways to offer the Dharma for a child to be born in his or her spiritual life, but the most usual is to share the Dharma through words. I try to practice in a way that allows me to touch my blood ancestors and my spiritual ancestors every day. Whenever I feel sad or a little fragile, I invoke their presence for support, and they never fail to be there.

—Thich Nhat Hanh, from *Living Buddha, Living Christ*

I respect

I never would have noticed
The first white snowdrop
Pushed through dirty snow...
A clothespin nested in the grass...
    An ant within a flower...
        The pertness of a chickadee...
        Dust mice hiding
        in my closet...
        That penny lost a week ago...
    A hairpin lodging in the floor
(How many years?)...
The soggy pine cones tight
and narrow...
The dirty rocks gathered by
winter's plows...
They would have gone unseen

I would not have remembered
The coldness of fresh snow...
The delight of a sled ride...
The exuberance of spring's
first day...
The sadness of the day's end...
The hugeness of a house...
The longing in a rainy day...
The friendliness of a stray...
The kindliness of humanity...
They would have been forgotten,
If it were not for my child.

—Margaret Steele

I glow

*Be lamps
unto yourselves;
be your own confidence.
Hold to the truth
within yourselves.*

— THE BUDDHA

She walks in beauty, like the night
Of cloudless climes and starry skies;
And all that's best of dark and bright
Meet in her aspect and her eyes:
Thus mellowed to that tender light
Which heaven to gaudy day denies.

One shade the more, one ray the less,
Had half impaired the nameless grace
Which waves in every raven tress,
Or softly lightens o'er her face;
Where thoughts serenely sweet express
How pure, how dear their dwelling place.

And on that cheek, and o'er that brow,
So soft, so calm, yet eloquent,
The smiles that win, the tints that glow,
But tell of days in goodness spent,
A mind at peace with all below,
A heart whose love is innocent!

— Lord Byron

❖ In the Congo, a new mother leaves her hut one or two days after the child's birth. This is the time of life when she is reputed to look the most radiant — she shines with beauty and happiness.

I plant

My mother was the making of me.
She was so true and so sure of me,
I felt that I had someone to live for—
someone I must not disappoint. The
memory of my mother will always
be a blessing to me. —Thomas Edison

I can't imagine my life without the incredible experience of pregnancy and giving birth. I felt centered and was in touch with every part of my body, mind, and soul—even though I puked five times a day!... Getting older is so freeing and wonderful—you don't waste time being embarrassed, ashamed, or afraid. I try to explain this to my daughters when I see how many of their waking hours are spent worrying, but I don't think they believe me! When they are grown women, I hope my words come back to them like a soft whisper. Sometimes I try to shield my daughters, but I remind myself that part of being a mother is working yourself out of a job. If you've done it well, your children will be strong enough to stand on their own.

—Cheri France, from *The Right Side of Forty: Celebrating Timeless Wisdom*

FAMILYING

With *'ohana*, the Oceanic approach to "familying," the child or *keiki* is treated like a seedling (keiki also means a young plant). As they develop, keiki are to be protected and cared for by everyone, but their development also involves caring for other keiki and *makua* (parents). 'Ohana stresses a steady, leisurely, joyful approach to child-care. Mealtimes are sacred rituals during which lessons of respect are modeled and taught. Ancestors and living elders are revered, and children are expected to help and care for the family.

—Paul Pearsall, from *The Pleasure Prescription: To Love, to Work, to Play—Life in the Balance*

I am innocent

CONTEMPLATION

*Respect the mature innocence
in grown-up people you
know and, whenever you
can, look into the eyes of a
child so you might catch a
glimpse of theirs.*

Have you ever held a sleeping baby in your arms?
Felt a baby curl its tiny hand around your finger?... Has a baby patted your cheek and pulled at
your nose? If so, you are blessed, for you have
been touched by innocence.

Babies grow so fast. Soon they are walking,
pulling the books down from the shelves, and
jumping on your bed. Next thing you know,
they're catching bugs in jars and selling lemon-
ade from a stand. Just discovering something
new pleases and amazes them.

But it's not just babies. If you have ever
heard the voices of a first-grade choir, your
heart swelled up so big you thought it might
burst. And you've probably experienced a child
saying something so straightforward, so truthful,
that you're stunned. Such purity catches you off-
guard, and for a moment you know you're feeling
the presence of the divine....

To me the truly grown-up people aren't those
jaded by "maturity" but rather the ones who have
kept the innocence alive in their own heart. They
have a sparkle in their eyes and spring in their step.
Just being around such a person lifts you up; you
feel happy and inspired. Grandpa Simon was like
that—kids of all ages hung around him. He gave
them hard candy from his pockets and let everyone
pet his rabbits. He grew raspberries and he'd fed
you toast and jam. He knew when to talk and when
to keep quiet. He told stories that made you feel better even though you weren't feeling bad.

—Judy Ford, from *Wonderful Ways to Love a Child*

I am feminine

Wednesday, 5 January 1944
I think what is happening to me
is so wonderful, and not only
what can be seen on my body,
but all that is taking place inside.
I never discuss myself or any of
these things with anybody; that
is why I have to talk to myself
about them.

Each time I have a period—
and that has only been three
times—I have the feeling that in
spite of all the pain, unpleasant-
ness, and nastiness, I have a
sweet secret, and that is why,
although it is nothing but a nui-
sance to me in a way, I always
long for the time that I shall feel
that secret within me again.

—Anne Frank, from *The Diary of
a Young Girl*

*For me, this piece brings beauty and
meaning into the world; I hope she
will touch men and women's lives
deeply, remind them of the force of life,
the power of beginnings, the awe of the
bringer and the brought.*

—MAGGIE EOYANG, NEEDLEWORKER ON *THE
BIRTH PROJECT*, BERKELEY, CALIFORNIA

THE BIRTH PROJECT

In 1980, the artist, Judy Chicago, following up
on her much-acclaimed work *The Dinner Party*,
began a five-year collaborative piece called *The
Birth Project*. The project culminated in a series of
over 100 images rendered in various forms of
needlework designed by Chicago and crafted by
women from various parts of the United States,
Canada, and New Zealand.

Chicago's inspiration for *The Birth Project*
stemmed from a fascination with cross-cultural
creation myths, and a desire to portray conception, pregnancy, and birth as a metaphor for
human existence. Furthermore, she wanted to
create imagery that put women and childbirth
in a place of honor. The work is powerful,
beautiful, and often graphic. Her colors are
intense, and the compositions
dramatic and forceful with a
radiant use of nature elements, inspired by the art of
tribal cultures. Each piece,
whether uplifting or jarring,
whimsical or sad, depicts the
woman as an intelligent, universal, and courageous being.

I am contentment

ACTIVITY

Once your doctor has given you a "due date" for your baby, take a box of paper clips and count out a number of them equal to the number of days remaining until your due date. Link them all together in a long chain. The repetition is a wonderful meditative opportunity! Hang the chain where you can easily remove a paperclip every day. How satisfying to watch the chain become shorter, and what fun for soon-to-be siblings!

Do Listen.
Do be assured of it in your heart.
My Littlest One
that nothing at all should alarm you,
should trouble you,
nor in any way disturb
your countenance, your heart…

For am I not here,
I, Your Mother?
Are you not in the Cool of My Shadow?
In the breeziness of My Shade?

Is it not I that am
Your Source of Contentment?
Are you not cradled in My Mantle?
Cuddled in the crossing of My Arms?
Is there anything else for you to need?

—Our Lady of Guadalupe

SONG OF THE LONG HAIR KACHINAS

*At the edge of the cornfield a bird
will sing with them
in the oneness of their happiness.
So they will sing together in tune with the
universal power, in harmony with the
one Creator of all things.
And the bird song, and the people's song, and
the song of life will become one.*

I illuminate

As the sun illuminates the moon and stars, so let us illumine one another. —ANONYMOUS

At what point do we see our mother's face and realize that she is a unique person who gave us birth, loves us, is beautiful in our eyes and vulnerable, and know that time and work have taken a toll on her and that someday she may need us to look after her?

Not until we could venture into outer space and look back upon the Earth could humankind have a similar experience of Mother Earth. The beautiful blue and white planet that is Earth, a sphere glowing with light, silhouetted against the blackness of space, is a gorgeous sight. She is beautiful and vulnerable, and the only Mother Earth we have.

In photographs, Earth also has the shape of a *mandala,* a circle within a square, the symbol of what Jung called the Self, an image of wholeness and the archetype of meaning. The Self is whatever we experience that is greater than our small selves through which we know that there is something meaningful to our existence. The round or the circle is a feminine symbol that represented the Great Mother before humanity could know that the Earth is round. The Earth is the Great Mother Goddess: she births us and breathes us and feeds us and holds us to her body with gravity, and we return to her in death.

—Jean Shinoda Bolen, from *Crossing to Avalon*

ILLUMINATED LIVES

In nineteenth-century Pennsylvania Dutch society, illuminated birth certificates called *Frakturschriften Taufscheine* were elaborately embroidered to honor a baby's baptism.

Ornate natural symbols of religious significance were lovingly and artfully rendered to mark this sacred and joyous occasion. Popular motifs included six-pointed stars to represent prosperity and fertility, hearts to portray God's ever-present and unconditional love, birds symbolizing Christ, and flowers adorning the piece to depict mankind's search for God and to signify hope.

I let go

We never did have tears over broken balloons because, knowing that they would rise when the string was released, the children always wanted to let go immediately. As parents we had a little trouble adjusting to this. While we secretly lamented the "waste" of our money, the children marveled at the freedom of each bright, rising thing. After a while they learned to hold on to their balloons a little more tightly and a little longer. So the kids are learning to hold on, while we are learning to let go.

—Anonymous

Every act of birth requires the courage to let go of something, to let go of the breast, to let go of the lap, to let go of the hand, to let go eventually of all certainties, and to rely on one thing: one's own power to be aware and to respond; that is, one's creativity. To be creative means to consider the whole process of life as a process of birth, and not to take any stage of life as a final stage.

—Erich Fromm

As each breath moves in and out of me, the mantra takes root in my soul and the wisdom of the ancients blossoms. I realize that I cannot will myself to stop breathing. I am not in control of this life. I am not even in control of the simplest act of life, breathing. I need not try to be in control. I need only to let go and become a part of that which is pushing to flow through me. Let go into the stream. Let go....

I know, too, all that is powerful and holy is here—breath and wind, stone and sky, trees and life. Here is God, the "Great I Am." If I flee this moment or fill it with fear and anxiety, I dishonor it, and miss a sweet touch of eternity. I will linger in this place for some timeless time, repeating the prayer, feeling the solid earth beneath my back and breathing the gentle incense of the woods.

—Karen A. Monk, from *Another Wilderness: New Outdoor Writing by Women*

I multiply

We two form a multitude. —Ovid

As children we were left pretty much to ourselves, since father was away most of the time. Mother was of course the center of the household, but in those years — and indeed, for a long time after — she was always either pregnant, or nursing an infant, so that she had little strength left for her growing brood. She bore my father fifteen children, of which three died in infancy, and twelve grew into full man and womanhood. She did not think childbearing a burden. She wanted as many children as possible, and she went on having them happily and uninterruptedly from her seventeenth year until her forty-sixth. She was already a grandmother when my youngest brother was born, and two of my oldest sister's children rejoiced in the birth of an uncle. I remember that Mother's constant childbearing was accepted in such a matter-of-fact way that when I was a schoolboy in Pinsk, and away from home, I saved up kopeck by kopeck, enough to buy a new cradle, the old one having become rickety; and I remember lugging it home on one of my visits, and proudly presenting it to mother for her "next."

—Chaim Weizmann, from *Trial and Error*

GIVING OF HER LIFE'S FRUIT

In India, Hindu mothers are provided with a ritual called phala dana trata *or "giving of her fruit to the world." This beautiful way of marking the painful and necessary release of her sons takes place over several years and involves the sacrifice of foods, metals and precious ornaments leading up to a final ceremony when the boys are five years old.*

"The last extreme stage of the sacrifice is a total fast: the woman presents fresh coconut milk to her guru and must then go thirsty all day. Brahmins, relatives and household attend this ceremony, representing the world to which the son must be given. At the end of the rite, twelve Brahmin and a few beggars are given ceremonial food: the highest and lowest caste, the summit and base of the social pyramid, symbolize the whole social world for which the matured boy must leave his home and sever his maternal bonds. At the end of the ceremony, the guru declares that the mother is ready to perform the act of giving her son to the world. And then silently and inwardly she completes the sacrifice of her life's fruit."

—Heinrich Zimmer, from *Spiritual Disciplines*

I am fertile

❖ Israeli Jewish women make pilgrimage to the tomb of Mother Rachel, beloved biblical matriarch, to pray for her intercession in the conception and birth of their children. After wrapping a red string seven times around the tombstone, they then wear it as a charm for fertility or to ease childbirth pain.

It is now, when the whole jar of humidity has been poured on me like wet petals, and there is no question of dryness anywhere, that I am most close to everything alive. The wet breath that links leaves and sky to my lungs reaches deep inside my body and stirs the silent seeds of all I hold dear, and you, like the powerful muscle we call heart, grow stronger with me.

—JOAN ROHR MYERS

Children are very special to Native American people. They're gifts and very precious and every child is to be loved and cared for by everyone. Mothers are special. The first important thing you learn about mothers in the Northeast is they have a gift of reproduction. Historically, the women farmed the land because they could make things reproduce, they had that special ability and it was recognized. Women owned the land, women owned the houses, the children belonged to the women. All of this has continued in New York State with Iroquois people, who have a very strong tradition and still practice their historical-religious traditions and maintain the language.

—Diosa, Native American artist, writer, educator, and mother, from *Mothering the New Mother: Your Postpartum Resource Companion*

I believe

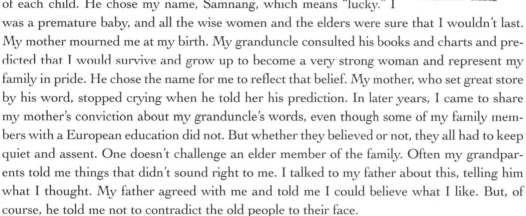

*My mother is my root, my foundation. She planted the
seed that I base my life on, and that is the belief that the
ability to achieve starts in your mind.*

—Michael Jordan

We asked for my granduncle's advice in the choice of name for every
newborn baby in the family. He decided on the name to suit the destiny
of each child. He chose my name, Samnang, which means "lucky." I
was a premature baby, and all the wise women and the elders were sure that I wouldn't last.
My mother mourned me at my birth. My granduncle consulted his books and charts and predicted that I would survive and grow up to become a very strong woman and represent my
family in pride. He chose the name for me to reflect that belief. My mother, who set great store
by his word, stopped crying when he told her his prediction. In later years, I came to share
my mother's conviction about my granduncle's words, even though some of my family members with a European education did not. But whether they believed or not, they all had to keep
quiet and assent. One doesn't challenge an elder member of the family. Often my grandparents told me things that didn't sound right to me. I talked to my father about this, telling him
what I thought. My father agreed with me and told me I could believe what I like. But, of
course, he told me not to contradict the old people to their face.

—Samnang Wu, from "A Lucky Woman," from *Women in Exile*

FERTILITY SEEDS AND SYMBOLS

The almond was revered as a fertility charm
and a blessing for marriages; in Italy
almonds were distributed at weddings as a
token of future fruitfulness for the union.
The roots of this ritual are the ancient pagan
symbolism of the *mandorla* or almond as
the female genitals and a sign of virgin
motherhood. Consequently, the almond was
adopted as an emblem of the Virgin Mary
and referred to as the "Womb of the World."

Pomegranates and oranges were also
symbolic of birth and fertility in many
cultures. The word pomegranate means
"apple of many seeds." The fruit, with its
red juice and numerous "offspring," was
almost universally known as a womb
symbol. In South America, pomegranates
were often used as fertility talismans.

nurture

Early morning,

moist and still mine,

       I greet the sun soaking a sleepy sky.

       Together we climb the towering tree

       clutching tender nest in crook.

       Shadows dapple

       where my arms hold steady

       two hearts,

       one pulsing eagerly

       one newly lit.

I wrap around the limber branch

below the swallow's patient perch

and listen to her mother dreams.

I know her song,

floating like gossamer on this bright day.

We bask

       sure with life and serene,

       while time unfurls our children.

       They face the sun guiding them home,

       where their hearts quicken

and we love.

ANDREA ALBAN GOSLINE

I nurture

Your rhythmic nursing slows. I feel
your smile before I see it: nipple pinched
in corner of mouth, your brimming, short, tuck
     cornered
smile. I shake my head, my *no* vibrates
to you through ribs and arms. Your tapered ears
quiver, work faintly and still pinker, my
nipple spins right out and we
are two who sit and smile into each other's eyes.

Again, you frowning farmer, me your cow:
you flap one steadying palm against my breast,
thump down the other, chuckle, snort, and then
you're suddenly under, mouth moving steadily, eyes
drifting past mine abstracted, your familiar
blue remote and window-paned with light.

—Anne Winters, "The Chair by the Window"
from *The Key to the City*

> *The Great Spirit is our father,*
> *but the earth is our mother. She nourishes us;*
> *that which we put into the ground she returns*
> *to us, and healing plants she gives us likewise.*
> *If we are wounded, we go to our mother*
> *and seek to lay the wounded part against her,*
> *to be healed. Animals too, do thus, they lay*
> *their wounds to the earth.*
>
> —Big Thunder (Wabanakis Nation)

✤ Women in tribal cultures often breast-feed their babies until the children are two or three years old. The Blackfeet of North America and the Jivaro of Ecuador are known to have nursed their children up to seven years.

I am the heart

It's a kind of love that lets you feel their pain, joy, disappointment. [Children] are such a part of you that no matter how old you are or they are, that feeling never dies. It's as if they are part of your soul and they are as "tied" to you as when they were first conceived. The only difference is in the way this love is expressed as time passes. On the outside you may be subtle, with just the words "I love you," but on the inside you still want to hold them close to your heart and never let go.

—from *The Motherhood Report: How Women Feel About Being Mothers*

The best and most beautiful things in the world cannot be seen or even touched. They must be felt with the heart.

—Helen Keller

GODDESS: THE NURSING MOTHER

The ancient hieroglyph *mena,* meaning "breast" and also "moon," is symbolized by a breast, reflecting the Egyptian belief that from the breast of the Moon Goddess flowed the Milky Way, the stars, and the life-giving waters of the universe. In nearly every known language, "Ma-Ma" means "mother's breasts."

Many other ancient traditions speak of the Goddess as a nursing mother to the world; the famous statue of Artemis at Ephesus, whose torso was covered with breasts, suggested overflowing nourishment for all creatures.

Enlightenment and even immortality were promised to those who discovered how to drink the Goddess' milk. According to a Tantric aphorism, "Deathless are those who have fed at the breast of the Mother of the Universe." Egyptian pharaohs believed they would become immortal infants, nursing forever at the Goddess' breast.

❖ The shamrock or three-leaf clover was a natural reference to the Three Brigits, the "mother-hearts" of Celtic tribes.

I am the sun

This is the spring there should be in the world, so I say to myself, "Lie in the sun with the child in your flesh shining like a jewel. Dream and sing, pagan, wise in your vitals. Stand still like a fat budding tree, like a stalk of corn athrob and aglisten in the heat. Lie like a mare panting with the dancing feet of colts against her sides. Sleep at night as the spring earth. Walk heavily as a wheat stalk at its full time bending towards the earth waiting for the reaper. Let your life swell downward so you become like a vase, a vessel. Let the unknown child knock and knock against you and rise like a dolphin within."

I look at myself in the mirror…I look like a pale and shining pomegranate, hard and tight, and my skin shines like crystal with the veins showing beneath blue, and distended…. I am a pomegranate hanging from an invisible tree with the juice and movement of seed within my hard skin. I dress slowly. I hate the smell of clothes. I want to leave them off and just hang in the sun ripening…ripening.

—Meridel Le Sueur, from "Annunciation," from *Salute of Spring*

This presence in my body is insistent, pulling me down below surface into deep water, warm earth water. Aware of my body. This presence stays with me always, quietly. I move in a dream of the presence, the earth of my body. Pregnant a month, two months. A long time. So now I find out what time is. The day comes around me like a coat. The sun is time. —MARILYN KRYSL

I am serene

Life is filled with suffering, but it is also filled with many wonders, like the blue sky, the sunshine, the eyes of a baby. To suffer is not enough. We must also be in touch with the wonders of life. They are within us and all around us, everywhere, any time. If we are not happy, if we are not peaceful, we cannot share peace and happiness with others, even those we love, those who live under the same roof. If we are peaceful, if we are happy, we can smile and blossom like a flower, and everyone in our family, our entire society, will benefit from our peace. Do we need to make a special effort to enjoy the beauty of the blue sky? Do we have to practice to be able to enjoy it? No, we just enjoy it. Each second, each minute of our lives can be like this. Wherever we are, any time, we have the capacity to enjoy the sunshine, the presence of each other, even the sensation of our breathing....I would like to offer one short poem you can recite from time to time, while breathing and smiling.

Breathing in, I calm my body.
Breathing out, I smile.
Dwelling in the present moment
I know this is a wonderful moment.

—Thich Nhat Hanh, from *Being Peace*

❖ **The Sea-Jakun of Malaya give birth on their boats, while lying facedown with their stomachs pressed onto a round piece of wood.**

*Stillness of body
creates quietness of breath;
quietness of breath creates
equanimity of mind, and
equanimity of mind creates
harmony of being.*

—Judith Lasater

*May serenity circle
on silent wings and catch
the whisper of the wind.*

—Cheewa James, Modoc

I protect

The angels whispering to one another, can find, among their burning terms of love, none so devotional as that of "Mother." —EDGAR ALLAN POE

Opening our hearts can mean letting our children make their own mistakes and learn from them. Opening our hearts to our children can mean loving them and ourselves enough to set boundaries that as adults we know they are unprepared to set. Opening our hearts to our children can also mean celebrating them, nurturing them, being literally, "in love" with them as we go through the day together.... I was beginning to understand that to open my heart was always a choice for me, moment by moment. Each time I did open my heart I was healed, as mother and as a woman, a little bit more. I had a choice, always, whether to contract into my old, small self or expand into the now, into grace, into new possibilities...Our spirituality may change in the process of opening. We find that sacredness does not lie in the past or the future, or in a particular place, or in what "should" be, but rather, simply and powerfully, in the present moment, in *kairos*. We find that as we open our hearts to whatever is happening at the time, not only does any difficulty become easier to deal with, but we also become reconnected to the Sacred, reconnected to the greatest web of life that holds us all.

—Melissa Gayle West, from *If Only I Were a Better Mother*

❖ The first record of a successful cesarean section is documented in the year 1500 on the wife of Jacob Nufer, a Swiss sow-gelder. After his wife had labored hard and long with no progress, Nufer stepped in himself, using the tools of his trade to deliver the baby. Both baby and mother thrived. Mrs. Nufer went on to have six more children, including one set of twins, all delivered naturally.

I reassure

FOOD CRAVINGS

Pregnant women of all cultures experience food cravings that may seem quite unusual, even bizarre, to non-pregnant folks. Fortunately, in most cultures, people are sympathetic and indulgent of a mother-to-be's food desires. Following is an international list of common cravings:

The Wayou of Malawi: shellfish and grain husks. **Turkey:** coffee grinds, soap, and cloves. **Ijaw of Nigeria:** oranges. **New Guinea:** coconut shells and bark. **Thailand:** uncooked rice, chalk, and charcoal. **The Bauris tribes of India:** sour fruits, such as green mango and plums. **Eighteenth-century United States:** coffee, chocolates, mud, and plaster. **Late twentieth-century United States** lemons, pickles, and ice cream (stereotype)

You start out eagerly, wide-eyed
With a singsongy humming
Punctuated with pleasured sighs

Gradually, the activity quiets
Eyes close and all is still
Save a tiny jaw, nibbling rhythmically

Soft lips soon draw out in a line
Sweet breath escaping gently
And the bedding embraces you

With a whispered kiss and a lingering touch
I slip away to leave you to sleep
And look back lovingly

—Elizabeth von Radics, "Nursing Clementine"

The earth is your mother,
she holds you.
The sky is your father,
he protects you.
We are together always.
We are together always.
There never was a time
when this
was not so.

—NAVAJO LULLABY

I praise

I was born in Nature's wide domain! The trees were all that sheltered my infant limbs, the blue heavens all that covered me. I am one of Nature's children. I have always admired her. She shall be my glory: her features, her robes, and the wreath about her brow, the seasons, her stately oaks, and the evergreen—her hair, ringlets over the earth—all contribute to my enduring love for her.

And wherever I see her, emotions of pleasure roll in my breast, and swell and burst like waves on the shores of the ocean, in prayer and praise to Him who has placed me in her hand. It is thought great to be born in palaces, surrounded with wealth—but to be born in Nature's wide domain is greater still!

I would much more glory in this birth-place, with the broad canopy of heaven above me, and the giant arms of the forest trees for my shelter, than to be born in palaces of marble, studded with pillars of gold! Nature will be Nature still, while palaces shall decay and fall in ruins.

—George Copway, (Kahgegagohbowh) Ojibwe

A child is fed with milk and praise.

—MARY LAMB

The world will be a better and a happier place when people are praised more and blamed less, when we utter in their hearing the good we think and also gently intimate the criticisms we hope may be of service.

—FRANCIS E. WILLARD

✤ Months before the birth of their babies, the Kalapalo women of Brazil make new hammocks and suspend them above the ones they usually sleep in. During labor, the women use both hammocks: the old one to lean back into, the new one for support and to raise their bodies. After delivery, the old hammock is thrown away and the mother and child sleep together in the new one.

I notice

"Flora and fauna reports," I used to call the long, winding letters from my grandmother. "The forsythia is starting and this morning I saw my first robin.... The roses are holding even in this heat.... The sumac has turned and that little maple down by the mailbox.... My Christmas cactus is getting ready...."

I followed my grandmother's life like a long home movie: a shot of this and a shot of that, spliced together with no pattern that I could ever see. "Dad's cough is getting worse.... The little Shetland looks like she'll drop her foal early.... Joanne is back in the hospital at Anna.... We named the new boxer Trixie and she likes to sleep in my cactus bed—can you imagine?"

I could imagine. Her letters made that easy. Life through grandma's eyes was a series of small miracles: the wild tiger lilies under the cottonwoods in June; the quick lizard scooting under the gray river rock she admired for its satiny finish. Her letters clocked the seasons of the year and her life. She lived until she was eighty, and the letters came until the very end.

—Julia Cameron, from *The Artist's Way*

EXPECTANT FATHER RITUALS

We need to further ritualize pregnancy and parenthood for both parents. Existing rituals such as visits to the doctor or midwife, baby showers, childbirth, and rooming-in need to be expanded to include the expectant father. To bring the father directly into his developing family we need to institutionalize more ways for him to participate openly in fatherhood as early as possible.

As couples, you can.... develop your own personal pregnancy rituals. Attending movies about childbirth; discussing books; sharing dreams, memories, and fantasies; keeping pregnancy journals; meditating together; and playing music for your developing child are some possibilities.

The ultimate task of pregnancy is to foster an atmosphere in which your differences and similarities are appreciated and supported. No doubt this takes a great deal of time and effort—realizing and identifying your feelings, sharing them, and trying to understand your partner's point of view. Take the time to work on these important issues together and alone. It will be well worth your time and effort.

—Jack Heinowitz, from *Pregnant Fathers*

I trust

One of the most important "moments" of my feminist education came in the contradictions of childbirth: a body swollen beyond recognition (the past body once so sexual, now spent and turned into a vessel, yes) now on the brink of a transformation from woman to mother/woman. The contradiction of the pain and the elation of seeing the child. The need to relax and be in perfect control. But these contradictions were small compared to the social one: the need to be self-absorbed and in complete partnership with my husband. When fear told me to stay put, to trust his urgings to squat or walk or lie down in a different position. To put a piece of ice in my mouth. Lean against his chest and cry. To shout during contractions—shout like this usually reserved but sassy body never shouts. My trust in him enabled me to relax. To focus the pain. To abandon pain. That depth of trust in the opposite sex is rare, profound, and ultimately necessary for political change.

—Kimiko Hahn, from "A Feminist Moment" from *Mother Journeys*

In soft whisperings from the heart,
The child within offers you always
The thread of your truth.

May you cherish that child, trust
That voice and weave that thread
Richly into the fabric of your days.

—ANONYMOUS

❖ During the 1940s, advocates for natural childbirth in the United States adopted a new and joyful attitude toward birth, viewing nature as orderly and benevolent.

Eagle Stones and Other Birth Aids

In eighteenth-century America, a popular amulet used to protect expectant mothers was a hollow stone, thought to be gathered from a raptor's nest, with smaller stones inside it that rattled when shaken. This represented the fetus moving within the mother's womb. The Eagle's Stone was a precious heirloom passed on through generations in wealthy families. It was usually worn high up on the woman's body during the early stages of pregnancy and was moved progressively closer to her abdomen as birth approached. During labor, the stone was tied around her left thigh.

Other childbirth "aids" of this era included placing the husband's nightcap on the mother's stomach, wrapping a snakeskin around her abdomen, having the mother pull on the father's clothing, wearing a red coral necklace, placing a magnet on her belly, and lighting a long candle that burned out by the end of labor.

I am the web

"What's miraculous about
a spider's web," said Mrs. Arable.
"I don't see why you say a web is
a miracle—it's just a web."
"Ever try to spin one?"

—E. B. White, from *Charlotte's Web*

Not until I heard her with her grandchildren did I remember the feeling of it, those invisible, constantly re-forming bonds which at the same time were roads to explore, teasing us along avenues of thought and imagination....

Mind you, even as a child you knew you were being led, and as you grew older you sometimes suspected you were being taken, but who could resist? Who wanted to miss anything? You knew she was building a glittering web to contain you but you knew you were always at its centre, and it was a throne, a chariot, as it became a rocket ship for her grandchildren, perhaps, and she might be controlling you but she was also completely at your service, helping you learn to work the controls that would take you farther, she promised, than even her dreams. She was artist, magician, slave and seer, counsellor, songbird, judge and peer.

—Adele Wiseman, from *Old Woman at Play*

I encourage

During my mother's pregnancy, everyone predicted that I would be a beauty. Then I was born and they perceived that I was not, was in fact quite the opposite. But, says my mother, they were all quite polite about it, said you were a healthy child. How I loved her. Every night and every morning she told me how much she loved me, a ritual I never tired of. And if an ugly child could be said to bloom, at each such declaration of her love, I blossomed. Her bedtime stories filled me with delight for they were mostly about mothers and children and she would demonstrate how much the mother loved the child by kissing and cuddling me.

—Anjana Appachana, from "My Only Gods" from *The Forbidden Stitch*

I did not have my mother very long, but in that length of time she cast over me an influence which has lasted all of my life.... If it had not been for her appreciation and her faith in me at a critical time in my experience, I should very likely never have become an inventor.

—THOMAS EDISON

...We call upon all those who have lived on this earth, our ancestors and our friends,
who dreamed the best for future generations, and upon
whose lives our lives are
built, and with thanksgiving, we call upon them to
teach us, and show us the way...

—CHINOOK BLESSING LITANY

I love

Love doesn't just sit there, like a stone, it has to be made, like bread; remade all the time, made new. —Ursula K. Le Guin

Mother is the home we come from, she is nature, soil, ocean. Mother's love is unconditional, it is all-protective, all-enveloping; because it is unconditional it can also not be controlled or acquired. Its presence gives the loved person a sense of bliss; its absence produces a sense of lostness and utter despair. Since mother loves her children because they are her children, and not because they are "good," obedient, or fulfill her wishes and commands, mother's love is based on equality. All men are equal, because they all are children of a mother, because they all are children of Mother Earth.

—Erich Fromm, from *The Art of Loving*

THE HEALING POWER OF TOUCH

Infant massage is a means of relaxing your baby and enhancing physical bonding. You do not need to learn any special techniques, just explore and stroke her spontaneously and you will be doing it right. Dr. Frederick Leboyer, an advocate of "gentle birth," believes all newborns should be lovingly massaged immediately upon their arrival, until they stop crying and are calm.

While infant massage is a relatively new concept to Western society, it has long been practiced in tribal cultures around the world where parents massage their infants regularly as part of daily care. Massage is also practiced to heal a weak baby. Tribal mothers believe that the healing properties of massage come not only from the power of their hands but from nutrients contained in the special oils they use. For example, vitamin D, which breastmilk lacks, is thought to be directly absorbed through the baby's skin from certain massage oils.

I am tender

*Dear Spirit, hear
and bless the beasts and
singing birds and guard
with tenderness small things
that have no words.*

— ANONYMOUS

Imagine your unborn child's hands are pressed against your abdominal wall and "touch" them with yours. Sing lullabies and read stories to soothe her. Tenderly rock your belly—your baby's house. Spending time with her now will give you a head start on your bonding experience.

Paris, November 1793
Sunday Night

I have just received your letter, and feel as if I could not go to bed tranquilly without saying a few words in reply, merely to tell you that my mind is serene, and my heart affectionate.

Ever since you last saw me inclined to faint, I have felt some gentle twitches, which make me begin to think that I am nourishing a creature who will soon be sensible of my care. This thought has not only produced an overflowing of tenderness to you, but made me very attentive to calm my mind and take exercise, lest I should destroy an object, in whom we are to have a mutual interest, you know. Yesterday—do not smile!—finding that I had hurt myself by lifting precipitately a large log of wood, I sat down in an agony, till I felt those said twitches again....

Write to me, my best love, and bid me be patient—kindly—and the expressions of kindness will again beguile the time, as sweetly as they have done tonight. Tell me also over and over again, that your happiness (and you deserve to be happy!) is closely connected with mine....

Take care of yourself, and remember with tenderness your affectionate, Mary

— Mary Wollstonecraft, from a letter to Gilbert Imlay

In its very name, the stork carries a tradition of love. The English word comes from the Greek *storge*, meaning "strong natural affection," and in Hebrew the stork means "the pious one."

Around the world, mothers tell their children that babies are brought by the stork and when depositing the baby the stork bites the mother's leg, causing her to stay in bed to heal.

The belief in the stork as the bringer of babies originated from observations of the bird's tenderness towards its young and old. Legends described how the young looked after their infirm and blind parents, carrying them around on their own wings and feeding them.

Also, the stork took great care in constructing its home and loved to return to

the same spot each year. Soon the stork's presence was considered a sign of good fortune. German peasants encouraged storks to build their nests on their roofs, putting a wagon wheel there for a foundation. The stork's natural habitat of swamps, marshes, and ponds gave rise to the ancient belief that it was in such watery places that the souls of unborn children dwelled.

I bask

I would like to tell a twenty year old daughter, if I had one, of my lifelong search to find peace and God and happiness.... I would stop and smile and sigh and probably start crying as I shared the extraordinary details of the day I had my first child, and of the chaos that came after when three more babies were born shortly thereafter. I would tell her how this puppy pack of boys would derail my career and link me inexorably to my soul and to the Almighty and to the present and to the forever. I would describe how these wriggly children captured me in the fleeting moment that is now, and ultimately drew me toward the peace I had tried desperately to reach....

I would tell her that should she decide to make children her priority she should never feel as if she was failing the feminist cause. Because her liberated mother had been independent and successful and had delayed marriage until the age of thirty-three, and here is what she had found: that after years of trying to find power in various gurus and exotic boyfriends, in interviews with movie stars, senators, and even a queen, surrendering to motherhood was the most liberating and powerful thing she had ever done in her life.

—Iris Krasnow, from *Surrendering To Motherhood*

I am the hearth

When I was a little girl, I lived on a farm in Wisconsin. On our back porch was a huge black iron pot, which had lovely rounded sides and stood on three legs. My mother made her own soap, so for part of the year the pot was filled with soap. When threshing crews came through in the summer, we filled the pot with stew. At other times my father used it to store manure for my mother's flower beds. We all came to call it the "3-S pot." Whenever anyone wanted to use the pot, he was faced with two questions: What is the pot now full of, and how full is it?

Long afterward, when people would tell me of their feelings of self-worth—whether they felt full or empty, dirty, or even "cracked"—I would think of that old pot....I am convinced that the crucial factor in what happens both inside people and between people is the picture of individual worth that each person carries around with him—his pot....

An infant coming into the world has no past, no experience in handling himself, no scale on which to judge his own worth. He must rely on the experience he has with the people around him and the messages they give him about his worth as a person. For the first five or six years, the child's pot is formed by the family almost exclusively.

—Virginia Satir, from *Peoplemaking*

Everywhere in the house is the need for order. The grandmother darns sheets before the children finish dreaming.

—ELIZABETH FULLIN-JONES

The only and absolute perfect union of two is when a baby hangs suspended in its mother's womb, like a tiny madman in  *a padded cell, attached to her, feeling her blood and hormones and moods play through its body, feeling her feelings.*

—DIANE ACKERMAN

Human beings need a secure base from which to start. It's built into our biology, unlike fish or insects, which develop rapidly, sometimes in constant motion; we mammals need to go through a relatively long period of secure housing before we're called on to start roaming around.

Your baby's house is the fluid-filled amniotic sac inside your uterus, built by the two of you out of the finest materials—your own cherished body. This home provides a period of security from which your baby will launch into the cool brightness of a world of infinite possibility.

All our lives, humans reach for some version of the warmth and flexibility of the womb. Many of us, if we're lucky, find it in our intimate relationships. The nourishment we get prepares us to meet whatever challenge greets us.

—Martha Vanceburg, from *A New Life: Daily Readings for a Happy Healthy Pregnancy*

I am comfort

As one whom his mother comforteth so will I comfort you. —ISAIAH

I love aprons. The large white ones with the broad bands and large square pockets. Before "The Lighthouse for the Blind" had them for sale, I used to buy nurses' aprons, the old-fashioned kind with all-around gathers. Pockets in a clinging apron don't mean much. A woman in an apron invites hugging. The apron of a woman flung over a kitchen chair is a wonderful still life. And the pockets of that apron, harboring sticky unwrapped candies, crumpled bits of paper, newspaper ads hastily torn out, pennies and nickels and a ribbon stuck to a band-aid, a baby's sock and a bottle cap, should be food for poets who are so easily tempted to linger on the treasures in a little boy's pants pocket.

—Marlene Dietrich, "I Love Aprons" from *Marlene Dietrich's ABC's*

❖ In Montana, women of the Gros Ventre tribe generally do not cook while pregnant. However, if they absolutely must cook, they wear a thick apron.

I replenish

Bring forth and multiply,
and replenish the earth.

—A KHARIA CHANT

When the moon appeared as a slender crescent, delicate and fine but firm in the promise of growth, Artemis roamed the untouched forests of Arcadia. On each night of the waxing moon Her animals and mortals came to dance with the Goddess. They encircled a large tree that stood apart from the others, its smooth bark and leaves seeming silver in the fresh moonlight. Artemis moved toward the tree and silence followed, but for her doves cooing softly in the boughs overhead. The Goddess crouched as the Great She-Bear She once had been and touched the earth. From the roots, up the trunk, along the branches to the leaves. She drew Her hands. Again. And again. With each pass She brought forth new life; pale blossoms unfolding and falling away, tiny globes of fruit shining among the branches, and finally ripe, glowing fruit

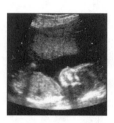

hanging from the sacred boughs. Artemis gathered the fruit and fed Her animals, Her mortals, Her nymphs, and Herself. The dance began.

—The myth of Artemis

Your tiny unborn baby inside the womb must adjust to your movements. The fetus uses its vestibular system for this purpose as well as to begin its own program of body-building. Long before you feel your baby's first nudge, he is engaging in regular exercise. Between ten and twelve weeks gestation, there is a sudden spurt of activity. The baby rolls from side to side, extends then flexes his back and neck, waves his arms, and kicks his legs. One of his favorite moves is to flex his feet, then extend them in a swift kick to the side wall of the amniotic sac.

Every one of the baby's muscles seem to be used during these "training sessions," according to doctors in Johannesburg, South Africa, who studied "womb exercises" in forty-six pregnant women. The most active babies exercised for seven and a half minutes straight; the longest "loungers" rested only five and a half minutes. Dutch scientists say that because these movements are graceful, voluntary, and spontaneous, they are an early example of initiative and self-expression on the part of the fetus.

I am gentle

The word "power" makes me gasp. Motherhood, more than my career as an inner-city school teacher or a wishful writer, has taught me that I am powerful because of my effect on others—a power I must accept and use consciously regardless of our culture's denial of feminine influence.

When my daughter was two (she's eleven now), she would sometimes put her hands on her hips (imitating me, I realize now), look at me defiantly and say, "Why do you say, 'Pick up your toys?' You should have said, 'Little Georgia, would you pick up your toys, please?' Then, Mama, I would feel happy."

Any mother knows that her inflections, gesticulations, mood, and facial expressions can create calm or havoc. Children respond to our actions, even our secret feelings, in utero, and most obviously within our everyday lives; our words and deeds strike our children like lightning or reassure like a favorite doll. My daughter's power is evident in her willingness to express her thoughts. I hope she will wield her power with great gentleness, as she is teaching me to do.

—Mary Hughes Lee

❖ In 1893, the Johnson brothers introduced American mothers to the fresh scent of Johnson's Baby Powder, including it as a giveaway item in the multipurpose Maternity Packets sold to midwives.

A mother's love is like the tree of life
Strong in spirit
peaceful, wise and beautiful
—AFRICAN PROVERB

YOM KIPPUR PRAYER

As we recall the compassion
shown us by our parents, so may
we dedicate ourselves to turning
that compassion towards all the
inhabitants of the earth.

I attend

Spoil your baby. During the first year give him all the attention he wants, because this is when he is learning to love and trust.

— LEE SALK

BIRTH STORY

There was a beautiful setup with mother and daddy when their baby was conceived. They enjoyed it. When she get in labor—another beautiful setup. I think the husband and wife should be by themselves durin the first stage of labor. That mother and daddy is together quietly by themselves at her beginnin of labor until labor get so severe.... Even though some of em get kinda skittish and want me to come right on. I tells em this. "It was you and yo husband in the beginning and it was fine. It's you and yo husband should be in the beginning at the birth a the baby, quiet and easy, talkin and lovin and happy with one another. You don't need nobody there. Me nor nobody else until a certain length a time." That's the reason I tell my patients, "When you get in labor, you call me when you think you in labor"—especially the ones right here in the city. "Let's have a telephone conversation befo I come cause that's beautiful for you and yo husband to be together. Then every so often befo I get there you call and let me know how you're coming on." And she will call me. Call me back in thirty minutes. Time yo pains and see how many you've had within the thirty minutes and if it be a good ways apart I says, "Well don't call me no mo until they start pickin up."

—Onnie Lee Logan, (midwife) from *Motherwit: An Alabama Midwife's Story*

✦ In colonial American villages and towns, childbirth was a strictly female ritual. The expectant mother would lay in a store of "groaning cakes" and "groaning beer" for the women who would gather when labor began. Midwife, neighbors, and kin stayed with her through her travail and for several days afterward, while her husband for once remained on the periphery.

The term midwife comes from the Anglo-Saxon *midwif* or "with-woman." In France, a midwife is *la sage femme*. Germans refer to her as *weise Frau* or *Hebamme*, mother's advisor, helper, or friend. In Portugal and Spain she is known as *comadre*.

The midwife's role is one of life-bringing import and her methods and techniques are as numerous and varied as the children she has attended over the centuries. Historically in the villages of Southeast Asia midwives delivered almost all the babies. Hawaiian midwives, called *kahunas*, can be  male or female. Some experienced kahunas were once believed to be able to project the labor pains onto another person, giving the mother a painless birth.

In Haiti midwives are attended by up to nine older women who represent the families of the mother and father. Nigerian mothers are attended by their grandmothers who act as midwives. In eighteenth-century Great Britain midwives were under the jurisdiction of the Church of England and had to take an oath before a minister to whom they were directly accountable.

I commune

Thoughts during the night before a planned cesarean section:

I wanted to focus my thoughts on what was going to happen, to direct my attention to childbirth and the experience of it. And so I spent a long evening happily studying…ancient birth incantations. As I read them, I felt the tradition of millennia of women who had given birth before me. I felt their strain and their joy and felt connected to the great cosmic process of renewal. My fears and anxieties about childbirth ceased to be the private emotions of an isolated woman and became, instead, a part of the grand challenge of human endeavors. My own short life span became extended by a spiritual communion with women past and future. I became tranquil and ready to marshall my will.

—Tikva Frymer-Kensky, from *Motherprayer: The Pregnant Woman's Spiritual Companion*

❖ **Martha Ballard, a midwife who kept an extensive diary of her life and work, attended 814 deliveries in the towns of Hallowell and Augusta, Maine. She began writing in 1785 at age fifty and continued until 1812. Her diary, kept during a period of time when few women left any written chronicles, is a heartfelt journal of the challenges of colonial American mothers.**

I cherish

We do not great things, we do only small things with great love.

—MOTHER TERESA

I cannot imagine a life without my children and that includes all six of them—those I gave birth to and those I didn't. I wouldn't want to live a life without them. Whoever they are, however many they are, they are different and special and unique and I love them. There is always room for them, and as much time as I can give them. Each one is special to me. If someone said you have two seconds to decide between your career and your kids, it wouldn't take past "one" to answer them: my children. May they always be as loved as they are now; it's the very best gift I can give them.

—Danielle Steel, from *Having a Baby*

MOTHERHOOD GODDESSES

In ancient Rome, a legion of goddesses presided over motherhood and childhood to protect the infant and assure the perpetuity of the race:
Abeona and Adiona: Protectresses of a child as he comes and goes. **Camoena:** Goddess who teaches children to sing. **Carna:** Goddess who strengthens the flesh of little children. **Cuba:** Goddess of children's sleep. **Cunina:** Protectress of the cradle and its contents. **Dea Mens:** Goddess of the child's mind. **Deus Catus Pater:** Father-god who "sharpens" the wits of children. **Diespiter:** Deity who brings the infant to the light of day. **Diva Edusa:** Goddess of the food of children. **Diva Potina:** Goddess of the drink of children. **Levana:** Goddess who lifts the child from the earth. **Minerva:** Goddess who gives memory to children. **Numeria:** Goddess who teaches children to count. **Ossipaga:** Goddess who hardens and solidifies the bones of little children. **Parca or Partula:** Goddess of childbirth. **Peragenor or Agenona:** Deity of a child's actions. **Rumina:** Goddess of the breast. **Dea Statina:** Goddess of a child's standing. **Venilia:** Goddess of hope, of "things to come." **Voleta and Volumnus:** Goddess and god of will or wishing.

I am new

Create each day anew by clothing yourself with heaven and earth, bathing yourself with wisdom and love, and placing yourself in the heart of Mother Nature.

—MORIHEI UESHIBE

RITUAL

Your needs as a woman are important to the well-being and growth of your family. Write down five activities, pursuits, or interests that you feel are important to maintain in the year following childbirth. Promise yourself that you will look at this list again in the months after your baby is born. This way you will not lose sight of the personal interests you want to integrate with motherhood.

We're connecting,
          foot under my rib.
I'm sore with life!
At night,

          your toes grow, Inches of the new!
The lion prowls the sky
and shakes his tail for you.
Pieces of moon
          fly by my kitchen window.
And your father comes
riding the lion's back
          in the dark,
to hold me,
     you,
          in the perfect circle of him.

I am new

Voluptuous against him, I am
nothing superfluous,
but all —
bones, bark of him, root of him take.
I am round
with his sprouting,
new thing new thing!

He wraps me.
The sheets are white.
My belly has tracks on it —
hands and feet
are moving
under this taut skin.
In snow, in light,
we are about to become!

—Kathleen Fraser, "Poems for the New"
from *In Defiance of the Rains*

❖87❖

I am family

For days, the woman wandered in and out of the slick rock maze. She drank from springs and ate the purple fruit of prickly pears…. All along the wash, clay balls had been thrown by a raging river. The woman picked one up, pulled off the pebbles until she had a mound of supple clay. She kneaded it as she walked, rubbed the clay between the palms of her hands, and watched it lengthen. She finally sat down on the moist sand and, with her fingers, continued moving up the string of clay. And then she began to coil it, around and around, pinching shut each rotation. She created a bowl.

The woman found other clay balls and put them inside the bowl. She had an idea of making dolls for her children, small clay figurines that she would let dry in the sun. Once again, she stopped walking and sat in the sand to work. She split each clay ball in two, which meant she had six small pieces to mold out of three balls she had found. One by one, tiny shapes took form. A girl with open arms above her head; three boys—one standing, one sitting, and one lying down (he was growing, she mused); and then a man and a woman facing each other. She had re-created her family.

—Terry Tempest Williams, from "The Bowl" from *Pieces of White Shell*

Family faces are magic mirrors. Looking at people who belong to us, we see the past, present, and future. —Gail Lumet Buckley

RAISING PARENTS

The word parent used to be considered a noun, but popular psychology has turned it into a verb. Adults used to "be" a parent rather than "do" the job, but today "parenting" has become a skill to master that results in successful children who are able to compete with other children. Our ancestors did not "parent"; they created a mutually responsible family based on reciprocity of caregiving. Children were not "raised"; they lived, worked and absorbed their values from within the family system. They were expected to contribute to the family and were obligated to help their parents, grandparents, and siblings to develop even as they themselves were cared for into maturity. In Polynesia this is still the approach to parenting. Hawaiians call it "family-ing," or *'ohana*.

—Paul Pearsall, from *The Pleasure Prescription: To Love, to Work, to Play—Life in the Balance*

I am protected

Sometimes, when I'm half-asleep or just waking up, I feel like a baby's spirit is hovering around me. I've never felt anything like this. No one I know has ever talked about it. Is it this baby's spirit? If so, I want it to know that I'm so glad it's chosen to come to me. I promise I'll be the best mother I can.

What will this baby be like? When we look at each other the first time, will we already know each other?

Just before sunset I saw a flock of geese flying north in a perfectly straight line. Sometimes I wish I could fly.

I wonder if every woman who's pregnant with her first baby feels like I do, that I'm the very first woman ever to feel what I am feeling?

I want to know what pregnancy is like for women in other parts of the world—not the modern world, but in tribes and villages. I don't feel like I belong where I am right now. So much pavement. Having to leave my home five days a week to go to work, where nobody talks about the kinds of things I want to talk about now, all the things I'm thinking and feeling.

I'm in a magic circle. No one can touch this life inside of me. We're protected.

—Suzanne Arms, from *Seasons of Change*

She made me a security blanket when I was born. That faded green blanket lasted just long enough for me to realize that the security part came from her.

—ALEXANDER CANE

❖ Among the prehistoric Batak tribes of Sumatra, a girl who was pregnant for the first time received a cloth made specially for her from her parents. Called a "soul cloth," it was covered with tiny designs that were used to foretell her future. She would rely on this cloth throughout her life, "as a guardian of her well-being." Its inherent revitalizing and protective powers were sought in the time of childbirth.

I renew

Whatever we cultivate in times of ease, we gather as strength for times of change.

—JACK KORNFIELD

❖ The word "obstetric" comes from the Latin word *obstare,* a verb meaning "to protect or stand by."

Most cultures have this concept: rest the body, hold the baby, stay in, let the milk flow. Strange day, when women expect to get back into slim clothes, at once, when nursing ties you down.

"Just stay right there," said my mother, bustling off to boil water for tea. In the next few days, she brought me tea with lemon, tea with milk and sugar, herbal tea, hot water with milk, barley soup, vegetable soup, chicken broth, seltzer and water and ginger ale and buttermilk and eggnog and chocolate milk shakes. Whenever she saw me pick up the baby to nurse, she pulled up a footstool for me. She brought a pillow. She positioned a makeshift table nearby and set a drinking vessel thereon.

"You have to get your strength back," my mother said.

"You have to keep up your fluids…" said my mother.

"…replace your calcium…"

"…keep your insides warm…"

"…make plenty of rich milk for the baby…"

"…she's on her schedule, not yours. Every twenty minutes if she wants it!"

"Let the laundry sit there," my mother said.

"Have some nice warm tea."

"Just get into bed and rest," said my mother.

"Take the baby with you."

These were the things her own mother, I believe, had said to her when I was born. I could liken the *bubbe*, my mother's mother, to a telegraph, transmitting information from a distant place: Poland, the *shtetl*, the old country. *Lign in kimpet*—that's what a woman did after childbirth, and the whole community mobilized to make sure she didn't have to do else but this.

—Elizabeth Ehrlich, from *Miriam's Kitchen*

I cradle

For the longest time I would wake up and go in to get her every morning. I'd stop at the threshold of her room and just look at her, at her skin, her hair, her eyes. I'd smile at her, and I'd wait for her to smile back, and it didn't matter how tired I was. I felt like I had won the lottery. It's like having a dream that something wonderful has happened to you. You wake up, and it hasn't, but this was like waking up and finding that something wonderful really has happened, and it keeps on happening.

The satisfaction is partly physical. Taking care of a baby means constant touching. In our culture you're almost never allowed to touch someone except in a sexual context. This is the one time when you can get enough of what you can never get enough of in the whole rest of your life—the holding, the kissing, the nuzzling, and the stroking. Not only that, you can get it in public. It's completely sanctioned.

The love is utterly uncomplicated. There are no strings attached. You can't give too much. You don't have to think about whether it is appropriate behavior. It's what

Above the rocking heads of the mothers
the blossom branches of the shepherds' stars
open again at night
singing in the warm sleep of children
the eternal transformations up to God
The homeless millennia
which since the burning of the temple roamed about
unloved in the hourglass of dust
break forth in new glory
in the children's beds
fresh branches of the trees surviving winter.

—Nelly Sachs, "Above the Rocking Heads of the Mothers," from *The Seeker and Other Poems*

you should be doing. Your complete mandate in the world is to hold this soft, cuddly, sweet little baby, and it just feels so good, the weight of a baby on your shoulder, or the way she fits against your body when you're nursing her. You get the feeling of union you long for your whole life. A baby is someone you can let your boundaries down to.

—Christina Day, from *Mothers Talking Sharing the Secret*

I receive

BIRTH STORY

I was practicing as a naturopath in my small clinic in one room of my two-room home in Solosa, Guatemala, 1973. I knew midwifery was next. My midwife and I were the only ones present at my son's birth the same year. She had arrived just in time to catch him. It was, and remains, the most precious moment of my life. I knew I had more karma with that. I had spoken with my neighbors about the local *comadrona.* One day I was walking back from the market with my son, Dov, on my back and she approached me. She was tiny, maybe four feet eight inches tall, thin, her unwrinkled skin tight across her high cheekbones, her grey hair in thin braids, and her sparkling black eyes meeting mine. She wore *traje* [traditional woven Mayan dress] from Solola. We were the only people on the path. An ancient comadrona and a gringa medicine woman. An odd couple.

Without an introduction, she grabbed me with her eyes and said, *"Tienes que aprender a recibir el nene."* "You will learn to receive the baby." (Not deliver, but receive!) And that's what we spent the next two and one-half years doing together.

—as told to Latifa Amdur and C.H., (Guatemala), *Native Wisdom for White Minds*

May your road be fulfilled.
Reaching to the road
of your sun father.
When your road is fulfilled,
In your thoughts
may we live.
May we be the ones whom
your thoughts will embrace,
For this on this day,
To our sun father,
We offer prayer meal.
To this end:
May you help us all
to finish our roads.

—FROM A ZUNI PRAYER, SPOKEN WHILE PRESENTING AN INFANT TO THE SUN

I am reborn

I am a woman giving birth to myself.

—Anonymous

[A]nd now I am very old, gently traversing my sixty-fifth year.... My old age is as chaste in thought as it is in deed. I have no regret for youth, no ambition for fame, and no desire for money, except that I would like to have a little to leave to my children and grandchildren. I have no complaints to make of my friends. My one sorrow is that humanity does not go forward fast enough.

My plan in jotting down these thoughts and feelings was based on a theory I once believed in. I used to imagine that I could pick up my own identity from time to time and carry it on. Can one thus resume one's self? Can one know one's self? Is one ever somebody? I don't know anything about it anymore. It now seems to me that one changes from day to day and that every few years one becomes a new being.

—George Sand, from *The Intimate Journal* *(1869)*

Their faces will shine like the sun, *and they are to be like the light of the* *stars that never die.* —2 Esdras 7:97

❖ The Hopis of North America believe that human beings first entered the world at an opening called *sipapu*. This event is reenacted in a celebration of rebirth called *wuwuchim,* held in secret every four years in a dome-shaped structure called a *kiva.* The kiva, considered to be Mother Earth herself, has a hole or sipapu in the center and a ladder leading up to an opening in the roof (the umbilical cord) and into the next world.

I am divine

If grains of sand can become a reflection of the divine, just think what can happen to the human being. —THE DALAI LAMA

The months of pregnancy are an ongoing experience of a truly awesome dimension of reality. Inside, beyond our sight, our bodies are doing something that is not quite within our ability to control....This our body does without conscious direction, through a power that transcends our cognitive mind. To me, this power is the immanent force of God, the presence of divine Presence....The making of another

human being should be an occasion for realizing the sacred holiness of all life. Pregnancy is an intensification of life itself, and all the many experiences of the Holy in human life are sharpened and condensed into the short months in which we engage the future within ourselves.

—Tikva-Frymer-Kensky, from *Motherprayer: The Pregnant Woman's Spiritual Companion*

✣ An old story links Maya, the mother of Buddha, with the sacred Sala tree. It was said that the tree recognized Maya's divinity and bent down to offer her its fruit and to support her while she brought forth her holy child.

General rules: To check her passions, not to sleep on one side but on both in turn, to wear a belt twelve or fourteen inches wide, sufficiently tied to support the hips without injuring the child and to take it off the moment she feels the first pains of childbirth; not to pay too much attention to the advice of the midwife who is always anxious to exaggerate the gravity of the case and to display her skill: for the child grows and falls like a ripe cucumber in due season. The child turns round in the womb and we must follow its movements. To have bread, we must let the corn grow. The accouchement may be rendered complicated by the weakness of the child, in that case the mother must lie in a horizontal position as being the most conducive to repose.

—from *Chinese Medical Review (1852)*, translated by Leonard Hegewald

I allow

Do not force nature, do not insult it, for it is as if you were to open the ears of corn to make the stalks grow. —CHINESE MEDICAL REVIEW (1852)

"You know how to act." For as long as I can remember, these are the words my mother would use whenever I left home. Whether it was to attend a seven-year-old's birthday party, a roller-skating night at twelve, my first date at sixteen, or even when I left home for college—that phrase, along with "I love you," always saw me on my way. In many ways the words symbolize the best apects of our relationship—trust, respect, and love.

As an adult, I think back on how amazing it is that this simple parting ritual so greatly impacted me. While many of my friend's mothers would send them off with mini-lectures extolling the virtues of etiquette and proper behavior, my mother only had to say one sentence. Those words held a sacred understanding and promise that my mother trusted me and believed in my ability to make good decisions. I know now that she worried every moment until she heard my feet crunching up the driveway, but she did not cloud my world with that fear and dread. She gave me the gift of freedom and self-assurance—a gift I hope to pass on.

—Ame Mahler Beanland

RITUAL

Wishing pod: Find a seed pod from any tree, or an eggshell. Write down your wishes for your baby on a piece of paper and decorate it to your liking. Place the paper in the pod or shell and bury it in a potted plant or under a tree, letting the wish go.

❖ In Japan, women who wish to conceive a child may be visited by the older women in their community, who mime the process of labor and birth. A doll is triumphantly held up at the moment of "birth" in this ritual beseeching the gods for the blessing of conception.

wonder

I see you salute
           from the skies
to the shimmering valley at dawn.
And I hear the long song of the rose-throated bird;
           your blessing for birth echoed clear.
           I know your sweet breath in the billowing clouds,
           swift whispers of daughters who mothered before.
           I sense every moment your spirit surrounds,
           where you end I begin, and my child begins, again.
           I run by the water emerging from far
           away where you waltz in my dreams
           and I shed, and I swim
           belly down near the shore,
           applauding, you rock us to sleep.

When I wake, I am born
           a mother today;
you cradle our child's first breath.
And I wonder how long you have traveled with me
and I bow with the trees
to your light   to your voice   to your wings   to your soul
           to your hands holding mine,
           remembering your walk on this earth.

ANDREA ALBAN GOSLINE

I wonder

A child's world is fresh and new and beautiful, full of wonder and excitement. It is our misfortune that for most of us that clear-eyed vision, that true instinct for what is beautiful and awe-inspiring, is dimmed and even lost before we reach adulthood. If I had influence with the good fairy who is supposed to preside over the christening of all children, I should ask that her gift to each child in the world be a sense of wonder so indestructible that it would last throughout life, as an unfailing antidote against boredom and disenchantments of later years, the sterile preoccupation with things that are artificial, the alienation from the sources of our strength.

— Rachel Carson, from *A Sense of Wonder*

Birth is the sudden opening of a window through which you look out upon a stupendous prospect.

—William Dixon

AMERICAN BIRTH AND INFANCY SUPERSTITIONS

❖ If a married woman is the first one to see a newborn baby, that woman will become a mother.

❖ If one finds a baby pacifier, there is going to be an addition to the family.

❖ A bright star in the sky means there will soon be a birth.

❖ Conceiving under the increase of the moon or in the moonlight means there will be a girl.

❖ A woman with child is always lucky.

❖ If a pregnant woman steps over a rope to which a horse is tied, she will be late delivering.

❖ Heartburn while pregnant means your child will have a full head of hair.

❖ If she is born on Christmas Day, your daughter will be able to speak with animals and spirits.

❖ A baby speaks with angels when it smiles.

❖ A daughter will be lucky if she resembles her father.

❖ If a baby teethes early, it is making way for a new baby.

I am freedom

I sat alone before my campfire one evening, watching, as the sunset colors deepened to purple, the sky slowly darkened, and the stars came out. A deep peace lay over the woods and waters. All at once the silence and the solitude were touched by wild music, thin as air, the faraway gabbling of geese flying at night.

Presently I caught sight of them as they streamed across the face of the moon, the high-excited clamor of their voices tingling through the night, and suddenly I saw, in one of those rare moments of insight, what it means to be wild and free. As they went over me, I was there with them, passing over the moonlit countryside, glorying with them in their strong-hearted journeying, exulting in its joy and splendor.

The haunting voices grew fainter and faded in the distance, but I sat on, stirred by a memory of something beautiful and ancient and now lost—a forgotten freedom we must all once have shared with other wild things, which only they and the wilderness can still recall to us, so that life becomes again, for a time, the wonderful, sometimes frightening, but fiercely joyous adventure it was intended to be.

—Martha Reben, from *Night Song*

Trusting that larger forces
than yourself are at work in your life,
you will give up the demand for
the outcome you think you want
and learn to appreciate whatever it is
you get. This is true freedom.

—Carol Orsborn

❖ When a woman is about to go into labor in households in Ireland, India, Siberia, and the Americas, family members set animals free, loosen their hair, and leave pots uncovered. These acts symbolize the removal of any obstructions during birth.

I am enlightened

Ahhh.... The sweet aroma of incense.... It beckons my memory to when I was little, watching my great grandmother burning incense and praying to Quan Yin (the Chinese Goddess of Mercy), Sahm Bo Fut (the Three Gods), and for the loss of her husband, Chung. She would put a little tiny spoon of cooked rice in three tiny bowls, and she would put tea in three other tiny cups. Also, she would put fruits and steamed chicken on the altar to pay her respects to the gods and goddesses of the kitchen. Gracefully, she would lean down and chant these words over and over again, holding her prayer beads: *"Na Mo Au Lae Tau Fut."* These words tingled in my ears so peacefully, and they sounded like a soothing lullaby.

I was determined to understand what she was doing. So I asked her what those peaceful words meant. [She explained:] The enlightenment and energy within....She said that she was praying for me to have health, happiness, and a good education.

—Jessica Oliver (age 11), from "Remembering MA-MA," from *Making More Waves*

Enlightenment is like the moon reflected on the water. The moon does not get wet, nor is the water broken. Although its light is wide and great, the moon is reflected even in a puddle an inch wide. The whole moon and the entire sky are reflected in dewdrops on the grass, or even in one drop of water.

Enlightenment does not divide you, just as the moon does not break the water. You cannot hinder enlightenment, just as a drop of water does not hinder the moon in the sky.

The depth of the drop is the height of the moon. Each reflection, however long or short its duration, manifests the vastness of the dewdrop, and realizes the limitlessness of the moonlight in the sky.

—Zen Master Dogen

✢ Egyptians and Babylonians considered it essential to step on sacred ground with bare feet, so as to absorb the holy influences from Mother Earth.

I am blissful

Many a summer morning have I crept out of the still house before anyone was awake, and, wrapping myself closely from the chill wind of dawn, climbed to the top of the high cliff called the Head to watch the sunrise. Pale grew the lighthouse flame before the broadening day as, nestled in a crevice at the cliff's edge, I watched the shadows

draw away and morning break. Facing the east and south, with all the Atlantic before me, what happiness was mine as the deepening rose-color flushed the delicate cloudflocks that dappled the sky, where the gulls soared, rosy too, while the calm sea blushed beneath. Or perhaps it was a cloudless sunrise with a sky of orange-red, and the sea-line silver-blue against it, peaceful as heaven. Infinite variety of beauty always awaited me, and filled me with an absorbing, unreasoning joy such as makes the song-sparrow sing—a sense of perfect bliss. Coming back in the sunshine, the morning-glories would lift up their faces, all awake, to my adoring gaze. Like countless rosy trumpets sometimes I thought they were, tossed everywhere about the rocks, turned up to the sky, or drooping toward the ground, or looking east, west, north, south, in silent loveliness. It seemed as if they had gathered the peace of the golden morning in their still depths even as my heart had gathered it.

—Celia Laighton Thaxter, from "Childhood on White Island," from *Among the Isles of Shoals*

Now may every living thing,
young or old,
weak or strong,
living near or far,
known or unknown,
living or departed or yet unborn,
may every living thing
be full of bliss.

—THE BUDDHA

❖ In ancient Greece, the moment a baby emerged into the world and the umbilical cord was cut, astrologers charted the lines into the heavens that connected the newborn with the primordial womb. Because astrology was connected with the moment of birth, and it was women who attended the birthings, it is surmised that many of the early astrologers were women.

I worship

Let the beauty we love be what we do.
There are a hundred ways to kneel
and kiss the ground. —RUMI

In Athens, where I grew up almost half a century ago, children were always the center of the household—worshiped by all in the family, treated, day in and day out, like extraordinary treasures bringing meaning to life.

My mother, whose family had fled Russia during the 1917 revolution, was captured by the Germans when she joined the anti-Nazi Greek resistance during World War II. She has never stopped being grateful for little things.

She always has had a passion for marathon midnight cooking—culinary binges that range from Russian piroshki to Greek stuffed grape leaves—and marathon reading sessions in psychology and the Greek classics.

"Angels fly because they take themselves lightly," she used to tell me.

After she left my philandering father, she sold everything to pay for our schooling—from the heirloom carpet spirited out of the Caucasus to her last pair of gold earrings. She sent me to Cambridge and my sister Agapi to the Royal Academy of Dramatic Arts. But far beyond an education, she gave us what I now know are the greatest gifts a mother can give her child: her attention, her energy, her unconditional loving.

—Arianna Huffington, from "For daughter and the grandkids, it's Yaya Day"

Remember, remember the sacredness of things
Running streams and dwellings
The young children within the nest
A hearth for sacred fire
The holy flame of fire

—PAWNEE SONG

I rejoice

Let thy father and thy mother be glad,
And let her that bore thee rejoice.

— PROVERB

BIRTH STORY

The last stages [of labor] were spectacular. Ah, what an incomparable thrill. All that heaving, the amazing damp slippery wetness and hotness, the confused sight of dark gray ropes of cord, the blood, the baby's cry. The sheer pleasure of the feeling of a born baby on one's thighs is like nothing on earth....

After the surprising delight of birth, other pleasures followed in their multitudes. Feeding, smiling, gazing. I actually remember feeling delight, at two o'clock in the morning, when the baby woke for his feed, because I so longed to have another look at him. Comfortable holding and carrying; babies fitted so well against one and seemed to like it there so much, how could one not enjoy it oneself? And when they are a few months old, they lie and look around and wave and smile and undergo a constant gentle agitation, as though they were sea anemones, gently waving in some other element, delicately responding to currents we cannot feel.

— Margaret Drabble, from "With All My Love, (Signed) Mama"

PAGAN BLESSING OF THE CHILD

FATHER: Behold this lovely child, conceived and brought forth in love. Bless and protect her and grant her the gifts of wisdom, inspiration and wonder.

MOTHER: Hail Earth, Mother of all, this is my infant, my love, and my jewel. Bless and protect her; Grant her your eternal strength. May she have a spirit that seeks the stars, and keeps its roots within your breast. May she never know hunger of body, heart, or soul. May she have the life force always strong within her. May she be infused with love for all living things. Protect her and bless her with wisdom, courage, and a sense of humor.

FATHER: The atoms from which you are made were forged in the heart of vanished stars. Always remember this, and know how small you are, how fragile, and how short the sum of human years. But stand in awe of life; the wonder of its complexity, the miracle that it exists, and remarkable human capacity to contemplate its mysteries.

ELDEST MOTHER PRESENT: We welcome this child into our midst, and welcome this mother into the company of mothers — givers of life and preservers of our species.

NEW MOTHER: I am blessed today with this child and take my place in the company of mothers.

— adapted by Anne Carson, from *Spiritual Parenting in the New Age*

I marvel

In all things of nature there is something of the marvelous. —ARISTOTLE

BIRTH STORY

Immediately on our arrival in Hamburg I became with child, and my mother along with me. In good time the Lord gracefully delivered me of a young daughter. I was still a mere girl, and unused as I was to bearing children, it naturally went hard with me; yet I rejoiced mightily that the Most High had bestowed on me a healthy, lovely baby.

My dear good mother had reckoned her time for the same day. However, she had great joy in my being brought to bed first, so she could help me a little, young girl that I was. Eight days later my mother likewise brought forth a young daughter in childbirth. So there was neither envy nor reproach between us, and we lay next to each other in the self-same room. But, Lord, we had no peace from the people that came running in to see the marvel, a mother and daughter together in childbed.

—Gluckel of Hameln, from *Fragments from Her Memoirs (1646-1724)*

❖ The analogy of a person's lifespan to a thread goes beyond length and fragility to the very act of creation. Women create thread from the raw material of wool or cotton; they seem to pull it out of nowhere, just as they produce babies seemingly from out of nowhere. The same image is latent in the term lifespan: span is from the verb spin, which originally meant to "draw out, stretch long."

I am the mystery

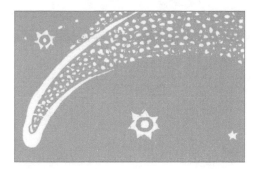

The mystery of conception has puzzled humans since the dawn of time. Ever since our hairy ancestors on the savannah plains first scratched their heads with emergent philosophical musings, people throughout history and all over the world have come up with answers that poetically express the sense of miracle we still feel when we realize we have made a baby.

In rarefied moments of silence, when dawn light filters gently through the canopy of an Amazon forest, or grey mist hangs thick and heavy on a Scottish coast, or an African night sky explodes with a flurry of shooting stars over a parched desert, simple questions can resonate in the wind: Where do we come from? Are we sent by God?... Do we come from the sky or from the earth?

—from *Mamatoto: A Celebration of Birth*

Before the seventeenth century, the scientific community felt that a woman could not conceive unless she achieved orgasm during intercourse—a woman's pleasure was tied to the viability of the sperm and successful fertilization. But during the seventeenth century scientists discovered that fertilization happened independently of a woman's sexual pleasure. Men were let off the hook, much to the dismay of their wives!

Later in the century, doctors "discovered" that women could be impregnated by the wind. One aristocratic woman of the time claimed she gave birth to a son she conceived during a dream while her husband was away. She was accused of infidelity, but a doctor came to her defense, explaining, "Her window being open, her blanket in disorder, the zephyr from the southwest, regularly impregnated with the organic molecules of human insects, of floating embryos, had fertilized her."

I know

Every birth is a getting to know.

—PAUL CLAUDEL

Learn to respect this sacred moment of birth, as fragile, as fleeting, as elusive as dawn. This child is there, hesitant, tentative, unsure which way he's about to go. He stands between two worlds.

For heaven's sake don't touch him, don't push him, unless you want him to fall. Let him wait until he feels the time is right.

Have you ever watched a bird take flight? As he's still walking, he's heavy, awkward, his wings drag, and then suddenly he's flying, graceful, elegant and free. He was the son of earth, now he's the child of the skies.

Can you say when he left one kingdom for the other? It is so subtle, the eye can hardly catch it. As subtle as stepping in, or out, of time, to be born, or to die.

What of the tide, which imperceptibly, irresistibly rises, only to fall. At what moment did it turn? Is your ear sharp enough to hear the ocean breathe?

Yes, this birth, this wave parted from wave, born from the sea without ever leaving her. Don't ever touch it with your rough hands. You understand nothing of its mysteries. But the child, the drop from this ocean, knows.

—Frederick Leboyer, from *Birth without Violence*

MOTHER KNOWS

haha ga ima yu-koto
sono uchi ni
wakatte kuru

What your mother tells you
now
in time
you will come to know.

—MITSUYE YAMADA, "WHAT YOUR MOTHER TELLS YOU NOW" FROM *CAMP NOTES AND OTHER POEMS*

RITUAL

Give the gift of your self to your child. As you continue to grow in self-knowledge and awareness, share with your children what is best in you. Make time for quiet meditation to see and feel what you want to share right now.

I bond

The sweetest flowers in all the world – a baby's hands.

—SWINBURNE

Exploring feelings and memories of your own birth may help you welcome your baby to life. Write your own birth story, including your impressions of your mother's experience of childbirth. After your baby's birth, compose the story of his arrival and its impact on your body and spirit. Write the story as a letter to your baby, describing images and feelings of your bonding time.

Women sit upon the moss
cleansing their bodies
of monthly bleeding
to bond with Mother Earth.

They used to sit in lodges
for revered privacy
to relish their time
with the Earth Mother.

Afterbirth was returned
to the Earth Mother
to bond with whom
we had come from.

A child's umbilical cord
was buried in Mother Earth
to bond the child
to its true Mother.

Such bonding made us one
with the Creation
and gave understanding of
the Sacredness of Mother Earth.

—SkyBlue Mary Morin (Cree ancestry), from "Bonding with Mother Earth," from *Writing the Circle: Native Women of Western Canada*

I am open

I was long and slender like a tube, except around that magic place where it was dense and packed. There was a tenderness, a tenuousness, a tenseness there. Some new muscle was working to hold me open. I could feel the hardness of my baby's head against my stretched skin. I wasn't worried anymore. I was hard at work. Pushing. Pushing my baby out, down the birth canal and into the world. Everything is compressed for maximum energy. I merge my nose with my mouth my chin with my neck my breasts with my stomach merging them all into a great pushing machine. Work and rest. Puffing and panting like a locomotive, trying to coordinate my pushing with my breathing. The heat of work. I can smell myself. Know nothing. Feel pressure below. I lift myself up and onto the pressure and push on it, bear down on the hard thing inside me that wants to come out. Once, twice, three times. And collapse. I make many mistakes until finally it is going like a great machine; steaming, driven. PUSH HERE. PUSH NOW. GOOD. GOOD. HOLD IT. DON'T PUSH. I pant, pant, pant, pant blow out a pellet of wind, out out out out. I hold the head with the thin, stretched muscles I've found, feeling it, actually feeling the presence of my baby's head at my core. I have stretched wide as the room. I'm completely open. I am the Birth Window and everyone is looking in.

—Stephanie Mines, from *Two Births*

Where does one read a deeper tale than upon the most perfectly printed page of the most precious book? Upon the blank page. —ISAK DINESEN

I introduce

First keep the peace within yourself, then you can also bring it to others.

—THOMAS À KEMPIS

When Charlie first saw our child, our Mary, he said all the proper things for a new father. He looked upon the poor little red thing and blurted, "She's more beautiful than the Brooklyn Bridge." On subsequent viewing when we three were alone, he stared at her long and solemnly and then said an odd thing, "We have given her birth and death and that's about all we can give her, really." I thought it morbid at the time because I was feeling all-powerful, as women do after childbirth. He was right, of course. It was life that would give her everything of consequence, life would shape her, not we. All we were good for was to make the introductions. We could introduce her to sights and sounds and sensations. How these reacted on her we must leave to her own private self. It is hard to accept this back-ground position, and like most parents, we do not do it very well at all times. But we did at least understand our roles, and that is a step toward a passing performance.

—Helen Hayes, from *A Gift of Joy*

GOOD-LUCK CHARMS

❖ The portuguese sew bits of garlic into the hems of a baby's clothes as a way of protecting her against evil.

❖ Bavarians throw a gold coin into the infant's first bath to ensure future prosperity.

❖ In Yorkshire, England, when a newborn first visits someone's home, the host sprinkles salt on the tip of the baby's tongue for good luck.

—Colleen Gardephe, from *Parenting*

I celebrate

My first child was a son, tiny and pink with a dear little head covered with red-gold fuzz. Nothing compared to the heart-tugging sweetness of cradling my newborn son—unless it was the equally lovely feeling of cuddling my little golden, brown-eyed daughter.

Now parents themselves, those two have brought me little but happiness, pride, and satisfaction. With my sixtieth birthday fast approaching, I reflect on a life immensely enriched by their gift to me of their own small children. Here truly is happiness beyond measure.

When he was less than two hours old, I held my only grandson—my son's first child. I cannot express the utter fullness of that moment. And later my daughter and son-in-law asked me to be with them when their two little girls were born. How does a mother—a grandmother—explain the ineffable joy of helping her daughter deliver a daughter of her own?

For grandmothers, the happiest reward is shedding the responsibility of seeing to the teeth-brushing, room-tidying, and rule-abiding; these duties dissolve, replaced by giggling, cookie-making, and tea-party planning. A grandmother gets to share the delight and wonder of watching the little ones grow and learn, stretch and explore—with the lagniappe of time to enjoy, to indulge, to say Yes! And to simply stop and hug them. Our years, and the sleepless nights and mistakes in our own child-rearing, have taught us the importance of stepping away from our chores to listen. In understanding this, we reap the blessings of a richer life. If my children are my life's golden diadem, my grandchildren are the jewels in that crown.

—Barbara Brock Moller

❖ Ancient Egyptians were the first to adopt the idea of birthday celebrations, which later became a part of Greek culture. The Persians, renowned among ancient confectioners, added the custom of a sweet birthday cake to commemorate the occasion. The writer Philochorus reported that worshipers of Artemis, goddess of the moon and the hunt, celebrated her birthday on the sixth day of every month by baking a large cake of flour and honey, topped with lighted candles. This signified moonlight, the goddess' earthward radiance.

The custom of serving a birthday cake reemerged among German peasants in the Middle Ages. The cake became part of their Kinderfest, held specifically for a young child, or *kind*. The Kinderfest began at dawn when the birthday child was awakened by the arrival of a cake topped with lighted candles. The number of candles totaled one more than the child's age, the additional one representing the "light of life."

I am intuitive

Standing up in her lodge, Thea could with her thumb nail dislodge flakes of carbon from the rock roof—the cooking-smoke of the Ancient People. They were that near! A timid, nest-building folk, like the swallows. How often Thea remembered Ray Kennedy's moralizing about the cliff cities. He used to say that he never felt the hardness of the human struggle or the sadness of history as he felt it among those ruins. He used to say, too, that it made one feel an obligation to do one's best. On the first day that Thea climbed the water trail she began to have intuitions about women who had worn the path, and who had spent so great a part of their lives going up and down it. She found herself trying to walk as they must have walked, with a feeling in her feet and knees and loins which she had never known before—which must have come up to her out of the accustomed dust of that rocky trail. She could feel the weight of an Indian baby hanging onto her back as she climbed.

—Willa Cather, from *The Song of the Lark*

✤ When an infant laughs for the fist time, the Navajos exchange gifts to mark the occasion. The person who made the baby laugh hosts the party.

Learning to understand our dreams is a matter of learning to understand our heart's language.

—ANN FARADAY

✤ A newborn knows many ways to share her thoughts with you. Pay close attention to the way she reaches out to you, looks inquisitively, protests, gurgles joyfully. These subtle movements and expressions will teach you much about her inner life. Notice how intently she listens to the stories you read and prefers to hear over and over those you read during the weeks before her birth.

I am complete

RITUAL

Place the ultrasound picture of your baby where you can look at it every day. Repeat this affirmation: "My baby is whole and healthy." Picture your vital baby in your mind's eye. Envision all his body parts moving synchronously and with vigor.

You appeared before me, so secure in the support of our doctor's lean hand that it was quite invisible. You alone were there, pale and composed, your flesh undisturbed by the short journey you had just made, even though it was the most important of your life. Yellow moisture clung to the down of your tiny forehead, and yet your brown hair, so surprisingly abundant, curled dry, close against your ears. Your fists were pressed at your chest as if you did not yet know you could open out the fingers. It was the movement of your lips that most impressed me. They curved in a small bow. You seemed to turn your head — although it must have merely bobbed away from the finger bracing it — and as it moved your lips curled upward in discovery, suddenly aware of the feel of some new element. Your tongue made a smack inside, and your lips parted and admitted your first breath of life. You sucked the air inside, and released it with a vocal sound.

—Charlotte Painter, from *Who Made the Lamb*

Motherhood is the most striking and beautiful aspect of the female character, providing the fulfillment of a woman's physiological and moral destiny.

—*GODEY'S LADY'S BOOK*, NINETEENTH CENTURY

Native Americans teach that we are linked to the earth through an invisible umbilical cord centered in the belly, one or two finger-widths below the navel....By practicing a breath exercise called "toning the belly," we can increase our receptivity to the subliminal messages constantly entering us through this psychic channel:

With your mouth closed, inhale through your nose to the bottom of your lungs, then expel the air....

Center your awareness in the belly and begin sensing the subtle impressions of the world around you. When you encounter a hummingbird or a willow tree, for example, let your awareness descend from the intellectual, observing mind to "Mother's Mind" below the waist, where you will effortlessly receive intuitive knowledge....

In a related exercise, lie in a prone position on your stomach on a favorite plot of ground for 15 minutes while visualizing a golden cord running from your belly into the heart of the earth. Afterward, turn over on your back for the same period of time, experiencing the sky realm of wind and sunlight through the belly.

—Ronald S. Miller, from *As Above, So Below*

I am mindful

As a woman lives so shall she give birth.

—GAYLE PETERSON

Pregnancy is a natural time to begin or deepen the practice of mindfulness. The increasingly dramatic changes that occur in our bodies and in our very perceptions, thoughts, and emotions invite new degrees of wakefulness, wonder, and appreciation. For some of us, being pregnant may be the first time we experience being fully in our body.

The changes in our body are of interest not only to ourselves but often to people around us. We are constantly reminded of our special state of being by the reactions we get from other people, ranging from warm inquiries to unasked-for advice to sudden pats on the belly.

The myriad physical and emotional changes we experience give us unique opportunities throughout pregnancy to work intimately with many aspects of mindfulness practice—paying attention to our experience, being fully present, being aware of our expectations, cultivating acceptance, kindness, and compassion, particularly toward ourself and our baby, experiencing feelings of deep interconnectedness.

—Myla and Jon Kabat-Zinn, from *Everyday Blessings*

I evolve

Where the day takes you. This is life as a mother.
For my children have taught me that what evolves on
its own is usually far more interesting than anything
I might have thought to plan. —Jennifer Graham Billings

❖ In Korea, certain dream symbols are said to suggest the sex of the fetus. A boy is sure to be born if the mother dreams of suns, persimmons, red peppers, carp, dragons, snakes, tigers, horses, or pigs. It's a girl if the dreams contain flowers, apples, butterflies, cherries, strawberries, shellfish, owls, rabbits, jewels, or hens.

Having grown up in Hawaii, a land of perpetual summer, it was only upon being schooled in New England that I came to experience four seasons. When my first-born arrived thirty days before a Columbus Day due date, it wasn't so much fall that I noticed. Rather, it was the surprise of his early appearance. Afterwards I gained a whole new view of the linear calendar brought alive by baby's first smile, baby's first tooth, his crawling, talking, walking, and all the precious moments in between. Not until the April birth of my second son did I begin to knowingly resonate to the circular rhythms of seasonal time.

To give birth in the spring is to be at one with Mother Nature herself, for no matter where the new mother looks, she is in the company of birth and rebirth. It is an alignment which causes her to know first-hand that her task is to bring forth the species. The awareness is both breathtaking in its magnitude and humbling in its generosity. It assures her place in the universe, a link in the chain unbroken since human life began. The ongoing gift of a spring-born child is that his every birthday reminds his mother of the life cycle of which she is an integral part. It is the birth that continues to renew.

—Yvonne Mendonca Johns

I am curious

I have seen
A curious child, who dwelt upon a tract
Of inland ground, applying to his ear
The convolutions of a smooth-lipped shell,
To which, in silence hushed, his very soul
Listened intensely; and his countenance soon
Brightened with joy, for from within were heard
Murmurings, whereby the monitor expressed
Mysterious union with its native sea.
Even such a shell the universe itself
Is to the ear of Faith; and there are times,
I doubt not, when to you it doth impart
Authentic tidings of invisible things;
Of ebb and flow, and ever-enduring power;
And central peace, subsisting at the heart
Of endless agitation.

—William Wordsworth, from *The Excursion*,
Book IV, Line 1132

*There is an amazed
curiosity in every young
mother. It is strangely
miraculous to see and to
hold a living being formed
within oneself and issued
forth from oneself.*

—Simone De Beauvoir

MOON TIME

My woman's blood and the moon have been linked since the beginning of time. It was most likely the congruence of moon cycle and women's bleeding cycle that birthed the idea of marking time.

Time (bleeding time), moon and women have been connected since ancient days. Bleeding, whether monthly or at birthing, was a sacred time in women's lives. A time in which women attended and nurtured each other. A time for connection with the divine—with the Earth who birthed us all and with each other. Such a sacred time was a holy day (holiday). Women rested from everyday activity and gathered in the woods to give their blood back to the Mother Earth. If there were those for whom bleeding was uncomfortable, these women were tended to, comforted and touched by others. It was a time for fun, for celebration, for silence, for being with oneself, for being with other women whose bleeding was also sacred. This was a holy time in their lives.   —Antiga, from *The Goddess Celebrates*

I imagine

I once read that a prospective parent becomes pregnant from the very moment that he or she imagines conceiving a child. At first that sounded a bit obscure, but over time it made better sense. With the first thought of bringing a new soul into the world, the parent assumes the responsibility of bearing and rearing that soul. God entrusts each parent with that responsibility, as the ultimate goal of parenting should always be to raise the God consciousness of their child such that the child may find self-realization, love of god, and peace in the world. So upon the first thought of conceiving a child, the pregnancy or the process of birth begins, both for the parent and for the child.

—John-Ambarisa Mendell Shields, from "How Parents Can Help a Child's Understanding of Spirituality," from *Spiritual Mothering Journal*

RITUAL

Imagine the world as seen and heard through your baby's eyes and ears. Let go of your own viewpoint for a moment. Try this upon arising every day to remind you of who this baby is and how he will experience his world.

*Woman is
the artist
of the imagination
and the child
in the womb
is the canvas
whereon she painteth
her pictures.*

—PARACELSUS
(1493-1541)

I am solemn

I knew I was in for a new wave of missing him. Dad would have loved to have seen me pregnant, to have served me heaping platefuls of food and, down the road, to have tickled and teased a grandson or granddaughter....He'd have shown off baby photos. When they were old enough, he'd have even played monster with them....

He most certainly would have wanted to know. So I decided to tell him. Rob was making dinner, and I went into our room and sat up in bed.

"Dad?" I said. Was it softly or silently? "Dad? I'm pregnant." I looked at his photo on my night table. "I'm pregnant and you're going to live on in my child.... He's going to know what he's missing, but also what he has of you."...

I wished I could believe that dad could look out from the framed photos I have of him and see, not just that life goes on, but that his life would go on. That I was going to have a baby who would inherit his Russian blood....If only Dad could be there for the first smile, first word, first step—I wanted him to know how welcome he'd be.

I touched his photo and said, "Look down on us if you can."

—Carol Weston, *From Here to Maternity*

If one but realized it, with the onset of the first pangs of birth pains, one begins to say farewell to one's baby. For no sooner has it entered the world, when others begin to demand their share. With the child at one's breast, one keeps the warmth of possession a little longer. —Princess Grace of Monaco

I am the passage

I relive birth each time I go to the ocean. The rhythms are the same. The waves approach and crest and break just as labor contractions build and peak and subside within you. There is the same crash, a ritual violence. The shore, like the pelvis, is racked with each onslaught. But when the great ellipse recedes, the sand sparkles and throbs, bejeweled and enlivened. You, the woman, are strengthened and intact and are one wave-crest nearer to bearing a child. At the ocean's edge I also think of the microcosmic sea within the sac and the fish-amphibian-mammal journey traced in development by the growing fetus. Life is a sea and its theme, destruction and creation, pain and joy, is played over and over, exquisitely varied as in the process of birth.

—Melisa Cassell, from *Written by Parents, 9 months, 1 day, 1 year*

Birth is not a beginning… the true beginning is at conception. Nor is birth an ending. It is more nearly a bridge between two stages of life, and although the bridge is not a long one, a child crosses it slowly, so that his body may be ready when he steps off at the far end.

—ASHLEY MONTAGU,
FROM *LIFE BEFORE BIRTH*

CONTEMPLATION

The nine months of pregnancy are a perfect time to reflect on the common ground that you now share with your own mother. Even if your relationship is tenuous, you can still indulge in a heartfelt communion with her. Just as you excitedly anticipate your baby's arrival and dream about your family's future, so did your own mother. You are walking in her shoes.

If it is not possible to speak with your mother, choose another special woman in your life with whom to share this sacred time. Many of the issues you struggle with, your worries, hopes, and joys, are certain to be the same as those she experienced. Communicating your feelings can help you bond with your mother just as you are bonding with your baby, in a wondrous circular process.

You might want to write your mother a letter or share a poem with her to express your appreciation. Use this common ground to strengthen and deepen your friendship with her.

I am daughter

I knew a beautiful woman once. And she was my mother. I knew a tenderness once. And it was my mother's. Oh, how happy I was to be loved.

And now I mourn her. I mourn that cornerstone. I mourn her caring. I mourn the one who always hoped for me. I mourn her lost image of me. The lost infant in myself. My lost happiness. I mourn my own eventual death. My life now is only mine….

Every blade, every leaf, every seed in my portion of the world has shifted. Your presence hovers everywhere, over house, over garden, over dreams, over silence. You are within me. I'll not lose you.

Once I was born. Can I be born again? Oh, wean me from pain to love. Help me to use your love and strength in my own life. Help me to carry my world.

—Toby Talbot, from *A Book About My Mother*

❖ Ancient Egyptians worshiped the placenta "born" along with each pharaoh. It was considered the unformed twin of the baby. The royal placenta bore the name of the moon god, Khonsu, especially when the king himself bore the name of the sun. Special preparations were made for disposing of the placenta, such as burying it under the house in which it was "born" so that the women of the house would receive its spirit and give birth to more children.

Somehow it was like I had been born again. Maybe that's what gives a woman strength when she finds out she's pregnant. At least some part of her will go on.

—Ann Cornelisen

I release

In the pursuit of learning
one knows more every day.
In the pursuit of the way
one does less every day.
Less and less until one does
nothing at all. And when
one does nothing there is
nothing that's left undone.

—FROM THE TAO TE CHING

Newborn, on the naked sand
Nakedly lay it.
Next to the earth mother,
That it may know her;
Having good thoughts of her, the food giver.

Newborn, we tenderly
In our arms take it,
Making good thoughts.
House-god, be entreated,
That it may grow from childhood to manhood,
Happy, contented;
Beautifully walking
The trail to old age.
Having good thoughts of the earth its mother,
That she may give it the fruits of her being.

Newborn, on the naked sand
Nakedly lay it.

—Grande Pueblo song sung by the person who
first takes a baby from her mother

✤ In Bali, the baby's umbilical cord is
placed in a special carved box and kept
by the mother until the child is old
enough to leave home. At that time, the
cord is given to the grown child as a symbol of this time when the figurative cord
is cut between mother and child.

I am extraordinary

BIRTH STORY

"Did you hear what the doctor said, Maudie?" chattered Belva. "You've got a daughter." "Well, she's a little beauty, isn't she!" she cried. She had not expected a handsome child.

Maud Martha's thoughts did not dwell long on the fact of the baby. There would be all her life long for that. She preferred to think, now, about how well she felt. Had she ever in her life felt so well? She felt well enough to get up. She folded her arms triumphantly across her chest, as another young woman, her neighbor to the rear, came in.

"Hello, Mrs. Barksdale!" she hailed. "Did you hear the news? I just had a baby, and I feel strong enough to go out and shovel coal! Having a baby is nothing, Mrs. Barksdale. Nothing at all."

"Aw, yeah?" Mrs. Barksdale smacked her gum admiringly. "Well, from what I heard back there a while ago, didn't seem like it was nothing. Girl, I didn't know anybody could scream that loud." Maud Martha tittered. Oh, she felt fine.

The doctor brought the baby and laid it in the bed beside Maud Martha. Shortly before she had heard it in the kitchen—a bright delight had flooded through her upon first hearing that part of Maud Martha Brown Phillips expressing itself with a voice of its own. But now the baby was quiet and returned its mother's stare with one that seemed equally curious and mystified but perfectly cool and undisturbed.

—Gwendolyn Brooks, from *The Courtship and Motherhood of Maud Martha*

Rose says that this is the day. I'm dubious. After all, there have been no clarion cries from the heavens, no storks seen fleeting against the still wintery sky. It's much too ordinary a day for such a remarkable event as the birth of our baby.

—MARTIN PAULE

I am fire

I learned from the age of two or three that any room in our house, at any time of day, was there to read in, or to be read to. My mother read to me. She'd read to me in the big bedroom in the mornings, when we were in her rocker together, which ticked in rhythm as we rocked, as though we had a cricket accompanying the story. She'd read to me in the dining room on winter afternoons in front of the coal fire, with our cuckoo clock ending the story with "Cuckoo," and at night when I'd got in my own bed. I must have given her no peace. Sometimes she read to me in the kitchen while she sat churning, and the churning sobbed along with any story.

She could still recite [the poems in McGuffey's Readers] in full when she was lying helpless and nearly blind, in her bed, an old lady. Reciting, her voice took on resonance and firmness, it rang with the old fervor, with ferocity even. She was teaching me one more, almost her last, lesson: emotions do not grow old. I knew that I would feel as she did, and I do.

—Eudora Welty, from *One Writer's Beginnings*

❖ During the fifth month of gestation, Chinese babies are believed to receive the fire essence, which becomes the *qi*, or life-force. Pregnant women are advised at this time to awaken early, bathe, wear clean clothes, inhabit a clean house, and, in the morning, inhale the heavenly brightness.

FIRE REST

Tribal societies around the world have traditionally used heat to comfort and treat the post-partum mother. In Thailand, an intense form of heat therapy was practiced after childbirth in a ritual called the "fire rest." For one to two weeks after giving birth, the mother would stay in a secure room and lie by a fire day and night. The baby stayed with her in a crib away from the fire and was fed whenever he or she cried. In Vietnam, a small charcoal stove was put under the bed of the mother and child for a month. In the Solomon Islands, birth assistants wrapped warm leaves around the mother's midsection. Tahitians gave the mother a sweatbath two days after birth, followed by a bath in the ocean. The Hopi of Arizona heated sand, then covered it in sheepskin for the mother to relax on. Zuni mothers and babies were privy to fresh warm sand beds every day for up to twelve days.

I am the icon

Amid the nodding roses sits a slender girl in blue, the book of Isaiah on her knee. Under her foot, the serpent's head is bruised. The moon beneath her reflects the light above. Dawn entwines her hair. In the stillness, aromatic with cedar, a dove coos. Then, in the breeze of morning, in a flutter, Mary is not alone. She looks up, astonished. The seal falls away from the book. She understands.

Mary is the chosen one. She had learned the news. In a moment's hesitation, a line appears between her brows, for the end is nailed upon the beginning. Choice. She sees it plain. Must it be? Time stands still. The dove is silent. Heaven and earth await her...

Yes!

Accepting her lot, she is transfigured. Gladly will she mother a baby. Her heart is full. With happiness she says yes to the white-lilied, winged messenger who interrupted her reading. Yes, I will. There is no withholding: her simple heart sings one note. She agrees. Blooming with yes, she is fragrant with grace. I accept. Thy will be done.

—Kathleen Riordan Speeth, from "The Madonna" from *To Be a Woman*

In [the] ages when women felt the religious significance of giving birth—just as men felt the religious significance of going into battle—they so frequently regarded the act as a great, mystical freeing of the life from the womb—not merely a birth but a resurrection—that they completely lost consciousness of pain, just as men were sometimes unconscious of their wounds in exhilaration of battle.

—CHARLOTTE, FROM
TELL GOOD HOUSEKEEPING, JULY 1915

I explore

[W]hen I think of the best things in life...I look back upon my almost couvade-like concern with our baby. You remember the discoveries we made (supposedly made by all parents): the perfect shape of the miniature fingernails of the hand you silently showed me as it lay, stranded starfishwise, on your palm; the epidermic texture of limb and cheek, to which attention was drawn in dimmed, faraway tones, as if the softness of touch could be rendered only by the softness of distance; that swimming, sloping, elusive something about the dark-bluish tint of the iris which seemed still to retain the shadows it had absorbed of ancient, fabulous forests where there were more birds than tigers and more fruit than thorns, and where, in some dappled depth, man's mind had been born; and, above all, an infant's first journey into the next dimension, the newly established nexus between eye and reachable object, which the career boys in biometrics or in the rat-maze racket think they can explain. It occurs to me that the closest reproduction of the mind's birth obtainable is the stab of wonder that accompanies the precise moment when, gazing at a tangle of twigs and leaves, one suddenly realizes that what had seemed a natural component of that tangle is a marvelously disguised insect or bird....

—Vladimir Nabokov, from *Speak, Memory*

Any adult who spends even fifteen minutes with a child outdoors finds himself drawn back to his own childhood, like Alice falling down the rabbit hole.

—Sharon MacLatchie

In Japan she was made as happy to see carrots and lettuce growing in the fields as she was to see sunlight, years earlier, pouring into the streets of New York City. Everywhere she's been she's seen people eating and sleeping and working and making things with their hands and urging things to grow.

—Carol Shields

I am the garden

Trust is the foundation of human relationships. This trust is generated not only by spoken messages but also by a meaningful look, a touch, a hug, a kiss, lifting a child on your lap, holding his hand, or simply laying your hand on her shoulder. In the photograph of the mother cradling her infant against her face, I note the gentleness with which the child is held and see the unconditional love reflected in the mother's eyes. I can almost feel the baby's sense of well-being and contentment. Properly and lovingly nurtured, this bond of trust between parent and child begets a spirit of compassion and kindness and a sense of security that grace a lifetime.

We all need to know that we can depend on someone. This is especially true of children, who trust adults for their well-being. Their trust, however, evokes from us a responsibility. One doesn't plant a garden and sit back and watch it grow. The plants need patience, care, watering, and weeding. Children likewise need protection, shelter, clothing, nourishment, guidance, encouragement, and love. They need an environment where they are comfortable, are not afraid to take risks, can develop self-confidence, are able to interact with others, and can enjoy life.

—Sister Carol Ann Nawracaj, from *Treasures from Heaven, The Gift of Children*

According to many of the world's myths, Paradise was a garden and the human race originated in that sacred place. According to the Bible, Adam and Eve, the first parents, inhabited the lush Garden of Eden. A more ancient creation myth tells of the first man and woman, who were born from trees and resided in a heavenly garden.

Other legends speak of a divine tree whose branches composed the sky and whose fruits formed the stars. The sacred literature of India tells of the Garden of Indra, where the gods reposed among celestial trees, lustrous flowers, and radiant fruits that bestowed immortality upon those who consumed them.

What was Paradise? But a Garden, an Orchard of Trees and Herbs, full of pleasure, and nothing there but delights. —WILLIAM LAWSON

I discover

I been a midwife ever since I was seventeen. I uster tend all the women around where I lived in the Bahamas. I've tended me own girls as well as meself. I still go when I'm called ere in Riviera, but if it gits beyond me I always calls a doctor. Most of what I know I owe to me aunt, for it was er what ad the books although she kept them under lock and key, cause she didn't want us childrens to read them. I uster steal the key and then open the case what she kept the books in, and sneak them out and ide until I could read them. As I growed up, I got more and more interested, so after reading them books I decided I'd be a midwife too, and sure enough that's what I did.

I was seventeen when I took my first case....This woman ad given birth at about six o'clock in the morning and by four o'clock that afternoon the afterbirth adn't come and she was dying from the poison that set in. There warn't a soul around that could do nothing about it, so remembering what I could, I took two pounds of onions and pulverized them; then soaked it in a pint of gin. Then I took it all and put it in two cloth bags. One bag I put to the lower part of the woman's stomack and the other to er back. Inside of a alf hour it ad come and she was gitting along fine.

—Izzelly Haines, from a 1939 interview collected by Ann Banks in *First-Person America*

A name without a life to live it is a restless, wandering thing

—ANONYMOUS

I am tradition

In the Flathead [c. 1910], children were named a few days after birth, usually by the father or grandfather, in the presence of the family and relations. The name chosen was that of a deceased person, either an ancestor or a well-known personage. Since a name was regarded as part of the individual, it could not be given to a child or assumed by an adult without his permission. A "good name"—one believed to be capable of bringing its bearer good fortune—was sometimes "sold" for as much as a horse.

On the fourth day after the birth of an Apsaroke child, a man of prominence, or in some instances a woman, was called in to bestow a name, which, as a rule, was one that he had heard called among the spirit-people in one of his visions, or perhaps one referring to some good deed of his own. Incense was made, and the child raised four times in the cloud of smoke to symbolize the wish that it might grow tall and vigorous.

—Christopher Cardozo and Edward S. Curtis, from *Native Family: Native Nations*

Pregnancy is one of those funny times in life, like weddings or funerals, when childhood superstitions and family folklore peek like ghosts from under the most rational people. I know this side of my mother appears whenever she brings up her old aunty.

"When I gave birth to you," my mother announced one day, "old aunty told me not to bathe for twelve days. After those twelve days were over, my first bath was full of herbs." She looked at me hesitating. "Maybe you shouldn't take a shower for a few days after you give birth."

The idea was absolutely shocking. "Mom," I tried to reassure her, "that probably was because the water wasn't clean enough in your village."…

When I came home from the hospital in the middle of summer, my mother wouldn't let me drink anything cold, but insisted I drink hot tea with ginger and roasted rice, "to bring my heat back." Other special foods were cooked and prepared to preserve my "heat" and keep away the "cold." For two weeks, I was not to do anything but rest and care for my new son—the Chinese call this "sitting for a month." Her behavior, as inexplicable as it seemed at times, comforted the two of us. I am sure her mother and her old aunty, in a different place and a different time, did the same things for her.

—Shu Shu Costa, from *Lotus Seeds and Lucky Stars*

voice

Mother's voice
hidden in bells

rings,

seeping beautiful earth sowed with seed

dreams me, opens me

with every tender sound of her.

Mother's melody

alive in tendrils

curves,   reaching graceful trellis arched for sun

sings me, releases me

with every loving song of her.

Mother's story

woven in wood

echoes,   spiraling wise tree lined for time

whispers me, breathes me

with every small step of her.

She is silent

touching life with lips

loudly radiant,

kissing me, searching me

for words; there are none.

ANDREA ALBAN GOSLINE

I voice

Sometimes there is one magic moment in our lives when the voice of Mother Earth calls to us, reminding us who we are, where we came from and what our essence is….

When my daughter was about three days old and we were still in the hospital, I wrapped her up one evening and slipped outside to a little garden in the warmth of late June. I introduced her to the pine trees and the plants and the flowers, and them to her, and finally to the pearly moon wrapped in a soft haze and to the stars. I, knowing nothing then of nature based religious ritual or eco-feminist theory, had felt an impulse for my wondrous little child to meet the rest of cosmic society.

—Charlene Spretnak, from "Ecofeminism, Our Roots and Flowering"

VOICE: SYMBOL OF CREATION

In old Eastern traditions, the female voice was an important symbol of creation: the source of the original creative word.

❖ In an ancient Indian myth, the Goddess of the Voice created everything in the universe by speaking its name in Sanskrit, her primordial language. To them, she was *Vac*—meaning "the sound of the Voice." They likened her to the wind, blowing from heaven and bringing the essence of soul to all things. She created the gods by speaking their names and revealed the holy mantras by which the gods could be controlled. Vac was the first, the queen, the greatest of all deities.

❖ Another female deity, Bath Kol, Daughter of the Voice, appeared in early Hebrew mythology. She was known as the divine afflatus, source of the prophets' inspiration, a mysterious female voice of God personified. Sometimes she was called "the last echo of the Voice," meaning that there was little left to be heard of the creative Logos. The Greek Goddess Echo was a similar conception, though reduced to a mere water nymph in the classical story of Narcissus.

❖ In Gnostic literature, the female Logos said, "I am the Mother of the Voice, speaking in many ways, completing the All. It is in me that knowledge dwells, the knowledge of things everlasting. It is I who speak within every creature…. I am the Womb that gives shape to the All by giving birth to the Light that shines in splendor."

I am harmony

If the family were a container, it would be a nest, an enduring nest, loosely woven, expansive and open. If the family were a fruit, it would be an orange, a circle of sections, held together but separable, each segment distinct. If the family were a boat, it would be a canoe that makes no progress unless everyone paddles. If the family were a sport, it would be baseball: a long, slow, nonviolent game that is never over until the last out. If the family were a building, it would be an old but solid structure that contains human history, and appeals to those who see the carved moldings under all the plaster, the wide plank floors under the linoleum, the possibilities.

—Letty Cottin Pogrebin, from *Chop Wood, Carry Water*

RITUAL

Sing your favorite songs to your unborn baby. Tell her enchanting stories. Take her on a tour of your daily activities. Let her hear your precious voice directed at her many times every day. After she is born, sing the same songs and tell the same stories. Watch how attentive and soothed she will be at the familiar sound of your voice and words.

Here is calm so deep, grasses cease waving…wonderful how completely everything in wild nature fits into us. The sun shines not on us, but in us. The rivers flow not past, but through us, thrilling, tingling, vibrating every fiber and cell of the substance of our bodies, making them glide and sing.

—JOHN MUIR

I am the gift

Too hot for her to come outside to greet me,
    I pull my car onto her circular driveway and look
      for her gray head inside the screened porch.
      She waits for me there, with arms extended, and I bend
      to hug her while she stands on tiptoe, whispering how
      she's missed me, how much she's looked forward to our visit.
    When she takes my hand to go inside, I see the brown bags
    brimming with oranges: small and round and ripe,
  picked, I know, by her own small hands
when the sun was slowly setting the night before.
And I imagine her, out in the yard, balancing on the ladder by the fence
poking orange after orange with the handle of a broom, watching
as each piece of fruit drops onto the moist earth.
Bent over her trimmed lawn she stood counting, figuring
how many it would take for me to have fresh juice for another week.
Now, on her front porch, we look at the bags lined neatly in rows
but she only shakes her head, trying to convince me there aren't that many
as I stand thinking of all the trees my grandmother has picked for me
the last thirty years, how she was the one who taught me
to thank the tree for giving us fruit, and so I do, listening to her
generous laugh as she pats my hand to come inside and eat.

—Karen Benke, "Oranges"

The mother's service is nearest, readiest and surest:
nearest because it is most natural, readiest because it is
most loving, and surest because it is truest.

—Juliana of Norwich (1342-1417)

I reflect

On interpreting the inner thoughts of an infant engaged with its mother: I enter the world of her face. Her face and its features are the sky, the clouds, and the water. Her vitality and spirit are the air and the light. It is usually a riot of light and air at play…. All her life is concentrated into the softest and hardest points in the world—her eyes.

They draw me in, deep and deeper. They draw me into a distant world. Adrift in this world, I am rocked side to side by the passing thoughts that ripple the surface of her eyes. I stare down into their depths. And there I feel running strong the invisible currents of her excitement. They churn up from those depths and tug at me. I call after them. I want to see her face again, alive.

Gradually life flows back into her face. The sea and sky are transformed. The surface now shimmers with light. New spaces open out. Arcs rise and float. Volumes and planes begin their slower dance. Her face becomes a light breeze that reaches across to touch me. It caresses me. I quicken. My sails fill with her. The dance within me is set free.

—Daniel Stern, from *Diary of a Baby*

I was fifteen when my brother was born. He was a child of light, while I was a child of shadows… I even forgave him for inheriting my mother's beautiful singing voice.

—CANDICE BERGEN

❖ **Many Asians believe the moment of conception is so powerful that the pregnant woman experiences a profound dream about the gender or personality of the new being. She might also envision the "birth grandmother," who is said to deliver the child from the gods to her womb. Some believe this *Samshin Halmoni* will care for the child for forty-nine days before returning to the heavens.**

I tell

The voice of a woman? Does it belong to a particular time and place?
Is it not something much more eternal? Like the womb? Is it a soft, gentle fertility
of instinct? The gesture is new, but, the roots are the same. A woman sings of creation,
and of recreation. —Estela Portillo

I called my mother, and I called my best friend, Sandy. "We had the baby! We had the baby!" I gave them each a blow-by-blow description of the birth. I just had to tell the story. I think it's a cathartic thing. It's so intense. So much happens in such a short time that you have to talk about it to make it real. It's how you believe that this baby who has been in your womb, who has been a part of you, becomes a separate person in the world. There are other reasons why you keep on talking about it. Even ninety-year-old women still talk about childbirth. I think you tell the story over and over again to keep from feeling the loss of that experience. To have participated so directly in the creation of life and to have held that life within you is so exciting. Then once you've given life, it's not yours to give again. That's the way it has to be, right? But you don't ever, ever want to lose that feeling of having given life. And every time you tell that story, you're trying to get back to that miracle.

—Judy Myerson, from *Mothers Talking Sharing the Secret* by Frances Wells Burck

✤ In *Keys to the Open Gate*, Kimberley Snow writes about the way the Sufis measure their words. They do not speak unless their words manage to pass through three gates. At the first gate, they ask themselves, "Are these words true?" If so, they let them pass to the second gate, where they ask, "Are they necessary?" At the last gate, they ask, "Are they kind?"

I am blessing

The first time it happened, I blushed the color of a pomegranate seed. I was on a late evening pilgrimage to procure the necessary pregnancy food: Heinz ketchup, Paul Newman's popcorn, and a couple of garnet yams. While selecting my tubers, my eyes wandered down the aisle to a gorgeous, young Leonardo DiCaprio lookalike bagging a few oranges. The second my eyes fixed on him, he turned, walked straight toward me in a slow-motion trance, and, with a smile as bright as the noonday sun, reached out and touched my big round belly with a warm, firm hand. His eyes gleamed with a "Wow!" and off he strolled.

I was shocked. I felt invaded, violated. How dare a cute, male stranger touch my body! Hot as a hornet, I almost trotted after him to deliver the wrath of a pregnant woman scorned. And then suddenly I felt it: the baby turned inside of me and started to purr like a kitten. I felt like an angel was pouring warm honey over my heart: In that redeeming moment after "the touch," I was blessed, innocent, and so powerful.

It is a phenomenon like no other: when you are pregnant, strangers will come up to you and unabashedly—and joyfully—lay their hands on your tummy.

What is this touch? At first I thought these common folks were just trying to wish me well in a bizarre way. But then I

Of the sadness or joy, good fortune or tragedy that awaits every mother and newborn child in this life, we can never know in advance. But the birth journey is and will always be nothing short of heroic, for every child and mother, every time. —Kemp Battle

realized that they were actually drawn to us, just like the devoted are drawn to power places of profound healing such as Lourdes, Tibet, or the Pyramids of Egypt. The miracle of "the touch" was the innocence and joy the pilgrim received from it. We simply smiled and purred. So for the rest of my pregnant days, we walked the aisles as a team; I attracted the faithful miracle shoppers and my unborn belly-dancer blessed and healed them with an unutterable, sacred innocence.

—Margie Beiser Lapanja, teammate/mother of Lila Grace, author of *Goddess in the Kitchen* and *The Goddess' Guide to Love*

I give

Giving is the highest expression of our power. —VIVIAN GREENE

The nature of a parent's work is sacrifice, for you must necessarily take away from yourself in order to give your children what they need. This story illustrates:

One of the old men had just finished putting handles on his baskets when he overheard a brother voicing concern about his own unfinished work. "The marketplace is about to open," said the brother, "and I have no handles for my baskets. What shall I do?"

The old man quietly removed the handles from his baskets and gave them to his neighbor. "Please accept these handles," he said, "for I have no need of them."

In his benevolence the old man left his own work unfinished so that his brother's needs would be met.

Just as the old man willingly gave his brother the handles from his baskets, so does a mother offer the gift of her time, energy, and love to her children.

—Katherine Ketcham, from *In the House of the Moon*

MOM IN 25 LANGUAGES

Albanian: *nâna*
Arabic: *el-oum*
Bulgarian: *máyka*
Czech: *matka*
Danish: *moder*
Dutch: *moeder*
English: *mother*
Estonian: *ema*
Finnish: *äiti*
French: *mère*
German: *mutter*
Greek: *mite'ra*
Hungarian: *anya*
Italian: *madre*
Latvian: *mâte*
Lithuanian: *motina*
Norwegian: *mor*
Polish: *matka*
Portuguese: *mãe*
Romanian: *mamă*
Russian: *mat'*
Serbo-Croatian: *majka*
Spanish: *madre*
Swedish: *moder*
Turkish: *anne*

SEVENTEENTH-CENTURY CHILDCARE

[R]oul [the baby] up with soft cloths and lay it in the cradle: but in the swaddling of it be sure that all parts be bound up in their due place and order gently without any crookedness or rugged foldings; for infants are tender twigs and as you use them, so they will grow straight or crooked…lay the arms right down by the sides, that they may grow right. When the Navel-string is cut off,…bind a piece of Cotton or Wool over it…and if the child be weak after this, anoint the child's body over with oil of acorns, for that will comfort and strengthen it and keep away the cold…. Carry it often in the arms, and dance it, to keep it from the rickets and other diseases.

After four months let loose the arms but still roul the breast and belly and feet to keep out cold air for a year, till the child have gained more strength. Shift the child's clouts often….

When the child is seven months old you may (if you please) wash the body of it twice a week with warm water till it be weaned.

—Jane Sharp, from *The Midwife's Book or the Whole Art of Midwifery (1671)*

I echo

I think of my own mother, who has sewed me suits with hand-piped linings and hemmed my dresses with lace and knitted me heavy, intricate sweaters. And of my grandmother, whose recipes, written in her own hand, I treasure in my file, and who would not die until after she had poured the candied orange peel into the sterile jars to cool. And of my great-grandmother, whose language I never learned but whose crocheted coverlet lay in my cedar chest, safe from the claws of cats, until my daughter found a room of her own for it. And of all the spinners and weavers and Salem witches, lost to me and yet not lost: in me, speaking through me. I think, too, of my daughter, now embarked on a writing project, a teaching career, a marriage. And of the daughter I wish for her one day.

Spirit enters flesh
And for all it's worth
Charges into earth
In birth after birth
Ever fresh and fresh.

—ROBERT FROST

—Nancy Mairs, from *Voice Lessons*

I breathe

Things to do today: Exhale, inhale, exhale. Ahhhh.

—FROM BUDDHA'S LITTLE INSTRUCTION BOOK

As I lay in bed that first night, I listened to four separate breaths in our family bed. Mine was hoarse and ragged after the harsh breathing of second-stage labor. My son Nathan, two and a half years old, was still making the sucking sounds he had made since he was born, even though he stopped nursing seven months before when I was found pregnant again. My husband's breathing was deep and even, as usual. My newborn baby girl lay beside me. Her breathing was irregular as a newborn's always is. I lay there and thought, six hours ago I was pregnant and in the most intense part of labor, trying to push the baby out. Now I'm lying peacefully in bed enjoying the complete absence of pain, and everyone I love is within arm's reach of me.

—Susan Vaughn, from *Just in Time*

❖ Labor is naturally designed to stimulate your baby in preparation for breathing. As the baby comes down the birth canal, mucus is massaged out of the lungs so they will be ready to take in air at birth. The baby's circulatory system is stimulated by the friction of moving through the vagina, much as you stimulate warmth by rubbing your hands together on a cold day. This provides your baby with a fresh supply of blood, thus warming the skin, as it is born into a much cooler environment than it has known.

I am the wind that breathes upon the sea,
I am the whisper of leaves rustling,
I am the power of trees reaching,
I am the swiftness of salmon swimming,
I am the size of the mighty oak tree,
And I am the thoughts of all people
Who praise my beauty and grace.

—ADAPTED FROM THE ANCIENT WELSH,
BLACK BOOK OF CAMARTHAN

I thank

Gratitude is Heaven itself. —WILLIAM BLAKE

Because you showed me they were only flies outside our door that day
then mowed the over-grown grass back into itself
Because you watched as I skated a little longer at the edge
and let me go out into the world even when you were scared

Because splinters of darkness once made up my heart
and it was your voice that held me over the telephone
Because after I left, I found small prayers tucked inside my pockets
wrapped between pieces of sky
Because by listening you help me to name what I do not know
teaching me the difference between shades of gray
Because these windows look on to hills, the ocean beyond rolling far
I am sitting here with you always, safe inside my heart.

—Karen Benke, "Reasons Why" *for my mother*

IROQUOIS THANKSGIVING SPEECH

The Creator said we will have daylight and we will have darkness. The darkness will be for sleep and rest. But you will also have a night-sun which you will call the moon. The moon will be your grandmother. And she will have special duties also. She will give moisture to dampen the land at night. She will also move the tides. Along with the moon there will be stars. The stars help give us directions when we travel and along with Grandmother Moon, tell us when we should begin our ceremonies. The moon and the stars were put there for these purposes. And we see, last night, that the moon and the stars are still here doing their duties. And for this we are very grateful. So, in our appreciation, let us all put our minds together as one and give thanks to the stars and the moon. And let our minds be that way.

—from *Wisdomkeepers: Meetings with Native American Spiritual Elders*

I teach

*Our first teacher
is our own heart.*

—CHEYENNE SAYING

*If you want your
children to keep
their feet on the
ground, put some
responsibility on
their shoulders.*

-ABIGAIL VAN BUREN

My mother was twenty-three years old when she gave birth to me. Over the past forty years she has taught me many lessons:

❖ Nothing is as it appears.
❖ There are no calories in a broken cookie.
❖ When in doubt, throw it out.
❖ A stuffed animal is easier to care for than a baby.
❖ You can never own too many pairs of shoes.
❖ Once you start the container of ice cream you may as well finish it.
❖ If you wear shoulder pads under a T-shirt you'll be appropriately dressed for almost any occasion.
❖ Never trust anyone with a secret—except your mother.

More and more often I open my mouth and my mother's words come out. I've started to hold my hands and gesture the way she does, and I'm told that I now laugh with her laugh. Unfortunately, the old saying that a woman grows up to become her mother is not usually meant as a compliment, but I hope to be so lucky.

—Irene Zahava, from *My Mother's Daughter*

CONTEMPLATION

Babies are magnificent teachers. They take you—inexperienced and untrained—and transform you instantly into a parent. You make mistakes and you falter but they keep letting you know what they need. For example, babies instinctively know to express hunger and can teach you to understand their voice and gestures. Your need to learn may be your best asset. As your baby grows, so will your knowledge.

I share

Although the work was hard, Anna didn't mind. She had a feel for the summer nights and enjoyed being alone in the mountains. She felt that there was something special about such a time—it smelled nice, there were sounds that aroused her curiosity and a swarming life all around that made the hours interesting. The birds that flew around her seemed as busy as she was.

"I would smile at the sight of little birds working hard to take care of themselves and their families. You are a kind of bird too, Anna, I thought—you too have a family to take care of."

"Best of all, I liked comparing myself to a woodpecker. Sometimes I sat on a mound near the *seter* with the rake in my lap, vividly recalling a story my mother had told me when I was a little girl: While Jesus was still wandering among us here on earth, one day when he was hungry be came to a woman baking bread. The woman's name was Gjertrud and she wore a red kerchief on her head. Jesus asked for a piece of bread. The woman took a small piece and it turned into a large loaf. She took smaller and smaller pieces, and the loaves got bigger and bigger, but she gave none of it to Jesus. So Jesus said: 'Because you would not give me even one piece of bread, you will turn into a bird that must find its bread between the bark and the wood. You will only have water when it rains. Instantly, a bird flew out of the chimney, a bird with a red top—the woodpecker, or *gjertrudsbird* as we call it. I didn't understand the story very well when my mother told it to me, but now I do: Share the good things you have with others. The only good things I owned were my hands. I wanted to use them to help the people at Haugsetvolden."

—Dagfinn Gronoset, from *Anna*

✦ A Roman man, Soranus of Ephesus, [second century B.C.E.] is known as the first specialist in gynecology and obstetrics. Unlike his predecessors, he focused on the more obvious and logical aspects of care rather than the supernatural and traditional superstitions. Most of his writings disappeared and were not discovered again until the nineteenth century.

Time is the judge. If you manage to pass on what you have to the next generation, then what you did was right.

—Barbara Kingsolver

I treasure

What matters moment by moment [is] not a really appallingly frail and old-looking woman but the person within, seeing an awful lot, being aware of an awful lot—a friend's thick, savory soup, and Pierrot the Himalayan, who looks like a Roman emperor in cat form, and the house filled with dewy pale pink roses, purple anemones, white and lavender tulips, blue asters. — MAY SARTON

My children are small, still lap-sized with many years ahead in my care. And yet, already I know, and I feel that one day, no matter how many diapers changed, bottles fed, books read, hands washed, or faces kissed, it will never be quite long enough.

— JENNIFER GRAHAM BILLINGS

At first you might not recognize the rolling sensations, twitches, and tingles in your belly as the movements of your baby, but at around twenty-two weeks, your little one, who weighs slightly over a pound, can kick so vigorously that you'll begin to take bets on whether he's a soccer player or a ballet dancer. Your baby is having a rollicking good time jumping, rolling, and pushing you around and may surprise you by responding to your touch with a wiggle. She might have the hiccups — they feel like tiny thumps — and jump or jerk at loud noises. You're in touch with your baby, and his blows are reassuring.

Getting kicked by your unborn baby is a blessing in itself. When you feel it, tune in so you don't miss it. You knew that there was a baby growing in your body, but her kicking made it real. What a precious greeting! Cherish every tiny jiggle, every little ripple. Your baby might stretch so wide that you can actually see his foot or her hand bulging out your side. What could be more thrilling? Treasure all this motion; there's not another feeling like it!

—Judy Ford, from *Blessed Expectations*

I value

I promise not to forget you, my three favorite girls, my feline treasures. Dulcie, who knows and sees and guards us, teaching attention and elegance. Bella, with no sight but firm trust and sea-blue eyes that glow in the garden. And Sara, wild and gorgeous, mother of the others, a silent secret we now share. I promise not to replace you, my perfect works of art. I have learned my necessary lessons from you. I know who eats first in this house and who gets affection with the sunrise. Please be patient with our fragile new friend, for the friend will love you, if only at first by gazing upon you, lovely dark silhouettes in our family still life.

—Lisa Burnett Bossi

I LOVE BABY RICKY

1952 heralded a first for American television—the word "pregnancy" was spoken and the condition of being pregnant was portrayed on-air. Trailblazers Desi Arnaz and Lucille Ball, who was pregnant in "real life," thought incorporating her pregnancy into the show, *I Love Lucy*, was a very natural way to handle the leading lady's condition. CBS and the show's main sponsor, Philip Morris, vehemently opposed the concept and thought the proposition was scandalous.

Desi countered the heavy resistance with a letter to Philip Morris' chairman of the board, in which he explained the circumstances and reminded him of the show's high ratings.

The network eventually agreed to break the media barrier and Lucy's pregnancy was written into the show. It was agreed that the baby would be a boy regardless of the true sex of Desi and Lucy's baby.

The "birth of the baby" episode was filmed in October, featuring a hysterical Ricky nervously pacing the halls while Lucy gave birth discreetly offscreen. The episode aired on Monday, January 19, 1953. Most of America tuned in to experience the happy occasion, and Ricky fainting with joy upon hearing that he had a son.

Meanwhile, only twelve hours earlier, on the same day as this historic telecast, Lucille Ball Arnaz gave birth to a healthy baby boy, Desi Jr.

I am ritual

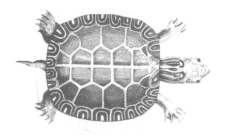

I always build a house
when I start something
new in my life.
That's my custom.
I'm like a snail crawling
along with a shell
on its back. I build a
house, and then I start
roaming around.

— CHIYO UNO

The women begin talking among themselves. They are together to perform a ceremony. Rituals of women take time. There is no hurry.

The magic things are brought out from pockets and pouches.

A turtle rattle made from she-turtle who was a companion of the woman's mother. It died the night she died, both of them ancient and tough. Now, the daughter shakes the rattle, and the mother and she-turtle live again. Another Grandmother pulls out a bundle that contains a feather from a hermit thrush. This is a holy feather. Of all the birds in the sky, hermit thrush is the only one who flew to the spirit world. It was there she learned her beautiful song. She is clever and hides from sight. To have her feather is great magic. The women pass around the feather. They tickle each other's chins and ears. Giggles and laughs erupt in the dwelling….

A woman gives a smile and brings out a cradleboard from behind her back. There is a nodding of heads and smiling and long drawn out ahhhhs. The cradleboard has a beaded back that a mother made in her ninth month. An old woman starts a song; the rest join in:

Little baby
Little baby
Ride on Mother's back
Laugh, laugh
Life is good
Mother shields you

A grandmother wipes her eyes, another holds her hands and kisses the lifelines.

— Beth Brant, from "Native Origin" from *Mohawk Trail*

I unite

*I remember all these primitive
feelings; I could see millions of
women throughout history in little
shacks by rivers, all alone, or
strapped down in hospitals.
That's one of the biggest things that
happened to me—that connection
with other women throughout time.*

—ANN, (AN ARTIST) ON HER WORK ON
JUDY CHICAGO'S *THE BIRTH PROJECT*

Being in a group with other people who were sharing the same experience put me in touch with the fact that I was part of a universal process. My words then come back to me now. I have never considered before that my mother had given birth, and her mother before her had given birth to her, that it was an endless stream. I suppose I felt like stepping over a barrier to be reunited with humanity—a totality was realized. That's where the group came into it.

Being with others who were going through the same thing, talking about our history…our parents' experience, even our grandparents' experience and about pregnancy and birth as an initiation rite provoked the image of stepping over a barrier. The barrier? Let's see, if it was in a dream, there would be a conveyor belt and several people along the side standing still, then one hopping in every so often…the belt would be endless.

—Jean, member of a birth support group

❖ Shu, the ancient Egyptian god of the air, and Tefnet, the goddess of moisture, were believed to have produced the earth god Geb and the sky god Nut. These deities embraced so tightly that there was no room for anything to exist between them. Nut became pregnant, but there was no space for the children to be born, until the air god Shu separated them.

I commit

Children are the
purpose of life.
We were once children
and someone
took care of us.
Now it is
our turn to care.

—CREE ELDER

Since you were born, your father and I have married again—our altar, your cradle—our church, this home. When we look down upon you, we silently recommit to vows made long ago. Only now, the promise we make to each other, we also make to you....

We want you to watch our love grow, as we hope it will. We want you to share in our joy. We want to show you that love can thrive over time, nourish and protect, urge gently onward.

We want to show you that it isn't always easy, that there are times when we all get scared. Like a teddy bear, love can slip behind the bedpost and appear to be lost. Rather than something one falls into, love is often a choice and an effort—to search until found. It is this choice that is our promise, to us and to you.

May your father and I plow a fertile ground within your heart, where love can be planted, struggle and grow.

—Mary Knight, *Love Letters Before Birth and Beyond*

RITUAL

Creating your own pre-birth ceremony is a wonderful way to bond with your women friends and family members, bringing extra support and love to you while you're expecting. ✣ Gather your favorite people together and form a circle. ✣ Have one person explain the intention of the gathering and ask each participant to share a wish for you and your baby. ✣ Pass an egg around the circle to represent the continuity of life. ✣ Create a welcoming gift for the baby, such as a quilt, painting, or poem. ✣ Close the ritual with a favorite song and a potluck meal.

I am spontaneous

When you are dealing with a child, keep all your wits about you and sit on the floor.

—AUSTIN O'MALLEY

I guess the best thing about having Hannah is that she helps me see the world through a child's eyes. I remember when I was small, it seemed that the things that made the world right were so totally simple—like the feeling of the sun shining on my face, or how cold and sweet an ice cream tasted, or how great it was to reach into a berry bush and cram berries into my mouth. This is all before I was old enough to think, "Gee, I really should have washed those berries," or "I can't eat that ice cream because it's fattening." When you're a kid everything is just there, you take it, and it's great.

—Judy Henry, from *Expectations*

VENUS OF WILLENDORF

The earliest images of the Goddess were sculptural icons known as pregnant "Venuses," of which the Venus of Willendorf is the most famous. Scientists date these small statues from 20,000 to 25,000 years old. These mystical figures have the voluptuous bodies of pregnant women, blank faces, and tapered legs so they could easily be placed into the ground as fertility offerings.

In *Shakti Woman*, Vicky Noble writes, "Since a woman's body, which is so like the earth, makes enough food for her offspring, our early ancestors learned to trust the Mother, fashioning images of this Great Mother with large, abundant breasts and a full, pregnant belly." According to archaeologist Marija Gimbutas, "Pre-industrial agricultural rites show a very definite mystical connection between the fertility of the soil and the creative force of women." That sacred connection is reemerging in our culture as women begin once again to honor the bond between their bodies and the living earth.

❖ In Vietnam, pregnant women are advised: "For your first pains, wait until the moon is full."

I am humble

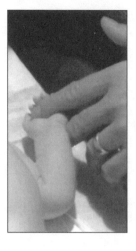

The little things. The click of your wife's makeup bottles and brushes in the bathroom in the morning, the subsurface sound of them, a kind of music. The accompaniments: the older boy's bedroom door opening and shutting in haste, a faucet running, a gust of wind in the eucalyptus, the last rain on the window. The little things are what we remember, what we know, of family life. Of life.

The large events have their place, but even the large events of a family's passage are assembled from little things. The rush to the emergency room and the way the air feels there and the brave little chin thrust up beneath the mask, the small choked cry and the sound—especially this sound—of the thread being pulled through the wound, and the way the little hand holds tight to your finger. The little things.

—Richard Louv, from *The Web of Life*

Don't limit a child to your own learning,
for he was born in another time.

—RABBINIC SAYING

The ancient forerunner to Mother's Day was a festival called Hilaria that began in third-century B.C.E. Rome. The celebration paid homage to the pagan goddess Cybele, known as The Great Mother of the Gods, and Mother of Nature. She was the symbol of fertility in all living things, and thus was honored with sensual reveling that featured loud music, dancing, and lustful endeavors.

The modern-day version of this tribute to mothers began unofficially on May 10, 1908, in Grafton, West Virginia, attended by 407 children and their mothers. Each was presented with a carnation, marking the beginning of the flower-giving tradition of this day. An ambitious letter-writing campaign garnered widespread national support for this lovely tribute, and on May 8, 1914, President Woodrow Wilson officially proclaimed the second Sunday in May as Mother's Day. The British had long celebrated Mothering Sunday on the fourth Sunday of the Lenten season, but it wasn't until the U.S. proclamation that countries worldwide adopted the idea.

I sing

I must be very young; my mother is still singing, all the time. I am the third of four living children, but at this moment we are alone. I play beside her on the couch while she dusts the sunroom windowsills. There are five round-arched windows. The woodwork is tawny, red gold. When my mother sings the neighbor comes out of his house and into our yard and stretches himself out on the lawn. I gaze at her fine, pink face, glowing in the window light. Her dark hair has small, tight tight tight waves. They glow in the light. Everything glows. I am aglow with the rapture of the revelation that she is the most beautiful woman in the whole world, my mother. I am too young to ask, "Why me? How come I am chosen?" I belong to what is given.

—Adele Wiseman, from *Old Woman at Play*

❖ **Mothers use special tones of voice to sing lullabies to their babies. Amazingly, when asked to replicate those sounds when their babies are not in the room, the mothers cannot!**

The miraculous moment was when I started singing as a continuation of the breathing. I sing to earn my living, and I sang to bring about this baby like I have never sung before. Imagine a labor room with singing women, what a chorus it would be! Singing was a great outlet for my emotions during pregnancy and at birth. It took the place of self-pity. So, when you are in doubt, keep on singing.

—Catherine Milinaire

I radiate

Poet and novelist Leopold Kompert (1822-1886), author of the classical Ghetto stories, chose, as the central figures of his fiction, mostly women. This passage was written by the poet in a remembrance book.

There exists only one source from which all the female characters I was able to form are derived:

my mother. A mere recollection of her, a submergence into one of her essential traits for minutes is sufficient to arouse in me the images of persons—and yet each of them is but a fragment, a spark of the flame emanating from one focus, a small piece of my mother's heart. You, my dear young lady, whose sincerity I have ever recognized, will understand what I mean when I say: my mother was my Muse!

—Leopold Kompert

The seasons and phases of the moon are the rhythms we live by, and they reflect the patterns of human life. When we feel part of this universal rhythm, we enjoy a greater sense of life's meaning. By celebrating the seasons, we connect more deeply with Mother Earth as she changes:
❖ **Midwinter:** God is born as the bright son of the Goddess. She can be seen as a magical maiden rebirthing herself. ❖ **Imbolc** (beginning of February): The Goddess has recently given birth and is fruitful and creative. God is young and growing. ❖ **Spring Equinox:** Both God and Goddess are youthful and vibrant with the excitement of their future. ❖ **Beltane** (beginning of May): God and Goddess, now mature, mate and joyously celebrate their love. ❖ **Midsummer:** The Goddess is fruitful as the mother of Nature. The God begins to change, turning his face towards the realm of quiet and shadows. ❖ **Lammas** (end of August): Earth Mother presides over the first harvests.

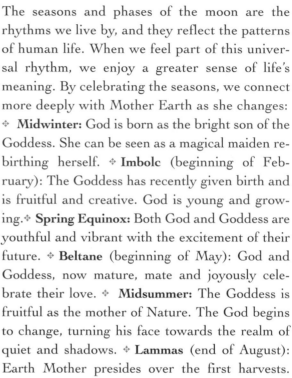

God dies, cut down with the corn, and is reborn in all the provisions reaped from the harvest. ❖ **Autumn Equinox**, the second of the "harvest" celebrations: The Goddess is still gentle Mother Earth and God is a shadowy presence. ❖ **Samhain** (end of October): God has become Lord of the Underworld and the Goddess is the Wise Crone. They are both old and mysterious. This is a time of death. ❖ **Rebirth** will occur once again at Midwinter, completing the circle of life.

I am rhythm

For it was then that the beautiful part transpired. I was alone and recently trained in natural childbirth. I knew what was happening to my body and it was incredibly beautiful. My body performed just as the teaching had said it  would perform. It was a cathedral of perfection. Muscles going into a pattern, reforming, regrouping and then forming another pattern of rhythm and pattern of the celestial movement of planets and stars and meteors—all was in rhythm, all was in tune. Nothing was discordant. All was profound beauty, the pattern and music of Nature. My body was a heaving symphony of movement. My hands on my abdomen caught the rapture of surging tidal waves. My brain luxuriating in my aloneness with this physical self that was *me*, heaving and moving and contracting and relaxing and pushing and sighing and waiting and moving again in the primeval rhythm of all living, pulsating heavenly and earthly beings.

It was sheer, unadulterated pleasure. Sheer ecstatic joy…. The goddesses of the universe gave these moments to me.

—Lolly Hirsch, from *Birthstories, The Experience Remembered*

And when I was born,
I began to breathe the
common air, and fell
upon the kindred earth;
my first sound was
a cry, as is true of all.

—WISDOM 7:3

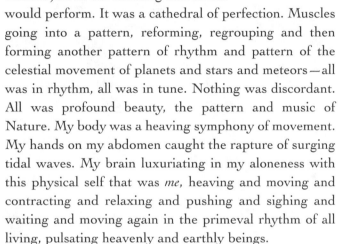

❖ In its primitive form, belly dancing was a form of worshipping the ancient earth mother goddess. It was a childbirth ritual: the dance mimes giving birth. The basic movements of the abdomen are similar to the natural-childbirth methods touted by Fernand Lamaze.

I am content

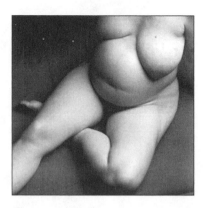

*I admire a
contented mind.
I revere enjoyment
of simple things.
I can imagine that
contentment
has a high degree
of truth.*

—FLORIDA SCOTT-MAXWELL

Insidiously, unhurriedly, the beatitude of pregnant females spread through me. I was no longer subjected to any discomfort, any unease. This purring contentment, this euphoria—how to give a name either scientific or familiar to this state of preservation?—must certainly have penetrated me, since I have not forgotten it and am recalling it now, when life can never again bring me plenitude....

Every night I bade farewell, more or less, to one of the happiest periods of my life, knowing well how I was going to regret it. But the cheerfulness, the purring contentment, the euphoria submerged everything and over me reigned the sweet animal innocence and unconcern arising from my added weight and the muffled appeals of the new life being formed within me.

The sixth month, the seventh month.... The first strawberries, the first roses.... Can I regard my pregnancy as anything but one long festival? We forget the anguish of the labor pains but do not forget the long and singular festival; I have certainly not forgotten any detail. I especially remember how at odd hours sleep overwhelmed me and how I was seized again, as in my infancy, by the need to sleep on the ground, on the grass, on the sun-warmed hay. A unique and healthy craving.

—Colette, from *Earthly Paradise*

I answer

Sometimes when Scarlett tiptoed at night to kiss her tall mother's cheek, she looked up at the mouth with its too short, too tender upper lip, a mouth too easily hurt by the world, and wondered if it had ever curved in silly girlish giggling or whispered secrets through long nights to intimate girl friends. But no, that wasn't possible. Mother had always been just as she was, a pillar of strength, a fount of wisdom, the one person who knew the answers to everything....

Scarlett regarded her as something holy and apart from all the rest of humankind. When Scarlett was a child, she had confused her mother with the Virgin Mary, and now that she was older she saw no reason for changing her opinion. [Her mother] represented the utter security that only Heaven or a mother can give. She knew that her mother was the embodiment of justice, truth, loving tenderness and profound wisdom — a great lady.

— Margaret Mitchell, from *Gone With The Wind*

I have called you by name, now you belong to me.

— ISAIAH 43:1

ESKIMO WOMEN VOICES

The Arctic wind takes possession of her, she claims. For brief spells she is no longer herself. She stands still, closes her eyes, lets her self rise, spread across the tundra, then fade away — the return to her body. She loves leaving, loves coming back. Her eyes see the wind approaching: the aroused waves; the grass bending; the birds tossing, riding their way on the currents, holding to a course. Her eyes contemplate the return of her "spirit": quiet water, a gentle flat land, a new stillness to the air. And always there are the sounds, which her ears crave — the whispers, whistles, strong voices.

— Robert and Jane Hallowell Coles, from "Eskimo Women Voices," from *Women of Crisis*

I am vulnerable

Red brought him into the labor room to sit with me. He wore a green gown to match his face. He took my hand in his, oh, so gently—he was so helpless, so sweet, so scared. As I took my hand away to hold on to the bars of the bed above my head as instructed, he turned even greener. He didn't know what to do—after a few minutes he asked if I minded if he waited outside, he couldn't bear to see anyone he loved in pain. Things happened very quickly after that—two hours later at 11:22 P.M., Stephen (after Steve in *To Have and Have Not*) Humphrey Bogart was born. Red showed him to me in the delivery room. He was beautiful—all six pounds, six ounces, twenty inches of him. Bogie was waiting for me when I was wheeled from the recovery room to my own room. So relieved to see me smiling at him, talking to him. I was still gaga from the anesthesia, but I knew my man when he looked at me with tears in his eyes and said, "Hello, Baby." It was the fullest, most complete moment my life has ever known.

—Lauren Bacall, from *By Myself*

I give you my naked soul
like a statue unveiled.

—JUANA DE IBARBOUROU, FROM
"THE HOUR," *DIAMOND TONGUES*

SOUL DOUBLE

The Dogon of Africa believe that the human soul has both feminine and masculine aspects. When a baby is born, the water spirit draws two shadows on the ground. The feminine shadow is created on the ground where the child is born. The masculine shadow is then outlined over the female shadow. By laying the baby face down on the shadows, he or she takes possession of the dual souls. The Dogon believe that the female part of the soul dwells in the foreskin of a boy's penis and that the male part of the soul will inhabit the girl's clitoris. The feminine and masculine energies are balanced in the child—one does not dominate the other. In order to instill the desire to procreate, they believe that both males and females must be circumcised to definitively establish their roles as men and women.

I speak

And the ground spoke when she was born.
Her mother heard it. In Navajo she answered
as she squatted down against the earth
to give birth. It was now when it happened,
now giving birth to itself again and again
between the legs of women.

Or maybe it was the Indian Hospital
in Gallup. The ground still spoke beneath
mortar and concrete. She strained against the
metal stirrups, and they tied her hands down
because she still spoke with them when they
muffled her screams. But her body went on
talking and the child was born into their
hands, and the children learned to speak
both voices.

She grew up talking in Navajo, in English
and watched the earth around her shift and change
with the people in the towns and in the cities
learning not to hear the ground as it spun around
beneath them. She learned to speak for the ground,
the voice coming through her like roots that
have long hungered for water. Her own daughter
is born, like she had been, in either place
or all places, so she could leave, leap
into the sound she had always heard,
a voice like water, like the gods weaving
against sundown in a scarlet light.
The child now hears names in her sleep.
They change into other names, and into others.
It is the ground murmuring, and Mt. St. Helens
erupts as the harmonic motion of a child turning

inside her mother's belly waiting to be born
to begin another time.

And we go on, keep giving birth and watch
ourselves die, over and over.
And the ground spinning beneath us
goes on talking.

—Joy Harjo, "For Alva Benson, and for
Those Who Have Learned to Speak" from
Birth Stories: The Experience Remembered

*It was my mother who gave
me my voice. She did this, I
know now, by clearing a space
where my words could fall,
grow, then find their way to
others.* —PAULA GIDDINGS

I savor

I yearn to be free enough to
spend all the time in the world
with the people I love, before they
grow up, grow old and die.
As we always thought we could
when we were children. Sometimes
I think I should have children
precisely in order to defy time and
reclaim the hearth. Maybe that is
what all mothers do . . .

—ALICE, FROM *BETWEEN OURSELVES:*
LETTERS, BETWEEN MOTHERS & DAUGHTERS

❖ **The umbilical cord is approximately twenty-six inches long, just the right length to allow the baby to be clasped to his mother's breast after delivery and still remain connected to a reserve supply of oxygen.**

I can still remember Danny, my firstborn, smiling at me with recognition for the first time, under a streetlight as we were wheeling him home one dark night in his baby carriage after visiting friends…. I can still remember my walks with Emily, each afternoon after she got home from nursery school, swinging hands and singing our own song with many verses that we called "Swing High, Swing Low." I can still remember rocking them on my lap in the middle of the night, to soothe them back to sleep after a stomach-ache or a bad dream, the songs I would make up, each a personal running commentary on each child's life….

There is so much I remember still of the vivid intensity of those days of my own motherhood, which comes back to me as I watch them with Rafi [my grandson] now—and so much I realize is gone forever, lost even in memory. The omnipresent daily details of those mother years, which seemed so pressing then, so harassing, and sometimes so clouded with guilts and conflict and that "problem that had no name," in those cramped apartments, those houses so vivid in my memory and theirs, so crowded with life—I only wish now that I'd savored them all more, at the time.

—Betty Friedan, from *Thoughts on Becoming a Grandmother*

I honor

When I became a Mom ten years ago, my daughter Antoinette's arrival opened up a whole new world to me. It truly awakened my feelings about babies and children and although I have always had the greatest respect for these little people, I never knew how much I would feel this. Her presence was astounding. She was so small, so helpless, yet when I looked into her eyes I knew immediately that she was here to guide me. I had read books that recommended sleeping with her, nursing her and keeping her very close by. I knew this was in her best interest and despite how tiring responsive mothering could be, I persevered. I listened to her and followed her cue.

I did the same with my second daughter Hannah. As a mother of two, I had the experience and insight into what babies like and what they need. I embraced the challenge because I knew that both my husband and I were responsible for doing our best to leave healthy beings on this planet. When my son Marcus arrived I was amazed that my heart had the capacity to divide again and feel such love. I nurtured this third child as the rest and realized after a decade of motherhood that parenting is all about respecting our children, being truly cognizant of how little they are, and championing their place in our world.

Mother is the name of God in the lips and hearts of little children.

— WILLIAM MAKEPEACE THACKERY

I believe our children will give back all the love and respect bestowed upon them. Without much effort, we could transform all of our communities into places that honor children and their families. Parents need the support to raise their children in a more enlightened and beneficial way. Children deserve and need this support too.

—Michele Mason

I am intimate

In a child's lunchbox, a mother's thoughts.

—JAPANESE PROVERB

Nurse Luella Hennessey, who attended the birth of twenty-seven of Rose Kennedy's grandchildren, claims that the Kennedy mothers have adopted a practice which, through the years, has become a family tradition. They have long "conversations" with their babies the first time they meet. Luella explains:

"When the babies are brought to them twelve to twenty-four hours after they are born, they start communicating with them intimately. They talk softly to them, pouring out their feelings, telling them the secrets they've had in their hearts the last nine months, explaining how much they were wanted, how much they will be loved, how anxious their brothers and sisters are to see them. It's real talk, not just a chucking under the chin or a few words about how beautiful they are.

"What astonishes me always is the reaction of the babies. They will look up at the faces of their mothers, as though seeing them and hearing their words. Actually, of course, they may not see at all, but they do hear. The soft, soothing tones, I am convinced, seep into some level of the babies' immature consciousness, and the babies respond.

"I don't know whether the Kennedy mothers passed this little custom on to one another, but they all do it."

—Liz Smith, from *The Mother Book: A Compendium of Trivia and Grandeur Concerning Mothers, Motherhood and Maternity*

TIP

During the last four to five months of pregnancy, lying on your side is the most comfortable sleep position and is healthiest for your baby. "Feather your nest" for the most restful sleep. Place two pillows under your head, another supporting your top leg, and a fourth behind your lower back.

BIRTH TALISMANS

Seventeenth and eighteenth-century European women relied solely on faith and magic to protect them through pregnancy and childbirth. The childbirth sachet, made of numerous paper or fabric panels intricately folded into a tight, thin packet, was a talisman believed to ensure health and well-being for mother and baby. Passed 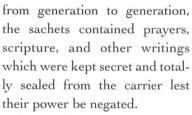 from generation to generation, the sachets contained prayers, scripture, and other writings which were kept secret and totally sealed from the carrier lest their power be negated.

Women who touched what was believed to be the sash of the Virgin Mary could expect miracles. King Louis XIII acquired the sash for his wife hours before labor began. After tying it on, she gave birth to a healthy son who later ascended the throne. Women of less aristocratic means would fill a large glass with water and submerge a tiny image of Mary or a piece of parchment with Bible verses written on it, and drink the water during labor.

I am strong

Child, be born when the moon is tender; even a tree must be pruned under the full moon so it will grow strong. —SANDRA CISNEROS

The Sioux language has a number of words for pregnancy. One of them means "growing strong." Another means "to be overburdened." I felt both strong and overburdened at the same time.

I was going to have [my baby] in the old Indian manner…. In the real ancient tradition, our women stuck a waist-high cottonwood stick right in the center of the tipi. Squatting, holding on to that stick, they would drop the baby onto a square of soft, tanned deer hide. They themselves cut the umbilical cord and put puffball powder on the baby's navel. Sometimes a woman friend was squatting behind them, pressing down on their stomach, or working the baby down with some sort of belt. They would rub the baby down with water and sweetgrass and then wipe it clean with buffalo grease. I did not think that I was quite that hardy or traditional to do it exactly in that way. And where would I have gotten buffalo grease?

When I say that I was determined to have my baby the Sioux way, I simply meant with an Indian prayer and the burning of sweetgrass and with the help of Indian women friends acting as midwives, having it the natural way without injections or anesthesia.

—Mary Crow Dog, from *Lakota Woman*

stand

Plant me in the forest
                on a hillock in the clear.
I belong to this circle
of redwoods gathering
sunlight ripples
and rain I drink.   Begin me then watch
                my shy uncurling;
                watch me spear busy earth
                toss my cocoon
                        lift slowly with the white fog
                        over fallen leaves and moss.

Watch my shadow stand
watch my roaming feet   see me   take my hand and taste
                        the sun of my skin. Glorious, I seek
                        the forest revealing
                        your face aglow, moon-calm
                        in the bathing pool.

                I hide among trees and watch
                your tears, sweet in the west wind
                falling for the harvest. Do not cry
                we will never part.
I belong to your circle.
                In your arms I stand.

ANDREA ALBAN GOSLINE

I stand

Parvis e glandibus quercus (Tall oaks from little acorns grow).
—ANONYMOUS

Through our journey of language, we, as women, must illustrate the great power of the quill and the strength it has woven within the quill's feathers, and within our own quilting of living. We, the mothers of life and the holders of the "seed within," must unite and carry for all, this gift of flight and breath into the nostrils of the winds. We must make our own stand on this path of the living and take the right to be the "keepers of our own gardens." Within each of us, we have the right to gaze upon a star and make a wish upon that star. Then, to be able to dream a dream—then, have the right to live it.

—Karen M. Watcheston, from *Writing the Circle: Native Women of Western Canada*

❖ Tribal women in Kenya, the Bongo district of Sudan, the Philippines, and India are known to give birth while standing. An ancient Japanese myth describes the Empress Jingo giving birth while standing and grasping a tree limb.

JAPANESE BIRTH CUSTOM

As soon as a child has come into the world, the father, or, as a rule, the grandfather, will go to the bank of a river, where he will seat himself upon the ground and pray to his gods. That done, he will cut a nice green stick of willow about a foot in length. This he will reverently bring home and, sitting down by the hearth, whittle into a fetish. When finished, he will worship it devoutly, offer prayers to the goddess of fire, and then, carefully taking it in both hands, carry it to the sleeping place and set it up there as the tutelary god of the new baby.

—practice of the Ainu people of Northern Japan

I am ancient

Every woman has a history
mother and grandmother
and the ones before that
the faces she sees in dreams or visions
and wonders Who?

—SHARON BARBA

Create a symbol commemorating your pregnancy that you can pass down to your children. Clay is the perfect medium because it is easy to work with and will last for ages. Flatten a large piece of modeling clay and form it into a circle the size of a plate. Embed nature elements, such as dried flowers and acorns, along with colorful, shiny objects such as beach glass and polished stones, into the soft surface. Sign and date the back of the piece for posterity.

she stays the night awake
often attentive
from changing to feeding to cradling to humming
she wanders into the room quietly
to check on the child sound asleep
her presence fills the room
o she is ani nah

leaning ever so gently
over the child coughing
how many times she comes by
in the night to pull up blankets
over the sleeping child
over the years
ani nah

the number of her footprints unknown
awaited often is her baking, her sewing,
her preserved berries
a rare treat, her bannock, her blankets,
she is growing beyond her years
her hair is getting thin with grey

wisdom speaks from the heart that greets
another small child's hands to cradle
yet another tiny hand
o they grow fast she smiles
o ani nah…

i look at the tiny spark of light flickering in her eyes
i cradled this bundle
in my now wrinkled hands
it is
motherhood

—Molly Chisaakay, from "Ani nah," *for my sister-in-law Debi*
(*Ani nah* means mother in the Dene Tha' language)

I am responsible

IRISH SONG

I arise each day
Through the strength
of heaven:
Light of sun,
Radiance of moon,
Splendor of fire,
Speed of lightning
Swiftness of wind,
Depth of sea,
Stability of earth,
Firmness of rock.

—ADAPTED FROM A SONG
ATTRIBUTED TO SAINT PATRICK

If there is a class of educators who need special education for their high and holy calling, it is those who assume the responsibility of parents. Shall we give less thought to the creation of an immortal being than the artist devotes to his statues or landscape? We wander through the galleries in the old world and linger before the works of the great masters, transfixed with grace and beauty, the glory and the grandeur of the ideals that surround us; and with equal preparation, greater than these are possible in living, breathing humanity. The same thought and devotion in real life would soon give us a generation of saints, scholars, scientists, statesmen; of glorified humanity; such as the world has not seen.

—from *Practical Housekeeping: A Careful Compilation of Tried and Approved Recipes,* (1881)

❖ Queen Maya, the pregnant mother of Buddha, reportedly dreamed that a rare white elephant with seven tusks, radiating light, entered her side while she slept. Her seers interpreted this as an indication that her baby would be the savior of mankind.

I overcome

"Nobody eber helps me into carriages, or ober mudpuddles, or give me any best place," said [Sojourner] Truth, and, raising herself to her full height, and her voice to a pitch like rolling thunder, she asked, "And Ar'n't I a woman? Look at me. Look at my arm," and she bared her right arm to the shoulder, showing its tremendous muscular power. "I have plowed and planted and gathered into barns, and no man could head me—and Ar'n't I a woman? I could work as much and eat as much as a man (when I could get it) and bear de lash as well—and Ar'n't I a woman? I have borne thirteen chillen, and seen 'em mos' all sold off into slavery, and when I cried out with a mother's grief, none but Jesus heard—and Ar'n't I a woman?"

—Sojourner Truth (1851), from "And Ar'n't I a Woman?"

How can you hesitate? Risk! Risk anything!
Care no more for the opinion of others,
for those voices. Do the hardest thing on earth
for you. Act for yourself. Face the truth.

—Katherine Mansfield

Sometime during the winter of 1797, two years before George Washington died on Mount Vernon, a black girl came into the world with only her mother present in the muddy cellar of Charles Hardenberg's inn in Ulster County, New York.

No one took notice.

After all, the birth of a black female slave was no earthshaking matter....

Who would have guessed that this wise and famous freedom fighter was that little girl, born between chores in a basement of a forgotten inn nobody even knows for sure when?

Somewhere, in some forgotten and unnoticed corner of the world, just as we read these words, there are other babies being born in hospitals, in alleys, in ghettos, and refugee camps, who are destined by circumstance and calling, by determination and courage, to be sojourners of truth; to dream dreams and to see visions. To change history.

We must listen out for them.

—Ina Hughs, on the life of Sojourner Truth, from *A Prayer for Children*

I am silent

As a child, I stood beside the railroad tracks that bordered the back of our two-acre lot. Caught up by the motion and sound of the rushing train. The magnificent steel turning, shifting, rumbling in the earth beneath my bare feet. Then bursting out of my child play, vanished on its way. I would sit in the grass and let the silence grow inside me. Let the quiet hold me. For in the quiet, the grass, the trees, the ants, the dirt would whisper to me. At least that is when I could hear them.

Silence is a wise sage who brings us knowledge to which our ears are deaf. The languages of creation are many and varied. We may hear them if we listen. Listen with our "very souls."

And so, led by the wisdom of our children, we turn to the whispering grass and talking trees. We clear the path for quiet. For if we have not paused with our children in silence this day, how will we know we are truly alive? How will we know, unless we have heard one another's breath and heartbeat?

— Shea Darian, from *Seven Times the Sun*

But I have calmed and quieted my soul,
like a child quieted at its mother's breast,
like a child that is quieted is my soul.

— PSALM 131:2

When God wants an important thing
done in the world or a wrong righted,
He goes about it in a very singular
way. He doesn't release thunderbolts or
stir up earthquakes, God simply has a
baby born, perhaps of a very humble
home, perhaps of a very humble mother.
And God puts the idea or purpose into
the mother's heart. And she puts it in the
baby's heart, and then…God waits.

— MCEDMOND DONALD

I dance

I like to go in among the rushes where the black birds with red upon their wings do go. I like to touch fingertips with the rushes. I like to listen to the voices that whisper in the swamp. And I do so like to feel the mud ooze up between my toes. Mud has so much of interest in it—slippery feels, and sometimes little seeds that someday will grow into plant-folk, if they do get the right chance. And some were so growing this morning, and more were making beginnings.

Most every day, I do dance. I dance with the leaves and the grass. I feel thrills from my toes to my curls. I feel like a bird, sometimes. Then I spread my arms for wings, and I go my way from stump to stump, and on adown the hill. Sometimes I am a demoiselle, flitting near unto the water. Then I nod unto the willows, and they nod unto me. They wave their arms, and I wave mine. They wiggle their toes in the water a bit, and I do so, too. And every time we wiggle our toes, we do drink into our souls the song of the brook—the glad song it is always singing. And the joy-song does sing on in our hearts.

—Opal Whiteley, from "The Joy-Song of Nature"

My way back into life was ecstatic dance. I reentered my body by learning to move my self, to dance my own dance from the inside out, not the outside in.

—GABRIELLE ROTH

THE NEWBORN DANCE

There is a dance that appears out of nowhere, steps we don't know we know until using them to calm our baby. This dance is something we learned in our sleep, from our own hearts, from our parents, going back and back through all of our ancestors. Men and women do the same dance, and acquire it without a thought. Graceful, eccentric, this wavelike sway is a skilled graciousness of the entire body. Parents possess and lose it after the first fleeting months, but that's all right because already it has been passed on—the knowledge lodged deep within the comforted baby.

Sometimes the dance returns, for moments, when one begs another's newborn child away from other ravished and exhausted parents, but it rarely works. The sway and hop and rhythm are peculiar to your own child, to his or her particular biology and stringed emotion, the harp of nerves.

—Louise Erdrich, from *The Blue Jay's Dance: A Birth Year*

I am supported

Now even as the world descends
my mother my mold my maker
Is with me to the end.

—PATRICIA GOEDICKE

❖ Buddhists have a tradition of tying a piece of red string around the neck or wrists of a pregnant woman's family members and close friends as a way of keeping vigil for the birth. The string is a daily reminder to hold the woman in their prayers as she approaches the moment of motherhood.

On Tuesday, June 17th, 1851 at eight A.M. was born our third daughter, Mary Brown. How glad and thankful were Mr. Maverick and I to have a daughter.... When Mary was seven weeks old, we had to commence feeding her, and I began drinking ale and porter myself to see whether I could provide the proper nourishment—and I recovered my strength rapidly. Baby however, was thin and fretful....

August 23rd. We call in the service of a goat—fed it well—and milk it four or five times a day for baby, and she improves some.

Bone Soup Bath. August 28th, Mrs. Salsmon, an experienced German nurse, came to see baby, and persuaded me to bathe her daily in bone soup. The bone soup is made by boiling beef bones four hours, and then cooling to a temperature of about one hundred, and the bath is ready. Daily I put her into the bath, and kept her there some time, and then, while wet from the bath, rolled her in a blanket and put her to sleep. And when she awaked, I rubbed her well and dressed her. At first the bath did not seem to do any good. But Mr. Maverick asked me to try it one month, and then we saw she had steadily improved. The treatment was kept up for about six months. Mr. Maverick bought a horse and buggy and drove us out into the country every evening.

September 28th, baby is rosy and playful and good.

—from the diary of Mary Ann Maverick, early American settler of San Antonio

I am determined

9 July 1969
Dear Blake,
I've written you no poems or letter while carrying you these past nine months, and some- how feel I can write you now only

I expect to pass through this world but once; any good thing therefore that I can do, or any kindness that I can show to a fellow creature, let me do it now; let me not defer or neglect it, for I shall not pass this way again.

—PROVERBIAL SAYING

because we know, [Kenneth] and I, that our labor with you has definitely begun, and so you seem finally very real, begin- ning your own struggle into the conscious universe.... We have no claims on you. We are your genetic mother and father, and beyond that, and more important, merely two people who will take the responsibility of you while you are still small and helpless, who will love you to the best of our ability, provide you with whatever tools of knowledge, skill, humor and emotional freedom seem to interest you, respect your own individuality, hope you dig us as people but hardly dare insist on that (only try to earn it)—and let go....

Of course, I already envy you. Despite the horrors that oppress people around the world, those people are rising up to fight for their freedom. You are born into the age of worldwide revolution. You will be thirty-one years old in the year 2000. You may well travel to other planets....

If you are a woman, you will grow up in an atmosphere—indeed, a whole Movement—for women's liberation, so that your life will be less reflective of sex- ual oppression than mine, more human.

If you are a man, you will also be freer; you will not need to live a form of stereo- typed masculinity which is based on the oppression of the other sex....

Dear Blake, I love myself right now.

Dear Blake, I love K. so very much.

Dear Blake, I love you, even though we've not been introduced.

Dear Blake, leave my body behind you quickly. K. and I, together throughout labor and delivery, will work hard to aid you in your struggle toward light and air and independence.

Dear Blake, welcome to the universe.

Dear, dear Blake, goodbye.

—Robin Morgan, to her soon-to-be-born child, from *Going Too Far: The personal chronicles of a feminist*

I adapt

Being a mother, as far as I can tell, is a constantly evolving process of adapting to the needs of your child while also changing and growing as a person in your own right.

—DEBORAH INSEL

✤ Native Californians used a rock pillow to flatten the back of their babies' heads, which was considered to be a mark of beauty. From the first moments of life, children were literally molded by cultural values.

Of course I wanted to be a mother one day, but I would be so different from any other mother because I WAS A BOOMING METEOR OF A WOMAN WITH A LIFE FOR GOD'S SAKE! I had energy! Ideas! Plans! No child was going to crash land my party. You wouldn't find me slaving over laundry or wiping sticky green stuff off refrigerator doors. I wasn't going to be like those other mothers who whined. "Oh! I cannot get a single thing done all day!" "You wimp," I'd think. Not me, I had it all planned out: I'd birth Ruby, bond with her, and then resume life as I knew it, writing, working, reading, going to movies and restaurants. Ruby would be nearby, strapped on to me like some exotic appendage, delightful, lovely, and obedient, living my life with me. "Wow!" people would exclaim, "And you're a mother, too!" "Yep," I'd grin, "Ain't I amazing?"... guess I imagined that my life would resemble [my mother's] to some extent, though of course I'd be so much better than she was. I wouldn't talk on the phone all day, wouldn't pick my kids up late from school, wouldn't grit my teeth, loose my cool, or slam my fists down on kitchen tables. I'd be the perfect fairy mom, so sweet and gooey with love and understanding that you could spread me over a muffin.

And then, one June, Ruby came.

—Laurie Wagner, from *Expectations*

I bear

The experience of bearing a child is central to a woman's life. Years after the baby has been born she remembers acutely the details of her labour and her feelings as the child was delivered. —SHEILA KITZINGER

BIRTH STORY

They said it's time to be born. I feel the pressure but I don't want to be born. I'm not ready yet. I'm just going to wait; it feels much better in here.

Now they are coming faster, faster; this way, that way. Oh, it's getting intense! It's pushing, pushing, pushing me out. I want to stay right here where I am, but they insist.

It feels like a tidal wave…I can see that I'm attached to the tidal wave. When it's ready to go, I guess I have to go, too…. Oh-oh, the tidal wave is coming again.

I'm still not ready. It's pushing, pushing. I'm going to stay right here. I don't want to go anyplace, but I have to…. Oh-oh, they are putting on gloves. They are getting me. Oh, goodness sakes, grrrr, that was a squeeze!

They are holding my head, but gently; they were gentle. And next thing I know, they're saying, "You just lie right here," and they wrap me up in something.

—Marianne, remembering her birth under hypnosis, from *Babies Remember Birth*

A WOMAN'S ANOINTING OIL

This recipe is from Margie Beiser Lapanja, author of *Goddess in the Kitchen* and *The Goddess' Guide to Love*. She swears by the "heavenly" effects of this body oil for smoothing skin while its aromatherapeutic qualities relax and calm the senses. She claims the oil will help prevent stretch marks as well.

3 ounces apricot kernel oil
2 ounces sweet almond oil
1 1/2 ounces aloe vera gel
1 ounce wheat germ oil
1/2 ounce rosewater
1/2 teaspoon *(approximately 24 to 30 drops)* lavender essential oil
(Note: there are 2 tablespoons in an ounce.)

Blend the apricot kernel oil, sweet almond oil, aloe vera gel, wheat germ oil, and rosewater together in an eight-ounce bottle. Shake well. Add the lavender oil. Shake well before using. Anoint your body with graceful blessings and thoughts of love after bathing or showering. You are loved. You are beautiful.

I am powerful

"Tonight, the world into which you are coming"—then I was speaking to the invisible child—"is very strange and beautiful. That is, the natural world is beautiful. I don't know what you will think of man, but the dark glisten of vegetation and the blowing of the fertile land wind and the delicate strong step of the sea wind, these things are familiar to me and will be familiar to you. I hope you will be like these things. I hope you will glisten with the glisten of ancient life, the same beauty that is in a leaf or a wild rabbit, wild sweet beauty of limb and eye. I am going on a boat between dark shores, and the river and the sky are so quiet that I can hear the scurryings of tiny animals on the shores and their little breathings seem to be all around. I think of them, wild, carrying their young now, crouched in the dark underbrush with the fruit-scented land wind in their delicate nostrils, and they are looking out at the moon and the greedy world. There is something wild about us too, something tender and wild about my having you as a child, about your crouching so secretly here.

"I put my hand where you lie so silently. I hope you will come glistening with life power, with it shining upon you as upon the feathers of birds. I hope you will be a warrior and fierce for change, so all can live."

—Meridel Le Sueur, from *Annunciation*

Whatever you can do, or dream you can, begin it. Boldness has genius, power and magic in it.

—Johann Wolfgang von Goethe

❖ In the traditional Apache way, the umbilicus was tied after birth and the infant was bathed in water in which the green part of the greasewood shrub had been boiled and then strained. For many weeks following, the child was bathed in this prepared water, especially where the cord had been cut. When the cord remnant dried up and fell off, it was wrapped carefully in beaded buckskin. It was believed to represent a turtle; turtle's power was strong in deflecting lightning.

I am heritage

A people without history is like the
wind on the buffalo grass.

—Sioux saying

My son had a very good singing voice,
even at a very young age (a special gift, I
always thought, but he said I just thought
so because he was my kid). He began, as
we sailed along the highway heading
east, to sing like a flute. Dad told him his
flute sounded beautiful, and it did. Dad
had never heard anything like it. My little boy kept his flute for a long while....
It was a happy flute, but subtle too, and
full of emotional intensity.

This was the first time I thought about
connections to people who had come
before, connections to the land—about
ancestral roots.... And this was the first
time I thought about my own posterity...of the possibility of my own bloodlines continuing down through the ages.

I had taken my camera along and I
took pictures of...my home, my first
home. The wild hills. The tall trees. The
snow. I took a picture of Dad too. I
insisted. In this photo he's standing
under a pine tree, its branches behind his
head and the snow is falling lightly. He's
still handsome at seventy-five, still looks
strong and vital.... This was the last picture that he would ever have taken.

—Janet Campbell Hall, a member of the
last family of the Turtle Clan, from
"Transitions," from *Bloodlines*

❖ At his death at age ninety-six on
October 15, 1992, Samuel S. Mast of
Fryburg, Pennsylvania, had 824 living
descendants: eleven children, ninety-seven
grandchildren, 634 great-grandchildren,
and eighty-two great-great-grandchildren.

❖ Jewish genealogists and religious lead-
ers have recognized the Lurie (or Luria)
family as having traced its genealogy back
to the tenth century
B.C.E. In January
1997, Chief Rabbi
Lau of Israel con-
cluded that the Lurie
family is directly
descended from the
royal house of the
biblical King David.

There are now approximately 800 members
of the original Lurie family, who arrived in
Palestine from Russia and Germany in 1815
and now live throughout the world.

I emerge

BIRTH STORY

When she called me again, it was 2:30 A.M. by my watch. This time she said that she felt like going to the toilet again and also complained of pain. I knew that this time, she was truly in labor so I rushed out for the old bucket and by the time I came back she was pushing. I got things ready as quickly as I possibly could, tidied her bed and then encouraged her to push having cleaned her up. Soon the head of the fetus was seen and in less than another ten minutes the baby was born. It was a girl. The cry of the baby was so strong that I suppose it woke

her husband who came flying into the apartment where we were. Soon he was dancing and shouting for joy and both his shouts and the cry of the baby brought the nearest neighbors in. Every place was full of joy.

—account from a young Nigerian nurse at the childbirth of her relative, as told to Iris Andreski, from *Old Wives' Tales: Life-Stories from Ibibioland*

Arise my beloved, my fair one
and come away
For lo, the winter is past.
Flowers appear on the earth.
The time of singing is here.
The song of the dove
Is heard in the land.

—SONG OF SOLOMON 2:10-12

POEM

Creation often
needs two hearts
one to root
and one to flower
One to sustain
in time of drought
and hold fast
against winds of pain
the fragile bloom
that in the glory
of its hour
affirms a heart
unsung, unseen.

—MARILOU AWIAKTA,
"MOTHEROOT" FROM *ABIDING APPALACHIA*

I am secure

TO MY MOTHER,

Lying here, curled up snugly inside your body, I feel peaceful. My entire surrounding area is love and warmth. I sense your emotions: happiness, sad-

ness, joy and pain. I feel the distinctiveness between day and night. In the day, you go about your business taking extra care so as not to harm me. I hear your gentle voice only utter caring words. At night I listen to the sound of your heartbeat, gently lulling me to sleep and I know that you are there....

The security you feel is the security I feel, the anger and hurt you feel are all passed on to me. But I have both comfort and peace knowing that you are not alone out there. I know because I hear the voice, the deep voice of the one who cares for you and also for me. My father.

This is my idea of peace, being cared for and looked after, feeling warm, secure and wanted and I owe all of these feelings to you. I am blessed with the knowledge that, one day in the not too distant future, I shall be able to see and touch the person who has given me this feeling of peacefulness and tranquility throughout the beginning of my life.... I hope that one day, in an effort to thank you, and also my father, I will do you both proud. I want you both to feel the peace that I feel now.

Love from your child.

—Samantha Williams, age 14, Manchester, England, from *Letters of Peace*

Oh little island,
How can you be so secure,
When countless great mountains
Have sunk in the sea?

—PING-HSIN

RITUAL

Creating or casting a circle around us provides a space where we can direct our energy toward a need, or seek refuge. Imagine a magical circle or ring around the space that you are in. Call on the four directions, saying: "I cast this magical space to create, may it protect me from unwanted energies and draw to me and in me only energy that works with light and love. All other energy be gone." Then imagine that you have a white light around you and know that this light can be called upon whenever you feel the need to have protection.

—ADAPTED FROM HELEN GLISIC, *SPELLBOUND*

I am grace

This little tiny light of mine,
I'm gonna let it shine.
This little tiny light of mine
I'm gonna let it shine.
Let it shine, let it shine, let it shine.

Hide it under a bushel? No!
I'm gonna let it shine.
Hide it under a bushel? No!
I'm gonna let it shine.
Let it shine, let it shine, let it shine.

May we walk with grace and may the light
of the universe shine upon our path.

—ANONYMOUS

The shape of my life today starts with a family. I have a husband, five children and a home just beyond the suburbs of New York. I have also a craft, writing, and therefore work I want to pursue. The shape of my life is, of course, determined by many other things; my background and childhood, my mind and its education, my conscience and its pressures, my heart and its desires. I want to give and take from my children and husband, to share with friends and community, to carry out my obligations to man and to the world, as a woman, as an artist, as a citizen.

But I want first of all—in fact, as an end to these other desires—to be at peace with myself. I want a singleness of eye, a purity of intention, a central core to my life that will enable me to carry out these obligations and activities as well as I can. I want, in fact—to borrow from the language of the saints—to live "in grace" as much of the time as possible. I am not using this term in a strictly theological sense. By grace I mean an inner harmony, essentially spiritual, which can be translated into outward harmony.

—Anne Morrow Lindbergh, from *Gift from the Sea*

I champion

What is astonishing, what can give us enormous hope and belief in a future in which the lives of women and children shall be amended and rewoven by women's hands, is all that we have managed to salvage, of ourselves, for our children...the tenderness, the passion, the trust in our instincts, the evocation of a courage we did not know we owned, the detailed apprehension of another human existence, the full realization of the cost and precariousness of life. The mother's battle for her child—with sickness, with poverty, with war, with all the forces of exploitation and callousness that cheapen human life—needs to become a common human battle, waged in love and in the passion for survival.

Adrienne Rich, from *Of Woman Born: Motherhood as Experience and Institution*

PRAYER FOR WORLD PEACE

We pray for the power to be gentle; the strength to be forgiving; the patience to be understanding; and the endurance to accept the consequences to holding to what we believe to be right.

May we put our trust in the power of good to overcome evil and the power of love to overcome hatred. We pray for the vision to see and the faith to believe in a world emancipated from violence, a new world where fear shall no longer lead men to commit injustice, nor selfishness make them bring suffering to others.

Help us to devote our whole life and thought and energy to the task of making peace, praying always for the inspiration and the power to fulfill the destiny for which we were created.

—from *A Grateful Heart*

Before you were conceived
I wanted you
Before you were born
I loved you
Before you were here an hour
I would die for you
This is the miracle of life

—MAUREEN HAWKINS,
"THE MIRACLE"

I live

We can catalog her being: tissue, fiber, bloodstream, cell, the shape of her experience to the least moment, skin, hair, try to see what she  saw, to imagine what she felt, clitoris, vulva, womb, and we can tell you that despite each injury she survived. That she lived to an old age. (On all the parts of her body we see the years.) By the body of this old woman we are hushed. We are awed. We know that it was in her body that we began. And now we can see that it is from her body that we learn. That we see our past. We say from the body of the old woman, we can tell you something of the lives we lived.

—Susan Griffin, "The Anatomy Lesson," from *Woman and Nature: The Roaring Inside Her*

I don't want to get to the end of my life and find that I just lived the length of it. I want to have lived the width of it as well. —DIANE ACKERMAN

TREE PLANTING CUSTOMS

Planting trees to commemorate special events is a timeless tradition in cultures throughout the world. Ancient cultures believed that trees were the domain of the gods or the spirits of nature, so it is natural that they were and still are chosen to mark important passages in life.

An old Jewish tradition is to plant a tree at the birth of a child—cedar for a boy and pine or apple for a girl. When a couple married, their respective trees were cut down and used in the construction of the *huppah*, or bridal bower.

In Switzerland, it is customary to plant an apple tree at the birth of a boy, a nut tree for a girl. In Sweden, an addition to the family is frequently marked by the planting of a *världsträd* "tree of destiny" at the child's home. From Germany comes the familiar story that on the day Goethe was born, his grandfather promptly planted a pear tree in his garden at Frankfurt.

Missionaries have attested to the prevalence of the custom in Java, Amboina, Guinea, the Fuji Islands, the Solomons, and New Zealand. On the Malacca Peninsula, there is a special semi-sacred enclosure in which birth trees are set up. The practice is inspired by the idea that the life and destiny of the newborn are bound up in some mythic fashion with that of the tree.

I am the beginning

The symbol of autumn is the seed, where future life lies compressed and perfectly ordered within a tender, flexible space.... "Here, in the seed," notes *The I Ching,* "in the deep hidden stillness, the end of everything is joined to a new beginning."

"From such small beginnings—a mere grain of dust, as it were—do mighty trees take their rise," wrote Henry David Thoreau in *The Dispersion of Seeds....* Drawn to the core, the inner substance and deeper meaning of life, Thoreau wandered through the woods and fields of his native Massachusetts, carefully observing how seeds were scattered by the wind or transported by birds, squirrels, foxes, and other forest creatures...."We find ourselves in a world that is already planted but is also still being planted as at first," he wrote. In the tiny, frail seeds of autumn, the wholeness and holiness of the world were revealed to him.

—Katherine Ketcham, from *In the House of the Moon*

✣ **Native American women wear birthing belts made from the skins of mountain lions, black-tail deer, white-tail deer, and antelope—all animals that have easy births. Medicine men are called in to pray to the spirits of these animals when a woman approaching confinement puts on the belt. It is worn constantly during the critical period, but only for a day or so, and is not removed until after the child is born.**

To everything there is a season, and a time to every purpose under heaven: A time to be born, and a time to die; a time to plant, and a time to pluck up that which is planted;...A time to weep, and a time to laugh;...A time to keep silence, and a time to speak; a time to love, and a time to hate; a time of war, and a time of peace.

—Ecclesiastes

Babies are a nice way to start people. —Don Herold

I am the gardener

Watching gardeners
label their plants
I vow with all beings
to practice the old
horticulture and let
the plants identify me.

—ROBERT AITKEN

They say a child is born
a blank shape to be molded,
a tabula rasa to be written upon.
But children come
like a plane with a rhizome—
its food source,
the genetic coding for what flower it will become,
how often it will bear fruit,
what its artistry is;
all of that born into it with the seed.
The role of the gardener, then,
is simply to discern the manner of the plant
or child trying to emerge.
The role of the gardener,
or parent then,
is simply to ask,
"How do I help it grow
into what it is in its roots?"

—Dawna Markova, from *Prayers for Healing*

CELTIC TREE ALPHABET

The ancients envisioned the entire cosmos in the form of a tree, believing that the earth's trees were keys to the mysteries of life. They sought to understand the essence of "the tree of life," certain that this was the same as understanding the mystery of women and the secrets of creation.

TREE	LETTER	SYMBOLISM
Birch	*Beth*	Birth and beginnings; connection with the White Goddess (life-giver)
Rowan	*Luis*	Sacred to Goddess Brigit (fertility); immortality
Ash	*Nion*	From roots came life-giving female lunar blood; universal mother, source of unborn souls
Holly	*Tinne*	From the Goddess Holle, universal mother and the patron of all newborn children. She had charge of naming them—which was the symbolic equivalent of giving a child its soul.

I am the tree

When the Civil War ended, the homeplace broke into fragments. So Little Grandma, the ninety pounds of her there were, took over. She taught her nine boys how to plow; they planted the fields together, they hoed and tended; and their mother was always there helping, making it seem like fun, while the two small daughters played dolls nearby and the baby lay asleep under a tree, near the branch.

One day, Little Grandma heard the snapping of twigs and saw, coming down the edge of the water, a swamp cat. He was almost as close as she; not quite, but he could spring swiftly and she knew it. She did not take her eyes off him as she started slowly towards the baby....

I have heard it all my life, this story. Little Grandma would sit by her hearth, stirring her fire now and then, and tell us. And while she told it, we would be roasting pecans in the ashes, or sweet potatoes. She would tell it and always it was a legend of reassurance, a story of human strength able to deal with what comes to a person day by day. Things are like that, she made us feel — This little lady who was more than eighty years old and still so slight and so strong. The swamp panther is always killed before it reaches the baby.

—Lillian Smith, from *The Journey*

Trees are not known by their leaves, nor even by their blossoms, but by their fruits.

—ELEANOR OF AQUITAINE

Tree...
He watching you.
You look at tree,
he listen to you.
He got no finger,
he can't speak.
But that leaf...
He pumping, growing,
growing in the night.
While you sleeping
you dream something.
Trees and grass same thing.
They grow with your body,
with your feeling.

—ABORIGINE SONG

I return

My mother is my mirror and I am hers. What do we see?
Our face grown young again. —Marge Piercy

29.8.44

The birth of a new member of the family always makes one feel reminiscent and remember one's childhood days and other births. I missed your birth for I was in England then, but when Nan came and Indu, I was very much there and I have vivid recollections of the events. And then the growth of the little ones, their childhood, girlhood, and womanhood. It is an unending panorama of human life with its sweet and bitterness, its ups and downs. One would think that with all this age-long experience and personal and racial memories, nothing very novel can be expected. The old cycle repeats itself again and again. And yet whenever a person arrives, it is something absolutely new, like others and still unique in its own way. Nature goes on repeating itself but there is no end to

its infinite variety and every spring is resurrection, every new birth a new beginning. Especially when that new birth is intimately connected with us, it becomes a revival of ourselves and our old hopes center around it....
Love,
Your loving brother,
Jawahar

—from a letter written by Jawaharlal Nehru while in prison to his sister Krishna Hutheesing, concerning the confinement of his daughter Indira Gandhi and the birth of his first grandson, Rajiv

Prayer for Clarity

May I enter this house
with clear thoughts, (touch forehead)
wise words, (touch lips)
kind heart. (place open palm over heart)

—Shea Darian, from *Seven Times the Sun*

I am sister

My sister, Margaret, was born during the early weeks of 1955. I was three and a half years old. My brother Allen was eighteen months younger than me. We'd prepared for the baby by helping our mother sterilize baby bottles and nipples; we were impressed by the tiny clothes. The bassinet took up the corner in my parents' room. My brother was moved to my room. I sneaked smells of baby powder and baby oil and imagined being sister to a girl, just as the doll in my cradleboard. My mother said we were ecstatic when she brought the baby home, for she'd told us Margaret was a gift for my brother and me. Margaret was the name bestowed on this gift of birth....

Sister is a new name, which I am fitting myself to. It means protector of this infant who still wears the stub of her birth cord, something I'm quite intrigued with—its appearance and smell remind me of the newborn puppies who abruptly disappeared shortly after our dog had given birth. Margaret's tiny hands are not much larger than the dolls my brother and I doctor and feed dirt, when we're not running or building worlds of sand and earth. I feel intimate and exposed by this little sister. Though I had been prepared in the weeks before her birth no one could precisely touch this feeling. I wonder now, how did I understand the role?

—Joy Harjo, "Gift of Margaret," from *Sister to Sister*

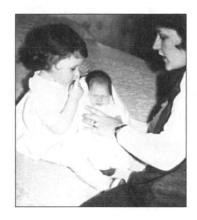

In thee my soul shall own combined
The sister and the friend

If from my eyes by thee detained
The wanderer cross the seas,
No more thy love shall soothe, as friend,
No more as sister please.

—CATHERINE KILLIGREW (1530-1583)

I am courageous

*Childbirth is more
admirable than
conquest, more
amazing than
self-defense, and
as courageous
as either one.*

—GLORIA STEINEM

In these past months, no matter how many books and articles I read on infant development, those first sparks of intelligence remain wonderfully mysterious. If you look into a newborn baby's eyes, those cloudy orbs that search your face as if trying to recognize you, inevitably the question will arise: what is the origin of its spirit?... Where her body came from is clear enough, but her little spirit—that invisible but no less real part of her being—where did that arise from?...

Is it true, as some of the world's people believe, that the laboring mother must descend into the underworld to fetch a new soul to inhabit her child? It was not until after Catherine was born that I read about this concept, yet it felt right. Those last ten or fifteen minutes, while I worked at pushing her out—each push was a plunge into black watery depth. The only way to get out of the depths was to dive back in.... Giving birth, even with an easy delivery, is a descent into the depths. It is an act of extra-ordinary courage that is performed by women thousands of times a day.

—Anne Carson, from *Spiritual Parenting in the New Age*

Hopi women experienced the moment of birth alone. Immediately after the newborn slipped from the birth canal, the baby's maternal grandmother joined the new mother and cut the umbilical cord. The paternal grandmother fastened a heavy blanket over the door to block out all light and created an atmosphere much like the darkened womb. The mother and child then spent a restful, eighteen-day "lying-in" period. Each day a ripe ear of corn was laid near the bed and on the nineteenth day, the mother rose to grind the corn into meal for the next day's celebratory breakfast.

The next morning, mother and child were purified with yucca suds and the baby was given a name by the mother's female relatives. In the predawn darkness, the women carried the baby to the edge of the mesa to meet the sacred Sun Father. The grandmother lifted the baby up just as the sun rose over the horizon, so that the first rays of light shone on its face. "Prayer meal" was sprinkled over the baby and a prayer was recited. After the ceremony, the newest member of the family took a nap while the rest of the group feasted.

I soar

There was a bird's egg once, picked up by chance upon the ground, and those who found it bore it home and placed it under a barn-door fowl. And in time the chick bred out, and those who had found it chained it by the leg to a log, lest it should stray and be lost. And by and by they gathered round it, and speculated as to what the bird might be. One said, "It is surely a waterfowl, a duck or it may be a goose; if we took it to the water it would swim and gabble." But another said, "It has no webs to its feet; it is a barn-door fowl; should you let it loose it will scratch and cackle with the others on the dung-heap." But a third speculated, "Look now at its curved beak; no doubt it is a parrot, and can crack nuts!" But a fourth said, "No, but look at its wings: perhaps it is a bird of some great flight." But several cried, "Nonsense! Can you suppose that a thing can do a thing which no one has ever seen it do?" And the bird, with its leg chained close to the log, preened its wing. So they sat about it, speculating, and discussing it: and one said this, and another that. And all the while as they talked the bird sat motionless, with its gaze fixed on the clear, blue sky above it. And one said, "Suppose we let the creature loose to see what it will do?"—and the bird shivered. But the others cried, "It is too valuable; it might get lost. If it were to try to fly it might fall down and break its neck." And the bird, with its foot chained to the log, sat looking upward into the clear blue sky; the sky, in which it had never been—for the bird knew what it would do—because it was an eaglet!

—Olive Schreiner, from *Woman and Labour (1911)*

✤ The Celts believed in fly souls and butterfly souls which flew about seeking a new mother. It was thought that women became pregnant by swallowing these souls.

Butterflies are colorful and bright and gentle and have no way to harm you. They go about their business and bring others pleasure while doing it, because just seeing one flying around makes people happy...I'm content with what I am, and butterflies seem to be content to be just what they are, too. They're gentle, but determined.

— DOLLY PARTON, FROM *DOLLY*

I am eager

What I wanted was to be where she was. Where she was the current was faster, the light more brilliant, the colors brighter. Air turned stale when she was gone, scintillant when she was there. She enhanced the ordinary present with her presence, made the quotidian more interesting than otherwise. I felt not that something was about to happen, but that something was happening now. I learned the reverberations of moment heaped upon moment. A word was important because she had spoken it, the vibrations of her voice continued to energize the local air indefinitely. A chunk of granite flecked with mica became a sacred stone because she picked it up, put it down. When she left a room, the space kept a faint residue of her presence. Nothing alive and touched by her hand could ever again be simply dull, dead matter.

She left dishes undone to help me perfect handstands, wrestling and giggling with me, tumbling me against her. She was lavish with hugs, making a big to-do lifting me to her lap, urging me closer, settling me against her. She read stories, taught me cat's cradle and witch's broom, laughed prettily at my remarks. She talked the butcher into giving her sheets of butcher paper for my drawings. And she got down on the floor on her hands and knees and admired the accumulating crayon, urging me on to grander sweeps all the way across that great, open field.

—Marilyn Krysl, "Mother" from *Mozart, Westmoreland and Me*

Children are the power and the beauty of the future. Like tiny falcons we can release their hearts and minds, and send them soaring, gathering the air to their wings, searching for the knowledge it is their right to want.

—SKIP BERRY

I dawn

You fall into your mother's womb, in your mother's womb nine months, ten days. The first month you are called Dot. The second month Light of Beginning. The third month Light of the Soul. The fourth month Light of the Countenance. The fifth month Light of the Womb. The sixth month Abdullah the Slow. The seventh month bow to the right, bow to the left, you are a daughter. The eighth month Light of Birth. The ninth month your outline and measure can be seen. The tenth out you come…you know your mother's body, you open your eyes and utter three prayers. The first utterance lifts the soul to the breast, the second utterance, the breath of life to the breasts. The third utterance lifts the vital force. May all your feelings be good. You let yourself breathe in the first five vital forces as you wave your arms.

—Malaysian song

That first night the three of us slept deeply and I had no dreams. I awoke at six in the morning and thought at first that it was Christmas. I felt as though there was something wonderful in the house, some great present. Then I remembered the baby.

—Janet Isaacs Ashford

PUEBLO VERSE

Hold on to what is good
        even if it is a handful of earth.
Hold on to what you believe
        even if it is a tree which stands by itself.
Hold on to what you must do
        even if it is a long way from here.
Hold on to life
        even when it is easier letting go.
Hold on to my hand
        even when I have gone away from you.

I sow

Sow the living part of yourselves in the furrow of life.
—MIGUEL DE UNAMINO

In my mother's garden, nothing lacks attention. Each stalk is carefully tended. Each lovingly nurtured. The stalks of the cabbages are always green, thick, and healthy. Their branches sprout out fully, not thinly and sickly. She always makes sure that all the weeds are plucked, that her babies are well nourished, and that the hard earth is softened. The soil of her garden, like her babies, glows with life and acknowledges her love....

I understand, now, that my mother's garden is more than a plot of land with growing vegetation. Her garden is about the power of love, faith, endurance, and vision. There, in her garden, I am showered with love and the history of our people—Hmong. Her view on gardening is rooted in our people's history. From our journeys from land to land, fighting for survival, Hmong had to envision the future existence of our roots. In order to make that vision a reality, our foremothers had to nourish and care for their garden the same way my mother has tended hers. They fought for the right to sow their garden—their roots and seeds. Their dreams and hopes for the future were all placed and mapped in their gardens. Without our mothers and foremothers, the history and existence of my people would have been lost in the shuffle of life's tragedies. They are the life-givers. Their garden is a symbol of their independence, vision, beauty, strength, perseverance, and courage. It is there in this garden that I am rooted and encouraged to spread—to multiply by leaps and bounds like dandelions.

—Ka Vang, from "Inheriting My Mother's Garden," *Making More Waves*

❖ Victorian women were urged to consider themselves "gardeners" whose duty it was to provide "good soil" for the baby.

I am the truth

My mother knew God. They were in constant touch. When I lied she would look into my eyes, then declare, you're lying…God told her everything. When I spoke the truth, He told her it was the truth. I was sure my mother was conspiring with gods in my grandparents' room, which had all their photographs and images. Were they all in league with her— Lord Rama, Lord Krishna, Lord Shiva, Lord Venkateshwara, Goddess Parvati, Goddess Saraswati, Goddess Lakshmi? I suspected it was Lord Rama who told my mother, for it was him she prayed to, his stories she told me every night. Or maybe it was Rama's devotee, Lord Hanuman. The more I pondered, the surer I was that it was Hanuman…. When we prayed to Hanuman on Tuesdays at the little temple outside our house, I placed extra hibiscus flowers at his feet in the hope that he would refrain from carrying tales to my mother.

—Anjana Appachana, "My Only Gods" from *The Forbidden Stitch*

Tell a pregnant woman that her unborn child hears her voice or senses her love, and she's bound to agree. For mothers intuitively know what scientists have only recently discovered: that the unborn child is a deeply sensitive individual who forms a powerful relationship with his or her parents—and the outside world—while still in the womb.

Now that you are pregnant, you may well have joined the ranks of women who understand the importance of communicating love and acceptance to the child you carry within. As you sing to, dance with, and massage your baby, you will stimulate his/her nervous system and communicate your love. And as you talk to, dream about, and even visualize your unborn child, you will strengthen forever your life-long bond, making your pregnancy a time of enormous joy and growth.

—Thomas Verny and Pamela Weintraub, from *Nurturing Your Unborn Child*

❖ Sprouting wheat, known as the "plant of truth," was cultivated in the famous gardens of Adonis, who was worshipped as a savior-god. Clay pots were used to symbolize the Mother's womb—a commonplace custom practiced into the twentieth century C.E.

I am the river

✤ The famous River Styx of Greek mythology, whose name means "fearful, magical, and taboo," was imagined as a river of goddess blood that emanated from Earth's womb. Its other name was the letter Alpha, meaning "birth."

You cannot step twice into the same river, for fresh waters are ever flowing in upon you. —ANONYMOUS

The moon calls to the sea and the sea calls to the humble stream, which flows on and on from wherever it springs in search of the sea, no matter how far away it may lie, and growing as it flows, the stream rushes on until no mountain can hold back its surge. The sun calls to the grapevine, which spreads and rises in its hunger for sunlight. The early morning air calls forth the smells of the awakening city, the aroma of newly baked bread, of newly brewed coffee, and the aromas fill the air and possess it. Night calls to the water lily, and at the stroke of midnight those white points of light burst open in the river, opening the darkness, penetrating it, breaking it apart and swallowing it up.

—Eduardo Galeano, from *The Book of Embraces*

WISH BLESSING

Just as water flowing in the streams and rivers fill the ocean, thus may all your moments of goodness touch and benefit all beings, those here now and those gone before.

May all your wishes be soon fulfilled as completely as the moon on a full-moon night, as successfully as from the Wish-Fulfilling Gem. May all dangers be averted; may all disease leave you.

May no obstacles come across your way and may you enjoy happiness and long life.

May those who are always respectful, honoring the way of the elders, prosper in the four blessings of old age, beauty, happiness and strength.

— The Buddha

I am bold

Falling on his knees by her bedside he held his wife's hand to his lips, kissing it, and that hand, by a feeble move-ment of the fingers, replied to the kisses. And meanwhile at the foot of the bed, like a flame above a lamp, flickered in Mary Vlasevna's skillful hands the life of a human being who had never before existed: a human being who, with the same right and the same importance to himself, would live and procreate others like himself.

"Alive! Alive! And a boy! Don't be anxious," Levin heard Mary Vlasevna say, as she slapped the baby's back with a shaking hand.

"Mama, is it true?" asked Kitty.

The Princess could only sob in reply.

And amid the silence, as a positive answer to the mother's question, a voice quite unlike all the restrained voices that had been speaking in the room made itself heard. It was a bold, insolent voice that had no consideration for anything, it was the cry of the new human being who had so incomprehensibly appeared from some unknown realm.

—Leo Tolstoy, from *Anna Karenina*

A MOTHER'S INSTINCT

Born in 1815, pioneering feminist Elizabeth Cady Stanton was known for questioning authority. She tells here how she not only ques-tioned the methods her doctors were employing to treat her four-day-old son's "bent" collarbone, but surpassed their remedies altogether:

I told them how badly their bandages worked and what I had done myself. They smiled at each other, and one said:

"Well, after all, a mother's instinct is better than a man's reason."

"Thank you, gentlemen, there was no instinct about it. I did some hard think-ing before I saw how I could get a pres-sure on the shoulder without impeding the circulation, as you did."

Thus in the supreme moment of a young mother's life, when I needed ten-der care and support, I felt the whole responsibility of my child's supervision; but though uncertain at every step of my own knowledge, I learned another les-son in self-reliance. I trusted neither men nor books absolutely after this, either in regard to the heavens above or the earth beneath, but continued to use my "mother's instinct," if "reason" is too dignified a term to apply to woman's thoughts, study first what relates to babyhood, as there is no department of human action in which there is such lamentable ignorance.

listen

I hush
the uproar rushing
your soothed room
and in the lull listen
to quiet sounds these walls whisper.
Drowsy flowers nod and the tempo begins
of another time. Another woman with child
unravels then weaves ecstatic in her sultry bloom.
I join her circle and round faster,
as your plush fingers nudge my womb
like the plump of a dandelion landing,
calling softly,

I am here
and I listen too,
for the hour you'll push the bold river
and meet the promising sea,
where your cries will bring touch,
your laughter will delight,
your thoughts will find home in my heart.

ANDREA ALBAN GOSLINE

I listen

--- SUGGESTION ---

When your baby has something to tell you and begins to fuss or cry, take a deep breath and relax. Will any negative feelings that arise to settle, and clear your mind. Look deeply into his eyes, hold him firmly but tenderly, and connect with him through your hands. Tell him with your voice, eyes and hands that you would like to hear what he has to say. Stay connected and receptive. The message you will be sending is: "I respect your feelings. I value you just the way you are." Invariably, your baby will grow more confident and trust that he has a very special place in the world.

For when you come to think of it, the only way to love a person is…by listening to them and seeing and believing in the god, in the poet, in them. For by doing this, you keep the god and the poet alive and make it flourish.

— BRENDA UELAND

Cool beneath melon-colored cloth, your belly—
a joyous ripening that happens & happens,
that gently takes root & takes over,
a miracle uncelebrated under an autumn dress
that curves & falls slowly to your ankles

As you busy yourself with backyard gardening,
humming, contained, I think of your tongue
at peace in its place; another kind of fruit,
mysterious flower behind two lips that open
for air & for exits & entrances.

       Perhaps if I placed
my hungry ear up next to a cantaloupe or coconut
(for hours at a time & enough),
I'd hear a fluttering or maybe a music almost like
the story I've heard with my ear to your belly,
a sea-shell history of evolution personified

Your womb is a room where it's always afternoon

—Al Young, from "For Arl in Her Sixth Month"

I am the wind

The heart of speech beats in your small chest, trying to get out. Like the ocean searching to escape through crevices of shore rocks fallen tightly together extending the land out to the sea. Your speech is breath. Air from your chest almost empty of sound, pushing hard as if to pick up tones like sediment stuck to the sides of your throat, jollying your voice box into activity. You are a gold digger panning for gold, scavenging the river bottom for the heaviest little sound, not the sand and silt that is silent but the nuggets, audible shapes of precious speech. I hear the iron pan scratching against the sand and mossy rocks but nothing shiny comes out; just a few squeaks, fool's gold. Your own little wind hurdles again from your gut through tubes, funnels into your throat, and blows out in small gusts of muted language. Your own breath is the eye of your storming mouth, pushing, pushing it out until suddenly there it is: a word that I cannot understand.

—Leslie Kirk Campbell, from
The Journey into Motherhood

Who has seen the wind?
        Neither I nor you;
But when the leaves hang trembling,
        the wind is passing through.
Who has seen the wind?
        Neither you nor I:
But when the trees bow down their heads,
        The wind is passing by.

—CHRISTINA ROSSETTI, FROM "WHO HAS SEEN THE WIND?"

BREATH OF LIFE

Breath has been synonymous with "soul" or "spirit" since women in ancient matriarchal societies believed that a woman not only forms her child out of her own uterine blood, but also animates her body. This theory may be the root of the habit of gently blowing into the mouth of a newborn to initiate breathing, rather than slapping the infant's bottom, as in the classical male-medical method. Brahman fathers gave their newborn children souls by breathing into their faces. Biblical scribes believed that God "mothered" Adam by breathing "the breath of life" into his nostrils (Genesis 2:7).

I am joyous

A MOTHER'S SONG

It is so still in the house,
There is a calm in the house;
The snowstorm wails out there,
And the dogs are rolled up with snouts under the tail.
My little boy is sleeping on the ledge,
On his back he lies, breathing through his open mouth.
His little stomach is bulging round—
Is it strange if I start to cry with joy?

—anonymous Eskimo woman

O, listen! Hear! Sing with me, for I am joy. —CHEROKEE SONG

THE BIRTH OF A PRINCE

Murasaki Shikibu lived in eleventh century Japan and wrote an epic novel, *The Tale of Genji*, which chronicled Kyoto life. The book was so successful and its author so famous that she was called to live in the court of Queen Akiko. From 1007 to 1010 C.E., Shikibu kept an elegantly calligraphed diary in which she chronicled court life in great detail. Here is an excerpt from her diary, recounting the birth of Queen Akiko's son:

Tenth day of the long-moon month.

…There assembled not only the priests who had been summoned here for these months, but also itinerant monks who were brought from every mountain and temple. Their prayers would reach to the Buddhas of the three worlds. All the soothsayers in the world were summoned. Eight million gods seemed to be listening with ears erect for their Shinto prayers. Messengers ran off to order sutra-reciting at various temples; thus the night was passed.…

Eleventh day.… The Queen was moved towards the veranda.… At noon we felt that the sun came out at last. The Queen was at ease!

She is now at peace. Incomparable joy! Moreover, it is a prince, so the joy cannot be oblique.…

The navel cord was cut by the Prime Minister's Lady. Lady Tachibana of the Third Rank gave the breast for the first time. For the wet-nurse Daisaemon-no-Omoto was chosen, for she has been in the Court a long time and is very familiar with it; the daughter of Munetoki, courtier and Governor of Bitchu, and the nurse of Kurodono-Ben were also chosen as nurses.

—from the *Diaries of Court Ladies of Old Japan*

I am connected

Extended family and community were strong in my upbringing. When my mother spent months in the hospital from an extended bout with poor health, her mother, my Grandma Angelique, became even more important in our lives. Dad used to pitch a tent in the back yard so we could sleep out with Grandma. "Look," she'd exclaim as we watched the Northern Lights flicker across the sky. "The ghosts are dancing."

I spent hours sitting beside her, drinking tea and watching her make birch bark baskets, decorating them with dyed roots and porcupine quills. It was from her I learned patience. She was the only one in the village that made baskets, whittling away at red willow, peeling the roots and collecting birch bark....

Our family is now scattered throughout the province. There are 45 of us and we are close, gathering frequently for holidays. Often, as I work in my chosen profession, I lose focus and get caught up with the daily realities and stress of deadline. That's when I head for my home in the north, to refocus, but most important, to renew my spirit.

—Joan Beatty, from "Cree Family," from *Catch the Whisper of the Wind* by Cheewa James

❖ **The virtues of rocking a baby were endorsed by Plato: "For the bodies as well as the souls of very young infants, it is beneficial for all, but especially for the youngest, to experience as much as possible during the night, as during the day, in addition to nourishment, a sort of swinging; in short, it would do them good to live, if possible, as if they had never stopped floating in the sea."**

To the mother alone it has been given, that her soul during the nine months should touch the soul of the child.

—JEAN BAPTISTE LACORDAIRE

RITUAL

Reflect on your surroundings. Are you native to your part of the world and do you feel at home there? Find out as much as you can about local folklore, history, and customs. Consciously put down roots and you will feel a greater connection with people and places when one day you walk around your neighborhood with your baby.

I learn

As anyone who has raised children can attest, motherhood is the world's most intensive course in love. We may experience it, by turns, as a state of grace or oblivion, entrapment or exaltation, profound joy or numbing fatigue. Sometimes we pass through all these emotions in the course of a single day. And yet, the next morning we are ready to resume. We bear our children, love them and struggle with them, learn to accept them as they are, and ultimately, learn to let them go. In the process, we learn much about ourselves. Some of these lessons have seemed to us, at times, too dark or painful to examine by the light of day; others we have shared easily. As Louise Erdrich wrote in her memoir *The Blue Jay's Dance: A Birth Year*, "Mothering is a subtle art whose rhythm we collect and learn, as much from one another as by instinct. Taking shape, we shape each other, with subtle pressures and sudden knocks. The challenges shape us, approvals refine, the wear and tear of small abrasions transform us until we're slowly made up of one another and yet wholly ourselves."

—Katrina Kenison and Kathleen Hirsch, from
Mothers: Twenty Stories of Contemporary Motherhood

*If you want to learn something well,
then teach it.*

—WALTER TROBISCH

SUGGESTION

Catching the baby as she slips warm and wet from your body can be a life-altering moment for both you and your partner. For many couples, the birth of their baby is accompanied by emotions that defy description. Touching the baby as she first enters the world offers a concrete sensory experience that can perhaps be more easily shared with loved ones.

I hear

As a young man, I was mystified by this unusual ability I had—to play certain pieces sight unseen. I'd be conducting a score for the first time and suddenly, the cello line would jump out at me; I'd know the flow of the piece even before I turned the page of the score. One day, I mentioned this to my mother, who is a professional cellist. I thought she'd be intrigued because it was always the cello line that was so distinct in my mind. She was; but when she heard what the pieces were, the mystery quickly solved itself. All the scores I knew sight unseen were ones she had played while she was pregnant with me.

—Boris Brott, conductor of the Hamilton (Ontario) Philharmonic Symphony, from *The Secret Life of the Unborn Child*

> *A wise mother learns each day*
> *from quiet listening.*
> *Her parenting springs from her*
> *children's changing needs.*
>
> —VIMALA MCCLURE

BABIES' EXPRESSION

Babies seem to act as individuals long before birth—they are spontaneously active and express preferences for certain sounds, motions, and tastes. They have even been observed to react to danger. Newborns engage in many complex activities, integrating sounds and sights, regulating exercise and sleep, and demonstrating true learning ability. Using their communication skills, babies will engage you in a sweet, simple dialogue (research films show that they lead as well as respond in dialogue with parents) and, if you watch closely, will express happiness, surprise, sadness, fear, anger, disgust, interest, and distress. Babies watch intently for changes in your face and can instantly mimic your expressions of sadness, happiness, or surprise. Unadulterated emotions are clearly reflected on their faces. Look and listen well, and your baby will be the first to teach you how to be a parent.

I am present

There is no beyond, there is only here, the infinitely small, infinitely great and utterly demanding present.

—IRIS MURDOCH

RITUAL

When you bring your baby home from the hospital, make time to marvel at his or her arrival into your life. Create a circle of calm for your family. The organizing, the unpacking, the day-to-day activities, can be suspended for a time. Count fingers and toes, trace eyebrows, look at every inch of your baby with love and admiration. Honor this unique time of your baby's brand-newness in your life.

We must have sat in that spot on the settee in the bay window for three hours. I held Gulliver and nursed him. He slept. It was very peaceful. Part of the pleasure for us of that pause was being back in our own home after two years abroad, being rooted. Everything we owned had been packed away. I enjoyed the sunlight on our pink Persian rug. I could see that beautiful fuchsia my mother had given me. The light was on that plant, and a cherrywood box of ivory dominoes from my great-grandmother....

But the embrace of all these things was not felt as much as a true sense of love in the house. A new person was entering our lives, a new person was making us three instead of two. We wanted him to feel at home. We wanted him to feel that he was surrounded by love. We wanted him to feel comfortable and harmonious. We didn't want to be tense and running around and worried.

We were entering a new era of our lives, and we wanted to start out on the right foot. Tom said later, "I'm so glad we did that, so glad we just sat there and enjoyed him and looked at him and were calm, because if we'd come in and immediately started organizing the stuff from the hospital and getting the diapers out, I don't think that would have been the right thing to do."

After three hours in that corner, in that lovely light, it began to get dark. We turned on a lamp, a favorite lamp with a rose-colored shade we had bought long ago. Then we carried him upstairs. That was it. After that moment of quiet and calm, we started the business of being parents.

—Meredith Hughes, from *Mothers Talking, Sharing the Secret* by Frances Wells Burck

Today many of the lifestyle changes suggested for contemporary pregnant women are based on sound medical research and common sense—no smoking, no alcohol, following a nutrient-rich diet, etc. But during the nineteenth century, and even into the twentieth century, the restrictions outlined for expectant mothers ranged from inconvenient to ludicrous. A European-based belief held that pregnant women were not supposed to leave their home after sunset. If a woman ignored this edict and ventured into the night, she must never urinate under a full moon for fear of being inseminated by the "celestial being" and thus liable to give birth to a supernatural creature. If she weighed herself during pregnancy she would jeopardize the health of the fetus. Waltzing, swinging, and singing were also off-limits. Expectant mothers were cautioned not to ride on streetcars, walk through stores, or organize their cupboards! In explaining the need to forgo sex during gestation, one doctor of the time wrote, "Let your lodger enjoy his apartment in peace."

I promise

I am with you always,
even to the end of the world.

—MATTHEW 28:20

It is time for the baby's birthday party: a white cake, strawberry-marshmallow ice cream, a bottle of champagne saved from another party. In the evening, after she has gone to sleep, I kneel beside the crib and touch her face, where it is pressed against the slats, with mine. She is an open and trusting child, unprepared for and unaccustomed to the ambushes of family life, and perhaps it is just as well that I can offer her little of that life. I would like to give her more. I would like to promise her that she will grow up with a sense of her cousins and of rivers and of her great-grandmother's teacups, would like to pledge her a picnic on a river with fried chicken and her hair uncombed, would like to give her home for her birthday, but we live differently now and I can promise her nothing like that. I give her a xylophone and a sundress from Madeira, and promise to tell her a funny story.

—Joan Didion, "On Going Home" from *Slouching Towards Bethlehem*

I am hopeful

Hope is the thing with feathers
That perches in the soul
And sings the tune without the words
And never stops at all

—EMILY DICKINSON

Dearest Minus Three Days,

My deep, sweet little love, the doctors
have decided your debut will be in
three days' time. Do you know that
Isaac means "he who laughed" and
Hannah means "grace" and Saul
means "deeply wanted?" You're all
of those, and boy or girl, I love you.
We love you. Good night, poppet.
I'll see you on Monday or Tuesday.
Love, Mother

—IRMA KURTZ, FROM WRITTEN BY PARENTS,
9 MONTHS, 1 DAY, 1 YEAR

THE GIFT OF HOPE

Upon winning the Antoinette Perry Award
for best performance by an actor in the
Broadway musical Raisin, Virginia
Capers shared the following about her
mother:

When I was small and she would
take me out for a walk where the cur-
tains were clean and things were nice
and pretty, she used to tell me that
hope lived in those windows. Her
teaching me that hope comes from
within, that it's something that grows
inside you, was one of the main reasons that I hung on for twenty-three
years until this moment.

—Virginia Capers

❖ Research reveals that newborns listen attentively as long as the caregiver
reads properly, but they stop listening
as soon as words are read backward (as
nonsense)—an indication of good
thinking skills.

The hope of the world—of birthing women, mothers, friends, and kin—rests in the newborn infant. The infant's hope resides in the world's welcome. As they take up the life that birthing labor has given, infants express what Simone Weil described as "this profound and childlike and unchanging expectation of good in the heart"—an expectation that she called sacred.

To respond to the promise of birth is to respect a birthing woman's hope in her infant and her infant's hope in the world.... A mother completes a birthing woman's labor by adopting her infant and thus protecting in the world the physical promise and vulnerability she has created. To "adopt" is to respond to an infant's trust that "good and not evil will be done to him." To adopt in and for the world means resisting "in the teeth of all experience of crimes committed, suffered, and witnessed" anyone or any policy that cruelly or carelessly violates that trust. To adopt is to make a space, a "peace" where the promise of birth can survive.

—Sara Ruddick, from *Maternal Thinking: Toward a Politics of Peace*

A mother understands what a child does not say.

—JEWISH PROVERB

I understand

I cannot recall what happened during the first months after my illness. I only know that I sat in my mother's lap or clung to her dress as she went about her household duties. My hands felt every object and observed every motion, and in this way I learned to know many things. Soon I felt the need of some communication with others and began to make crude signs. A shake of the head meant "No" and a nod, "Yes," a pull meant "Come" and a push, "Go." Was it bread that I wanted? Then I would imitate the acts of cutting the slices and buttering them. If I wanted my mother to make ice cream for dinner I made the sign for working the freezer and shivered, indicating cold. My mother, moreover, succeeded in making me understand a good deal. I always knew when she wished me to bring her something, and I would run upstairs or anywhere else she indicated. Indeed, I owe to her loving wisdom all that was bright and good in my long night.

—Helen Keller, from *The Story of My Life*

I am aware

When we are in touch with our bodies, we become in touch with the natural rhythms of life imbedded in our bones and tissues. The more aware of this we are, the more we begin to understand that our survival depends on nature, that we are supported by it. And if we listen to our bodies and the body of the Earth, we will know what is going on around us and in us.

It is humbling to be one with nature. Indeed, the root of the word humility is humus—Earth; to become humble is to get close to the Earth. Humility requires us to surrender and change, to focus on the nonmaterial gifts that life offers us every day.

A soulful life requires being aware that we are a soul in a body, which is connected to the bigger body of the Earth and the universe. At the same time, it is noticing the miracles of your functioning body, of your children or other loved ones, of how you are feeling and watching the changes in yourself from moment to moment.

—Robin Hereens Lysne, from *Sacred Living: A Daily Guide*

TRIBAL PREEMIE CARE

Cultural anthropologists have discovered that many early tribal cultures provided effective care to premature babies. They seemed to know that preemies needed to be kept especially warm as demonstrated by their "invention" of natural incubators. The Chukchee tribes of Siberia placed the baby in the soft skin of a seabird, which had been turned inside out so that the feathers encased the infant. The baby was then placed close to a warming lamp. The Thongas of South Africa swaddled preemies in the leaves of the caster-oil plant and put the bundle into a vessel that was placed in the sun. Zaire's Basongye tribe boiled a root in a pot of water, cooled the water to warm, then placed the baby in the pot. They put a lid on the container and actually "steamed" the infant for a few seconds. This therapy was administered six times a day for a week. In Africa the Akamba wrapped preemies tightly and secured them in a clay vessel to keep them warm. In Zimbabwe, where a premature baby was called the "unripe one," they made sure not to expose an infant to the outdoors until he or she gained more strength.

I am balanced

Blessings and Balance, Balance and Blessings, For from Balance comes all Blessings.

—Grandmother Keewaydinoquay, Ojibway Medicine Woman

When I think about moms in their power, I think of two things. One is actually being in a position of power. Moms are authority figures, managers of the home and children. Lots of responsibility, which many women enjoy. The downside is that it is easy to become so immersed in motherhood and those responsibilities that a woman's total identity is MOM. Her interests and hobbies and other things that nurture her often get shelved. She gives and gives, and suddenly wakes up depressed and wonders why. Why? She's neglected the things that feed her soul, that empower her.

Which brings me to number two. It is my theory that if a woman is nurturing herself—not as a mom, but as a person— she has a more balanced identity (i.e., I'm a mother and a musician). Therefore her mothering will come more from a place of power, because she will be happier and more balanced.

Empowerment Recipe for Moms

In a long day, mix:

- ❖ A walk in the park
- ❖ Ten minutes reading a positive book
- ❖ Uplifting and relaxing music
- ❖ Some time spent on a hobby or personal project
- ❖ A cup of tea in the afternoon
- ❖ A little quiet time alone
- ❖ A twenty-minute nap
- ❖ An adult conversation with your spouse
- ❖ Lots of hugs and kisses.

—Cindy Angell Keeling

CONTEMPLATION

Learn to live with tension without losing your balance. Surrender control over the outcome by bringing your full attention to the present moment. Your children need you to be centered and trustworthy. Their well-being and security are a direct result of the manner in which you walk through difficult times.

I am essential

She came to me in a fierce vision: rich dark hair and piercing green eyes, demanding to be born as my body began its monthly ovulation ritual. I felt so differently this time, as if every cell of my entire body was vibrating. I could feel a strange kind of pressure, almost painful, sending currents of energy to my fingertips and toes, and all while this amazing female figure danced before me.

I came home that evening and announced to my husband that I thought it was

ANIMAL FACTS

❖ New mothers among some species of dolphin may rely on another dolphin to help bring their babies to the ocean's surface for their first breath.

❖ Kangaroos can have overlapping pregnancies and are able to feed their babies in a developmentally appropriate manner by producing different formulas of milk through different nipples.

time: a child wanted to be born. He listened thoughtfully and then replied gently in a calm, logical manner that it was simply not "a good time": our finances were rocky at best, I had no health insurance and was in the throes of finishing graduate school.

My logical mind agreed with him, yet my heart felt deflated. Nonetheless, I vowed to make a "mature decision" and not succumb to my impulsive nature—and the call of this goddess.

The next morning the vision came again. I called my husband from work—feeling an anxious, irrational panic—and explained as calmly as possible that this was bigger than logic. Whether he truly understood me or was simply lured by the exciting prospect of an afternoon tryst, the Fates played matchmaker that day and a soul was given the life-form she so adamantly demanded.

Now three years old, our raven-haired daughter's eyes are changing from smoky infant blue to brilliant emerald green. She often sits between her father and me on the couch and wraps her chubby, possessive hands around our necks and pulls us closely together, amused. The proof is in her eyes; the Goddess understands so much more than we, and her timing is always perfect.

—Pamela Castle Alba

I record

And still she sings. [My grandmother] Casard's voice is backbone, nothing less. The story she tells is mine, though I believe there are other tales of families that pass every day along the invisible threads from mother to daughter to daughter. Our tales are what bind, they are the spiraling—the vicious, wondrous spiraling—

which, if never questioned, lock the generations in a web of infinite expectation, lies, shame, hope. For my unborn child, I am after hope. Hope, and the chance for a new story that will put to rest the lies and shame. And so I listen cautiously to Casard, who says: To make a new life, you must hope for the future, and you must remember what has already been. Hope I have plenty of to give Unborn. Hope grows inside me, it could pour any minute from my breasts, gold threads of light. It is that much hope.

—Carol Edgarian, from *Rise the Euphrates*

[My] mother's stories came as naturally as breathing…. I have absorbed not only the stories themselves, but something of the manner in which she spoke. Something of the urgency that involves the knowledge that her stories –like her life–must be recorded. —PHILLIS WHEATLEY

ST. BERNARDINO'S
INSTRUCTIONS TO HUSBANDS

Wherefore as thou seest that thy wife endureth travail on every side, therefore thou, O husband, if she falls into any need be sure thou help her to bear the pain. If she be with child or in childbirth, aid her in so far as in thee lieth, for it is thy child also. Let all help her whereinsoever they may. Mark her well, how she travaileth in childbirth, travaileth to suckle the child, travaileth to rear it, travaileth in washing and cleaning by day and by night….

I labor

*I could feel my blood
like a river inside me,
and my breast deep
and thigh and womb
ready for a new child,
and strong labor for it
and I liked it.*

—MERIDEL LE SUEUR

Rocking, breathing, groaning, mouthing circles of distress, laughing, whistling, pounding, wavering, digging, pulling, push-ing—labor is the most involuntary work we do. My body gallops to those rhythms. I'm along for the ride, at times in some control and at others dragged along as if foot-caught in a stirrup. I don't have much to do at first but breathe, accept ice chips, make jokes—in fear and pain my family makes jokes, that's how we deal with what we can't change, how we show our courage.

—Louise Erdrich, excerpt from *The Blue Jay's Dance: A Birth Year*

SONG OF
A WOMAN IN LABOR

*towering rocks
sound
in the evening
with them
I cry*

—ANONYMOUS
(PAPAGO, NORTH AMERICAN
INDIAN)

For centuries, water has been a familiar medium for labor the world over. Water relieves pain because it gives the pregnant woman a lift and applies counterpressure to her aching muscles. When a laboring mother gets into a deep pool of water she feels almost weightless, and her energy is spared for the uterus' hard work. As she relaxes her thighs, back, and abdominal muscles, the birth passage muscles also relax. This state of relaxation is good for the mother and consequently good for the baby; the baby receives more oxygen, contraction discomfort is eased, and the mind and body surrender more easily. According to Dr. William Sears in *The Birth Book*, "immersion in water acts like a continuous total-body massage…. It would take thousands of fingertips to reach the same number of receptor sites in the skin that can be stimulated by a nice warm soak."

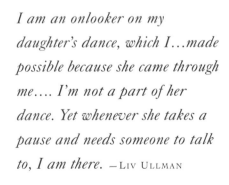

I emphasize

I am often asked if being a midwife has influenced the way I give birth. Really, very little — I am still a woman in an emotionally and physically vulnerable place who needs the support and love of my mate and friends. I need the reassurance of someone telling me I'm doing fine and that the pain is not going to continue forever. Of course, being so familiar with the birth process gives me confidence; my body knows how to birth as long as I surrender and let it happen. I have learned a lot from my recent pregnancies and births and now have a deeper understanding as a midwife. I feel a stronger empathy with the women I help; now I know how hard it is to do some of the things I have asked women to do in labor.

—Lily, from *Hearts Open Wide*

I am an onlooker on my daughter's dance, which I…made possible because she came through me…. I'm not a part of her dance. Yet whenever she takes a pause and needs someone to talk to, I am there. —LIV ULLMAN

I am perfection

The baby should be addressed in its own language. The language that precedes words. Are we, then, to speak in gestures, as we would to a foreigner? Of course not. We must go back still further and rediscover the universal language, which is simply the language of love.

—FREDERICK LEBOYER

A child is born with a perfect love and dependence on its parents. In the perfection of its love, it calls forth the perfection of yours. In its innocence, it opens up a place of innocence in you. Something pure is communicated that can never be understood by those who have never looked into the eyes of an infant whose very survival is in their hands....

When you experience parenthood, the whole world remakes itself before your eyes. Nature aligns itself. You understand your parents more and honor them more.... You feel the unity of generations cascading into generations from the beginning of time. You feel something in the world that is more important than yourself.

Your life suddenly becomes centered. Your own failings are cast in high relief, but so are your own strengths. You know what it is that you believe in and must pass along.

If you have a chance at parenthood, look upon it with a sense of mystery and awe. You are given the joy of watching life afresh, and the chance to help another being take flight into the richness and mystery of life. The very clay of which our world is made is, for a brief moment, placed in your hands....

A child, whether of your blood or someone else's, whether healthy or ill, whether beautiful or misshapen, is one of life's greatest miracles. It opens your world into a new sunlight and is a gift greater than a dream.

—Kent Nerburn, from *Simple Truths*

I am a legend

If newborns could remember and speak, they would emerge from the womb carrying tales as wondrous as Homer's. —ANONYMOUS

At three or four o'clock in the afternoon, the hour of café con leche, the women of my family gathered in Mama's living room to speak of important things and to tell stories for the hundredth time, as if to each other, meant to be overheard by us young girls, their daughters. In Mama's house (everyone called my grandmother Mama) was a large parlor built by my grandfather to his wife's exact specifications so that it was always cool, facing away from the sun....[N]o one could walk directly into her living room. First they had to take a little stroll through and around her beautiful garden where prize-winning orchids grew in the trunk of an ancient tree she had hollowed out for that purpose. This room was furnished with several mahogany rocking chairs, acquired at the births of her children, and one intricately carved rocker that had passed down to Mama at the death of her own mother. It was on these rockers that my mother, her sisters, and my grandmother sat on these afternoons of my childhood to tell their stories, teaching each other and my cousin and me what it was like to be a woman, more specifically a Puerto Rican woman....They told real-life stories, though as I later learned, always embellishing them with a little or a lot of dramatic detail, and they told *cuentos*, the morality and cautionary tales told by the women in our family for generations.

Don't be satisfied with stories, how things have gone with others. Unfold your own myth. —RUMI

—Judith Ortiz Cofer, from *Silent Dancing*

❖ Hellenistic Egyptian women wore rings portraying the womb as an upside-down pot with a toothed image near the neck, which represented the key to the womb.

I decide

*Making the decision to have
a child—it's momentous.
It is to decide forever to
have your heart go walking
around outside your body.*

—ELIZABETH STONE

The woman who has the fortune to plan a pregnancy also has the opportunity to experience rare pleasures. She can consciously participate in the evolution of her body from fecundity to its ultimate production stage, the delivery of a child. During the entire period, if she remains attentive, she will marvel at the emergence of new and delightful sensualities.

She must carefully prepare her mind in order to enjoy the parturition. She will spend time appreciating her body before conception. Knowing that her features will undergo dramatic changes, she and her mate will spend considerable time examining and enjoying her breasts and calves and arms and belly.

She will have photographs made for the months ahead, which will seem to stretch into years. When her belly extends so far that her feet disappear from her view, then the portraits of her lissome days will have the value of rare gems. If she and her mate do not consider pregnancy a common occurrence just because it happens all the time, if they are persistently imaginative, each stage can furnish them exquisite gratification.

—Maya Angelou, from *Wouldn't Take Nothing for My Journey Now*

❖ A set of Nigerian octuplets—the first born on December 8, 1998, the rest on December 20, were given names celebrating God's gifts, in the tradition of their parent's Igbo tribe. The translations of the names are: God is great (Chukwuebuka Nkemjika), God is beautiful (Chidinma Anulika), God thinks of me (Chinecherem Nwabugwu), God knows my way (Chimaijem Otito), God has my life (Chijindu Chidera), God is my strength (Chukwubuikem Maduabuchi), God is my leader (Chijioke Chinedum), and God is merciful (Chinagorom Chidiebere).

I am the cusp

You must teach your children that the ground beneath their feet is the ashes of our grandfathers. So that they will respect the land, tell your children that the earth is rich with the loves of our kin. Teach your children what we have taught our children—that the earth is our mother. Whatever befalls the earth befalls the sons of the earth. If men spit upon the ground, they spit upon themselves.

This we know. The earth does not belong to man: man belongs to the earth. This we know. All things are connected like the blood that unites one family. All things are connected.

Whatever befalls the earth, befalls the sons of the earth. Man did not weave the web of life; he is merely a strand in it. Whatever he does to the web, he does to himself.

—Chief Seattle

*We have been here before
and we'll be here again.
The circle remains,
though we all wander far.
So lift up your heart,
you will never be alone.
Let the earth be your
medicine forever.*

—DALE COLLEEN HAMILTON

CHEESE TRADITIONS

Cheese has long been associated with the mysteries of birth and lactation. The Egyptians pictured the human body as a product of mother's milk "curdled" into solid matter as the child grew and put on new flesh. A remnant of this idea occurs in the Bible: "Hast thou not poured me out as milk, and curdled me like cheese?" (Job 10:10). One of an Egyptian's seven souls was the ren or "milk name," given by the nursing mother. This is the root of the word rennet, a milk-curdling agent.

Cheese figured prominently in a traditional rite still practiced at rural British christening feasts. The newborn child is passed through a hole in the center of a large cheese known as the Groaning Cheese. In doing so, the cheese symbolically becomes a surrogate mother, "birthing" the child.

I deepen

*Little ancestor
sweet baby, how
you temper me,
deepen. Like an
ancient smithy
working slowly.*

—PHYLLIS CHESLER

❖ **In Uganda, Seibei women in the seventh or eighth month of pregnancy are massaged by an old woman "with knowledge." Butter is rubbed on their abdomens to determine if the baby is in an undesirable position. If so, through external massage the old woman manipulates the baby into a correct delivery position.**

My feelings for the power of the grandmother are rooted in my childhood. I remember when my brothers and I were children, how life seemed to shift and deepen when my grandmother, my mother's mother, came to visit. It was as though another element, a third perspective, was added to the everyday struggles between parents and children. We called her Oma, the German word for grandmother. She told us stories from my mother's childhood. Her eyes were violet, looking inward, looking backward. I remember how the soft folds of skin at her throat shook when she spoke. "Once I told the children that I too had had a mother. Your aunt was about four then, your mother three. Do you know what your aunt said to me? She looked me up and down, because of course she was very little, and I was very big, and she said: 'You had a mother? She must have been a giant!!'"

—Naomi Ruth Lowinsky, from *To Be a Woman*

I inspire

It was from my father that I inherited a gift of mathematics which in later years was to enable me to overcome some of the heaviest obstacles placed in the way of my education. My mother was, in every fiber of her being, a woman of mood and intuition. In all that she did or said—even if the matter was some daily commonplace—she made evident such depth of soul, such fineness of feeling, such sympathy and compassion, that she drew me to her with magic power. If it could be put so crudely, I would say that my father's influence was to intellectualize me, my mother's to inspire me: from my father streamed a cool, clear light; from my mother, warmth and emotion. My head was drawn toward my father, my heart toward my mother, and I was forever swinging like a pendulum between these two forces.

—Shmarya Levin (1867-1935), from his memoirs.

✤ Among the Tlinget tribes of Alaska, women are said to suffer very little during childbirth and some have been known to give birth while sleeping.

Was it her voice?
Did they like to listen
to her talk just to hear
the music sounds she made?
Was it because she was so
full of life that she made
things move inside you,
tears or laughter or anger,
and when she went out
of a room something
like something alive left
with her?

—DOROTHY WEST

I am the guardian

Each of us, as Spirit, has a Birth Guardian. She is with us as we travel from the spirit world, through the birth gateway, and incarnate into human form. We are never alone, for our Birth Guardian is beside us at all times, whether we are aware of her presence or not. She smoothes the way as we shift realities—from the formless nature of the spirit realm into the earthly-human world of form. The Birth Guardian knows the way, and offers guidance and comfort along this mystical journey. She is with us as our physical bodies grow and develop within our mothers' wombs, and remains by our sides for weeks or months after we have been born. She is the true spiritual midwife, with an expansive overview and deep love for every Spirit-child she is responsible for. Her energy is feminine, for this is what is most soothing to an incoming spirit. Our Birth Guardian visits us often when we are young children, and maintains an awareness of us throughout our entire lives. She is accessible whenever we might need her. We can always trust her.

Your Spirit-child, no matter what age, is always cared for. It is the same for all, for our Birth Guardians watch over us throughout our lives with the love of divine mothers. Fully embracing our eternal spiritual essence, they offer us warmth, insight, and unconditional love. Always.

—Ann Fuller

RITUAL

If you wish to know more about your child, speak with her or his Birth Guardian. She will gladly offer you guidance. Find a place where you won't be disturbed and sit quietly. Breathe into your heart. Use your breath to relax your linear mind, and allow your heart to expand. Call to your child's Birth Guardian. Ask her to come and visit with you. Allow yourself to feel the subtle or dramatic shift in energy as she appears. Speak with her. Open your inner ears, and hear or feel the answers to your questions or concerns. Trust yourself and your experience. When your visit is completed, give thanks to the Birth Guardian, and breathe into your heart once again. —Ann Fuller

It is not the Desert's charm that calls one. What is it? I know not; only that there is a low, insistent voice calling—calling—calling. Not a loud voice. The Desert proclaiming itself, speaks gently. And we—every child of us who has laid on the breast of a mother while she rocked slowly, and hushed our fretting with a soft-sung lullaby song—we know how a low voice soothes and lulls one into sleep....

When...your ear is attuned to catch the music of the plains or the anthems sung in deep canons by the winds; when your heart finds comradeship in the mountains and the great sand-seas, the sun and the stars, and the huge cloud-drifts that the Desert winds set a-rolling round the world—when all these reach your heart by way of...your ear, then you shall find one of the alluring ways that belongs to the Desert.... And when you can lay your head on its breast, and hear its heart-beats, you will know a rest that is absolute and infinite.

—Idah Meacham Strobridge, from "The Lure of the Desert," from *In Miners' Mirage-Land*

I am majestic

I see the forest for the first time.... Now I am overcome. I look up and around me. The trees are heavy with moisture; their canopies gaze down quietly, their trunks stand like the bare legs of grownups. Except for the downpour, the only sound is the croak of a tree frog hidden in a tangle.

Lush breath
and strength
in species
Heavy with birth
and rebirth
and rebirth,

I once wrote those lines as a love poem... describing myself as a teeming forest. I cannot fight the tightness in my throat. It is all there for me, I am not missing a detail: vulnerable, majestic, restorative. Cry, because it is beautiful and tears roll down and dry on my face as the clouds weep, because they have to. The wilderness is in me.

—Gabrielle Daniels, from *Another Wilderness*

In nature, nothing is perfect
and everything is perfect.
Trees can be contorted,
bent in weird ways,
and still they are beautiful.

—ALICE WALKER

I am flesh

This is flesh I'm talking about here. Flesh that needs to be loved. Feet that need to rest and to dance; backs that need support; shoulders that need arms, strong arms I'm telling you. —TONI MORRISON

Body within my body, I shape you out of almost nothing,
   give you a tight envelope to surround your soul.
      I deem you female— eyes cobalt blue, fingers long
         and translucent— without even realizing it. And after
            the quantum leap from single cell to complex organism,
         much of your body's life is beyond my conscious thought:
   your waking, your sleeping, the small objects of your
   complete desire. Complete as the perfect wings
of the jay above your head or the pale stars that mark
your birth with nothing but pure light. Daughter,
I cannot give you anything so complete or perfect or pure.
But I can give you something better. Your body,
which is your life. And the fierce love of it that no one
can take away. And these words that will remind you
of that love. And your father's broad hand that opened
the door to it. And the blankness of the rest of this page
for your own words, your own history.

—Linda Nemec Foster, from *History of the Body*

❖ **In Bang Chan, Thailand, during labor a woman leans back against her husband's body while he digs his toes into her thighs; perhaps this toe pressure, like oriental shiatsu, gives her some pain relief.**

I follow

Among all the uncertainties I have experienced about myself as a mother, of one point I feel sure: that I am not today the woman I would have been had Anne not been born one September evening almost nineteen years ago. I cannot prove this hypothesis, there being no control in this experiment. There is only this Nancy Mairs who, for nearly half her life, has in raising been raised by a daughter.

Anne can't have found her job an easy one. Raising a mother is difficult enough under the best of circumstances. But when you get one who's both crippled and neurotic—who doesn't do her fair share of the housework, who lurches around the house and crashes to the floor in front of your friends—then you have your work cut out for you. Of all the things Anne has taught me, perhaps the most important is that one can live under difficult circumstances with a remarkable amount of equanimity and good humor. It's a lesson I need daily. My education began, no doubt, from the moment of her birth.

—Nancy Mairs, from "On Being A Cripple," from *Plaintext*

Show me the path where I should go, point out the right road for me to walk. Lead me: teach me.

—Psalm 25:4-5

BIRTH MUSIC

Music can play an important therapeutic role in your birthing experience: it helps relax your mind and body. Selecting musical pieces for a birth tape is a wonderful preparatory ritual you can share with your partner. Here are some suggestions that will help you create a soothing, celebratory atmosphere in your birthing space.

Soothing and calming pieces: Chopin, *Polonaises;* Debussy, *Clair de Lune;* James Galway, *The Magic Flute, Annie's Song;* Mendelssohn, *A Midsummer Night's Dream*

Pieces to aid in focus and concentration: J. S. Bach, *Brandenburg Concertos, The Well-Tempered Clavier;* Baroque string music of Vivaldi, Albinoni, Corelli, Torelli, and others; Handel, *Water Music;* Tibetan bells

Timeless birth music: Brahms, "Lullaby;" Gluck, *Dance of the Blessed Spirits;* Handel, "Largo" (from Xerxes); Wagner, "Evening Star" (from Tannhäuser)

Spiritual music: Berlioz, Hosanna, Sanctus; Gregorian chants; Handel, "Hallelujah Chorus"; Mozart, *Laudate Dominum,* Psalm 116

I reveal

Enrich your pregnancy with preparatory activities that beautify your surroundings. Collect sacred objects such as decorative stones, necklaces, birthing garb, and wall hangings. Place them around your home to enhance your awareness of the soul of pregnancy.

If your most deeply held desire is to know God, to make all that you do an act of worship, then the guidance you give your child will be more like the light touch of a butterfly on a flower than the heavy hand of domination…Rather than dispensing rules, regulations, and righteuosness, you seek to assist your child to see the path clearly. After all, we are all on this journey together, regardless of our age.

As parents, we should consider ourselves more like a Sherpa guide than a trainer or commanding officer. As one who has greater experience, but not greater value, our function is to climb the mountain beside our child, providing direction whenever we can, but above all offering our constant support. Then as we near the peak—as the child becomes an adolescent and then an adult—we stay back and let her pursue the dream, asking not even for credit for how much we helped along the way.… Only peace leads our children to peace; only love can find the place of love.

—Hugh and Gayle Prather, from *Spiritual Parenting*

*With your hand in hers,
you will never stumble. With her
protecting you, you will not be
afraid. With her leading you,
you will never tire. Her kindness
will see you through to the end.*

—Bernard of Clairvaux

I remember

Before you were born, I knew you.

— JEREMIAH 1:5

There once was a goddess named Draupadi who was known in Indian legend as the daughter of fire. Her story was often told to Ana Gupta at bedtime who passed the story down to her granddaughter.

I smiled and brushed my granddaughter's hair away from her sleepy eyes. "No, Chand, I didn't forget about Draupadi. She gave birth to many, many daughters. She told them that they were beautiful and special. Draupadi taught them to be strong and courageous. She gave them the tools to survive the hardships that a new, darker era would bring. She helped them understand the injustices they would face as women. Draupadi made her daughters believe in themselves. Lastly, she made them promise to always remember that they were the daughters of fire, just like their mother. And those daughters gave birth to more daughters, who gave birth to more daughters…who gave birth to me and you."

— Ana Gupta, from "Storytime," from *Making More Waves*

LULLABY OF THE BENE-ISRAEL JEWS OF BOMBAY

Jo, jo, my child,
My seed of pearl,
Keep your eyes
From crying, my treasure, jo, jo.

I washed your flesh,
I pitied you dear;
In the name of the Lord,
I put you to sleep, jo, jo.

My milk has quietened you,
Has sweetened your lips,
And within the hand of God
I shall deliver your soul, jo, jo.

Your shirt is green,
Your matlet of silk;
The *pipalpan* is yellow,
And pure are the pearls, jo, jo.

Your cradle is of sandalwood,
Your cushion of silk;
Grandmother will come
And will sing you to sleep, jo, jo.

I'll thread pearls for you,
To decorate your neck;
Your mother will dress
Her head with flowers.

— from *The History of the Bene-Israel of India* by Haeem Samuel Kehimkar

I am glorious

When I was twelve, my grandmother told me that I would have a son, and that there was a very important tradition I must remember to follow with him when he first began to read. Having a son seemed a ridiculous thing to even think about, but traditions I liked. Traditions were candles, and feathers, and mysterious words and moving hands like flowers in wind. She placed her warm open palm on my forehead, and our minds became like two watercolors bleeding into one another.

"When your son learns to read, the very first time, you must give him some honeycake, something sweet to eat. His mind will tie the two things together from that moment on. Learning and sweetness. Don't forget this!"

—Dawna Markova, from *For She Is the Tree of Life: Grandmothers Through the Eyes of Women Writers*

❖ When a Wachagga mother in Uganda leaves the hut for the first time after birth, she emerges in special dress: she has in her hand a staff such as is carried by the elders, and is followed by the child who cooks for her. "Sedately they take their way to the market, where they are greeted with songs such as were sung to the warriors returning from battle."

The sun is the mother of earth and gives it its nourishment of heat; it never leaves the universe at night until it has put the earth to sleep to the song of the sea and the hymn of birds and brooks.

—Kahlil Gibran

BIRTH FLOWERS AND STONES

❖ **January:** Flower: Carnation, Birthstone: Garnet. ❖ **February:** Flower: Violet, Birthstone: Amethyst. ❖ **March:** Flower: Jonquil, Birthstone: Aquamarine. ❖ **April:** Flower: Sweet Pea, Birthstone: Diamond. ❖ **May:** Flower: Lily of the Valley, Birthstone: Emerald. ❖ **June:** Flower: Rose, Birthstone: Pearl. ❖ **July:** Flower: Larkspur, Birthstone: Ruby. ❖ **August:** Flower: Gladiola, Birthstone: Peridot. ❖ **September:** Flower: Aster, Birthstone: Sapphire. ❖ **October:** Flower: Calendula, Birthstone: Opal. ❖ **November:** Flower: Chrysanthemum, Birthstone: Topaz. ❖ **December:** Flower: Narcissus, Birthstone: Turquoise.

I like to use the term "rush"
in place of "contraction" because
I think it describes better how to flow
with the birthing energy.

—INA MAY GASKIN

I flow

This is a day when life and the world seem to be standing still—only time and the river flowing past the mesas....I go out into the sunshine to sit receptively for what there is in this stillness and calm...Just now it seemed to flow in a rhythm around me and then to enter me—something which comes in a hushed inflowing. All of me is still and yet alert, ready to become part of this wave that laps the shore on which I sit. Somehow I have no desire to name it or understand. It is enough that I should feel and be of it in moments such as this.

No, it is not what Ouspensky experienced when he was drawn by the waves into them, becoming all—mountain, sea, sky, ship. I am I and earth is earth—mesa, sky, wind, rushing river. Each is an entity but the essence of the earth flows into me—perhaps of me into the earth. And to me it is more than a few seconds experience.

Even in these rushed days there is such peace between. There are moments when two eagle feathers can fill me with joy; when the last rays of the sun touch my forehead as I stand by the kitchen door; when the outline of To-tavi is marked in rhythm against a clear western sky; when even the wind is part of it all.

—Edith Warner, journal entry from *The House at Otowi Bridge: The Story of Edith Warner & Los Alamos*

envision

We walk by their window

every night drawn
by the yellow glow brushing
an indigo sky.

Our eyes linger,
coaxed inside
to lively walls breezy
with leaf shadows
and a small silhouette.

There is a boy
in a worn chair cherished,
gazing his dreams
through the story rousing his mother's mouth.

Looking up, I squeeze your true hand;

we envision the words unearthing that boy,

his long, good life

glistening wonder
like starshine

on a still forest pool.

ANDREA ALBAN GOSLINE

I envision

*Your young shall
dream dreams and
your old shall see
visions.* —ANONYMOUS

December 26, 1919

There are days when Mother sleeps most of the time, murmuring softly in her dreams and daydreaming when she is awake. Always about children. Sometimes full of care and fear that they will not come home. But mostly the scenes she sees are very pleasant. The children sleeping in their room. Then she wants to go to wake them, and comes back wondering: where are they? It is really so sweet to see how the dreams and visions and fantasies of so old a mother always return to her children. So after all they were the strongest emotions in her life.

—Kaethe Kollwitz, from *The Diaries and Letters of Kaethe Kollwitz*

✛ The Minoans built palace shrines in Knossos, Gournia, Phaistos, and Mallia. All four were situated in a similar landscape: near a vast female figure, formed by a pair of mountains resembling breasts, beneath a rounded hill that represented a belly. This tribute to the female body suggests that the ancient Greeks recognized a sacred, female power inhabiting their living world.

*Little child! Your mother's
breasts are full of milk.
Go and be nursed,
Go and drink!
Go up to the mountain!
From the summit of the
mountain you shall seek health,
You shall draw life.*

—IGLULIK ESKIMO, TRANSLATED BY KNUD RASMUSSEN, FROM *INTELLECTUAL CULTURE OF THE IGLULIK ESKIMOS*

I am the mountain

One day, after my morning time with the children, I...accompanied my oldest, my eleven year old son, to a Dharma class for Westerners at a school for young Tibetan lamas. The English-speaking nun in charge was teaching and she said, "So countless are all sentient beings, and so many their births throughout time, that each at some point was your mother." She then explained a practice for developing compassion: it consisted of viewing each person as your mother in a former life. I played with the idea as I walked on down the mountain, following a narrow, winding road between cedars and rhododendron trees. The astronomical number of lifetimes that the nun's words evoked boggled my mind—yet the intent of this quaint practice, for all of its far-fetched fantasy, was touching.

—Joanna Macy, from "Three Lessons in Compassion," from *World as Lover, World as Self*

MOUNTAIN MOTHER

With their voluptuous shape and magnificent presence, mountains have long been linked with motherhood. In the Epic of Gilgamesh, Mashu, a holy mountain who gave birth to the sun, is described as having walls as high as heaven and "paps" reaching down to the underworld. Symbols inspired by this mountain mother's "breasts" resemble an "M" and were probably the first version of this alphabet letter. (The Japanese character for mountain is also an M-shaped brushstroke, with two breast-like peaks.) Sumerian myth tells of Ninhursag, a mountain mother who gave birth to the world and was known as a cow-goddess and milk-giver to the kings. The oldest deity in Greece was the Divine Mountain Mother, Gaea Olympia. She was called the Universal Mother and Deep-Breasted One. Chomo-Lung-Ma, "Goddess Mother of the Universe," is one of the oldest Indo-Tibetan deities whose mountain shrine is now known as Mt. Everest.

The universal idea of breastmilk flowing down from mountain peaks was common in both Eastern and Western cultures. Snowcaps melting into white glacial streams probably inspired this idea. The four rivers of paradise were equated with streams of mother's milk, as in the Iranian myths of High Haraiti, the birth-giving mountain at the earth's center.

I admire

The blossoming flower is an evocative symbol for both the dilating cervix and the widening vagina. Imagine your favorite flower in your mind's eye. Watch it open petal by petal—opening, opening, until it is open wide. See the shape of the colorful petals covered with dewdrops and lit by sunlight. Smell the flower's perfume. Listen to the birds singing, coaxing it to open fully.

Why was it that so many women artists who had renounced having children could then paint nothing but mothers and children?

—Erica Jong

When I open Mama's album of poetry and look on the southern letters of the words, on the poems written in exquisite fair blossoms and silk-like leaves, then I know: she was the poet, and I merely the teller of her rapturous thoughts. I did not yet go to school, and the instruction at home meant nothing else for me but playing, but when both of us, my very best friend, namely, my young, beautiful Mama, and I sat together at the table made of rosewood and wrote poems—that was for me the finest reward. Ah, she voiced her admiration endlessly. I was so proud, relying on her judgment, and when I created poetry in the bosom of my mother I succeeded in making the most difficult verses.

—Else Lasker-Schuler, from *Else Lasker-Schuler Remembers Her Mother*

❖ The Omphalos (navel in Greek) was a gigantic, sacred stone. One was located in Crete at the site where the umbilical cord of Zeus is believed to have fallen after his birth. Another omphalos site in Delphi honored Gaia, Goddess of the Earth. Together, these two stones symbolically brought together Zeus and Gaia as the dual source of life itself.

I relax

I was ready to have this baby. There was a new energy I was feeling. A week before I had cried because I was going to miss the aura of pregnancy and my relationship with my daughter in my womb. But I realized quickly that it was time to let her expand into a new space; so I said goodbye to my state of pregnancy, loving and blessing myself.

When I began to have expansions (this is what I prefer to call contractions: the muscles contract to make the cervix expand), I did not react to labor as is taught in some childbirth books, where they suggest doing a very fast breathing that will keep you above the pain. This creates a sensation of separation....

What I did is go deeper into my body and the sensation. My whole training in rebirthing taught me to go into the body. For me the ideal way to labor was not to avoid the pain but to go into it. As the energy of my labor progressed, I thought of my own birth and of my fear at my son's birth; so I just looked at each fear, knowing it had nothing to do with the present. I would take a deep breath, let go and relax into my body.

— Rima Beth Star, from *The Healing Power of Birth*

*Do as much as you can
and take it easy.* —TARA TULKU

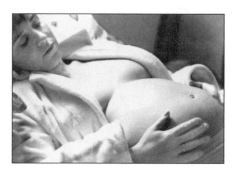

SINK INTO STILLNESS

*As you close your eyes,
sink into stillness.
Let these periods of rest and respite
reassure your mind
that all its frantic fantasies
were but the dreams of fever
that have passed away.
Let it be still
and thankfully accept its healing.
No more fearful dreams will come,
now that you rest in God.*

—FROM *A COURSE IN MIRACLES WORKBOOK*

I am celestial

Babies are bits of stardust blown from the hand of God. Lucky the woman who knows the pangs of birth for she has held a star. —LARRY BARRETTO

Once upon a time a beautiful young lady and a very handsome young man fell in love and got married. They were a wonderful, compatible couple, and God blessed their marriage with a fine baby boy (eight pounds, eight ounces). They loved their little boy very much. They raised him, nurtured him, and spoiled him. They raised him in the palm of the hand and gave him everything they thought he wanted. Finally, when he was about seven or eight, they let his feet touch the ground.

—Duke Ellington, from *Music Is My Mistress*

PREDICTING BABY'S DUE DATE

The night sky has always played a significant role in women's predictions of the time they will birth their children. In ancient times, Kwakiutl women of North America counted ten moon cycles after the date of their lasts period, to calculate the time of birth. At the first sighting of the new moon, in the last month of pregnancy, they went outside and prayed to the moon for an easy delivery. Similarly, in Morocco, if a woman's last day of menstruation was between the full moon and the new moon, she assumed the birth would occur nine moon cycles later; if it was between the new moon and the full moon, she added fifteen days. The Maricopa of Arizona counted nine lunar months (probably from conception) and some women knew they would give birth at a particular full moon. In the Philippines, mothers-to-be expected the birth to occur when the sun or moon was at a certain height in the sky. In Japan, birth was traditionally thought to be easier at high tide. The Navajo say that a child is born when the moon is straight overhead. In present-day Mexico, solar eclipses are believed to cause premature births, and phases of the moon to influence the length of labor.

I am the star

At first I couldn't make out what I was made for, but now I think it was to search out the secrets of this wonderful world and be happy and thank the Giver of it all for devising it. I think there are many things to learn yet—I hope so; and by economizing and not hurrying too fast I think they will last weeks and weeks. I hope so. When you cast up a feather it sails away on the air and goes out of sight; then you throw up a clod and it doesn't. It comes down, every time. I have tried it and tried it, and it is always so. I wonder why it is?

…By watching, I know that the stars are not going to last. I have seen some of the best ones melt and run down the sky. Since one can melt, they can all melt the same night. That sorrow will come—I know it. I mean to sit up every night and look at them as long as I can keep awake; and I will impress those sparkling fields on my memory, so that by and by when they are taken away I can by my fancy restore those lovely myriads to the black sky and make them sparkle again, and double them by the blur of my tears.

—Eve, from *The Diary of Adam and Eve* by Mark Twain

❖ The "river of stars" created by our cross-section view into the central portion of our galaxy was seen as a river of sparkling, life-giving Goddess milk by ancient civilizations.

My mother always seemed to be a fairy princess: a radiant being possessed of limitless riches and power.… She shone for me like the evening star.

—Winston Churchill

There is a star above us which unites souls of the first order, though worlds and ages separate them.

—Christina of Sweden (1626-1689)

I am the earth

Because we know ourselves to be made of this earth. See this grass. The patches of silver and brown. Worn by the wind. The grass reflecting all that lives in the soil. The light. The grass needing the soil. With roots deep in the earth. And patches of silver. Like the patches of silver in our hair. Worn by time. This bird flying low over the grass. Over the tules. The cattails, sedges, rushes, reeds, over the marsh. Because we know ourselves to be made from this earth. Temporary as this grass. Wet as this mud. Our cells filled with water. Like the mud of this swamp. Heather growing here because of the damp.... Places where the river washes out. Where the earth was shaped by the flow of lava. Or by the slow movements of glaciers. Because we know ourselves to be made of this earth, and shaped like the earth, by what has gone before. The lives of our mothers.

—Susan Griffin, from *Woman and Nature: The Roaring Inside Her*

We didn't inherit the land from our fathers.
We are borrowing it from our children.

—AMISH BELIEF

Holy Mother Earth, the trees and all nature are witnesses of your thoughts and deeds.

—WINNEBAGO SAYING

BIRTH ANNOUNCEMENTS

In nineteenth-century France, middle-class families sent a small card to family and friends announcing the birth of a baby. The announcement included a date and time in which people could call upon the family to extend good wishes and gifts. A common blessing was, "May God bless you and make you straight as a match, healthy as salt, full as an egg, sweet as sugar, and good as bread." During the visiting period, baby girls, dressed in ornate silk dresses given to them for this special occasion, were held by their nurses. The wet nurse also donned her finest attire. Everyone in the party wore pink. For a baby boy, everyone wore blue and all the child's furnishings were blue, to symbolize the color of divine protection.

I expand

While out driving many years ago, my small daughter asked me a question. "Why are boys called sons, and girls called daughters?" Dumbfounded, I hesitated. "It's very odd," she said, "because girls are warm and golden like the sun, but boys are white and distant like the moon." After a moment of shock, I comprehended. "Would you like me to call you a sun?" I asked her. She nodded.

The power of language is wonderful. Without it, we circumnavigate only feeling and image. Without it, there is no mythology, no history. Erase the words, and memory is random.

I write because I have an immense respect and gratitude for language.

—Ara Taylor, from *My Spirit Flies: Portraits and Prose of Women in Their Power*

AFFIRMATIONS

❖ *I am laboring in perfect harmony with nature.* ❖ *I am ready and able to have my baby right now.* ❖ *My cervix is expanding with each moment.* ❖ *My cervix is allowing my baby to emerge.* ❖ *I can push my baby into welcoming hands.*

*Suddenly many movements are going
on within me, many things are happening,
there is an almost unbearable sense of
sprouting, of bursting encasements,
of moving kernels, expanding flesh.*

—MERIDEL LE SUEUR

I am forever

All is mortal.
Only the mother
is destined to immortality.
And when the mother
is no longer among the
living, she leaves a
memory which none yet
have dared to sully.
The memory of a mother
feeds a compassion in us
that is like the ocean—
and the illimitable ocean
feeds the rivers that dissect
the universe.

—Isaac Babel

Children reinvent
your world for you.

—Susan Sarandon

I hear her circling
I open my arms
she is filling them
I am trembling
suddenly I hold her
she is crying and I have always loved her
she is my daughter and I am forever
her skin
I breathe it in
can you smell that
smells so sweet
don't you think
did you count her fingers
her toes
I'm counting
her hands rest
so beautiful
long tapered
   fingernails
     like a woman's hands
      seeing her hands
       I remember an astronaut quote:
       he walked on the moon
       he turned back to earth
      (he said)
     seeing Earth from the moon
  made him know there is God
made her know there is God

—Maureen O'Brien, from "Seeing the Earth from the Moon"

I leap

Crow women do not lie down when their babies are born, not even afterward, except to sleep when night comes, as others do. Two stakes had been driven into the ground for me to take hold of, and robes had been rolled up and piled against them, so that when I knelt on the bed-robe and took hold of the two stakes, my elbows would rest upon the pile of rolled robes.

While I stood by the door, Left-hand took four live coals from the lodge-fire. One of these she placed on the ground at the door, then one to the left,…one at the head, and one in front of the bed-robe.…

Then she dropped a little of the-grass-that-the-buffalo-do-not-eat upon each of these coals, telling me to walk to the left, go around my bed (as the sun goes), stepping over the coals. "Walk as though you are busy," she said, brushing my back with the tail of her buffalo robe, and grunting as a buffalo cow grunts.

I had stepped over the second coal when I saw that I should have to run to reach my bed-robe in time. I jumped the third coal, and the fourth, knelt down on the robe, took hold of the two stakes; and my first child, Pinefire, was there with us.

—from *Pretty Shield: Medicine Woman of the Crows*

INFANT CARRIERS AND MANIFEST DESTINY

Pioneer women were faced with the challenge of safely carrying their babies across the rugged western plains. One woman discovered that imported champagne baskets made excellent infant carriers. Since they were easy to attain, hundreds of infants crossed the United States in these sturdy containers. The wife of a cavalry officer transported her one-month-old infant across the desert in a basket strapped to a wagon seat. She claimed the rocking motion and sounds of the wagon soothed her baby. Some mothers made the arduous journey walking, carrying their infants in their arms. Others fared slightly better on horseback: holding their infants in one arm, clinging to the saddle horn with the other hand, bottles and other baby items attached by rope to the saddle, traveling across desolate wilderness for months on end!

I am focused

My mother's cool handling of childhood crises was one of my first lessons in how to live. Once I was bitten by a black snake…when I was about seven. Moving through deceptively soft-looking wild grasses that prickled my legs, and picking and eating [blackberries] as I went, I was pushing farther and farther into the thicket when suddenly I felt a blunt, muscular hit on my leg, a sharp pain, and in that second saw the snake's black body whip out of sight. I remember a moment of paralysis as my seven-year-old mind organized the facts. Then I ran, crying and calling for my mother, to the dark shingled, frightening house (overshadowed by tall pines, never sunlit), up the white steps onto the wooden porch, in through the wide front door and into the central hall. My mother, in her light cotton dress and white sneakers, was by that time running down the staircase to meet me.

With no loss of time whatsoever and with equally no hurry, she looked at the mark, asked a couple of clear questions about the snake's body, made me lie down on the black, horsehair sofa in the dining room, told the nurse to put some wet soda cloths on my leg, and called the doctor. I can see her now, dignified and reserved as always, with the telephone receiver shaped like a black tulip held to her ear.

—Anne Truitt, from *Daybook*

If it is true that we are mirrors to our infants and that looking forms the boundaries of a self, then perhaps we are also helping to form a spiritual soul self during those concentrated love gazes during which time stops, the air dims, the earth cools, and a sense of deep rightness takes hold of our being.

—LOUISE ERDRICH, FROM *THE BLUE JAY'S DANCE: A BIRTH YEAR*

❖ Dwellers on the Nile regarded the hippopotamus as a goddess form in the water. The divine Hippopotamus Mother, Taueret or Ta-urt, was associated with the *ankh,* or Key of Life, and the sign *ja,* meaning life-giving uterine blood.

I am timeless

Suppose time is a circle, bending back on itself. The world repeats itself, precisely, endlessly.

For the most part, people do not know they will live their lives over...Parents treasure the first laugh from their child as if they will not hear it again. Lovers making love the first time undress shyly, show surprise at the supple thigh, the fragile nipple. How could they know that each secret glimpse, each touch, will be repeated again and again, exactly as before?... In the world in which time is a circle, every handshake, every kiss, every birth, every word, will be repeated precisely.

— Alan Lightman, from *Einstein's Dreams*

*I can relinquish, perhaps,
the physical things of the past,
if I believe that their essence
continues through time.
I can go on with everyday
life in the company of ancient
values, insights, questions,
and doubts.*

—Elizabeth Ehrlich

SETTING THE EYES ON ONE

It is customary for Hawaiian families to gather on the day of a child's birth to support the parents and to perform specific duties. Sometimes the expectant mother is overwhelmed by a desire to see a certain family member or friend. This desire is called *kau ka maka* (setting the eyes on one) and it is believed that the baby will be very fond of this longed-for person. If the person cannot come, another relative places a rock in front of the door and loudly announces the person's arrival. The mother feels close to the absent person through the stone's presence. After the baby's birth, the proxy is thrown into the sea or another place considered to be safe from corruption.

I purify

"I like smokin' the baby," Betty said. "It's the start of her real life…. Got to make the fire with konkerberry. Get the dry wood first, then the green leaves. Wood to make the fire, leaves to make the smoke…. Gettin' smoked with konkerberry is the start of the baby's ceremonial life. It's a cleansing, a kind of purification."

The fire took hold, starting to crackle, but immediately Amy sprinkled mineral water over it from a plastic bottle, dampening the flames. Now she set a batch of green konkerberry leaves in the fire, sticking her head into the sudden white smoke and blowing mightily with wide-puffed cheeks. A cloud of white smoke arose and the pungency in the air increased tenfold.

"Now bring the baby!" Amy said. Vicki brought the wide-eyed Ashley, only in diapers now, and set her in Amy's lap. Pouring

To enter into this font is to plunge into the mythological realm…. Symbolically, the infant makes the journey when the water is poured on its head…. its goal is a visit with the parents of its Eternal Self, the Spirit of God and the womb of Grace. —JOSEPH CAMPBELL

PRAYER

Let the pure sky ahead, this sky of long and sweeping clouds, send to me a wind so strong, a wind the scent of joy; let all be born now, cleansed of dreams.

—SIMONE WEIL

water from the plastic bottle into her cupped hand, Amy applied it liberally to the baby's hair, head, chest, back, and legs.

"Don't wanna burn her," she explained. Ashley made no cry, not even a whimper. I'll never forget that look in her wide-brown Dreamtime eyes as Amy held her out directly into the perfumed smoke like a living sacrifice. The smoke enveloped her tiny form. For perhaps twenty seconds Amy held her there. Finally, she extracted the child from the smoke and rocked her in her arms. Ashley smiled sweetly, cooing.

"Done," Amy announced. "All done." It was over. No words, no prayers had been spoken. I suppose they would have been irrelevant. The act itself was the prayer.

—Harvey Arden, from *Dreamkeepers: A Spirit-Journey into Aboriginal Australia*

I soothe

BIRTH STORY

I had to write, I just had to write Pia to tell her I loved her, that even at this moment, if it should be my last, she would know I was thinking about her.... How to tell a ten-year-old child that I was expecting another baby.... I finally finished it, literally hanging over the chair. I wiped the sweat away and said, "All right, call the doctor now."...

The car arrived. I sneaked into it and off we went. Then when we were halfway there, I suddenly realized I wasn't wearing my green emerald ring which Roberto had given me, and which I never took off. I had washed my hands and left it in the bathroom. That really threw me. In the hospital I rushed for the phone. Poor Elena; there I was raving at her again: "I can't have this baby without that green ring on my finger! It is in the bathroom! Throw yourself in a taxi and rush it to the hospital. I shall not have the baby without it. Hurry! Hurry!"

The pains were now arriving so regularly that all my time schedules had gone astray. And I had gone astray too because the last thing I remembered was dear Elena slipping the ring on my finger and smiling at me. Then I was in the delivery room and Robertino was born at seven o'clock in the evening.

—Ingrid Bergman, from *Ingrid Bergman: My Story*

PAPYRUS EBERS

German archaeologist and Egyptologist Georg Ebers was on a dig in 1872 when an anonymous Egyptian man offered to sell him an artifact. Ebers raised the money to purchase the item, a huge papyrus wrapped in mummy cloth—the oldest medical work in existence, dating from the reign of Amenhotep I, ca. 1550 B.C.E. Ebers gave the papyrus his name and had it translated in 1890. These instructions on how to induce a speedy delivery were outlined in the text:

❖ *Remedy to cause a woman to be delivered:* Peppermint: Let the woman apply it to her bare posterior.

❖ *Remedy to loosen a child in the body of a woman:* Sea-salt, clean grain-of-wheat, female reed: Plaster the abdomen therewith.

Fennel, incense, garlic, sert-juice, fresh salt, wasp's dung: Make into a ball and put in the vagina.

Tail-of-a-tortoise, shell-of-a-beetle, sefet-oil, sert-juice, oil: Crush into one and poultice therewith.

I am a bridge

One day, Mother Woyengi stepped down to earth in a lightning flash. She began shaping the earth into people, lifting each one to her nostrils and giving it the breath of life. She whispered in their ears, "You can choose to be a man or woman. You can also choose the life you want." And so the new wise women, farmers, potters, musicians, fishers, weavers, hunters and mothers-of-families-to-be felt power and character stream into them. Woyengi then took them to two streams and said, "The stream on this side leads to luxury; the stream on that side leads to ordinariness. You've chosen the kind of life you want." When the people who had asked for riches, fame or power stepped into their stream, they found it fast-flowing and dangerous with weeds and currents. The people who had asked for humble, helpful or creative lives stepped into the other stream and found it shallow, clean and clear. So, one after another, Woyengi's children began floating or swimming in the stream of riches and the stream of ordinariness, and the waters carried them away to irrigate the world with the human race.

—story of the Nigerian Ijo people, from Hallie Iglehart Austen, *The Heart of the Goddess*

*The end of a thing
is never the end,
something is always born,
like a year or a baby.*

—LUCILLE CLIFTON

*I was the first midwife
in my family. And I loved
the job; you always need
to get somebody to help
when you have a baby,
and I was always the
woman they could get—
I could stand it. I had
a better nerve. You know
you can't deliver a baby
if you ain't got no nerve.*

—ANONYMOUS

I see

What most impresses me is my infant's eye...[which] sees no design, and has not yet begun the awesome task...of sorting reality from dream. No doubt has ever settled even on the surface of those dark blue depths, no doubt of self, of love, of form. They would change nothing in this world, not even next year's building blocks. They are less impressed by what appears before them than the baby lamb. It is as if, in these few weeks before they can identify my own, his eyes will be living out some final cycle in the story of the race, and still look only on the vast shapelessness of a primordial world.... But just after birth, the forest shadows linger in his eyes, even casting their grayness upon the whites. They have not yet made way for those shadows that seem to be in the nature of man, doubt and anxiety, though every other fiber of his being, from the high dome of his head down to his perfect foot, bespeaks intelligence of his kind.

—Charlotte Painter, from *Who Made the Lamb*

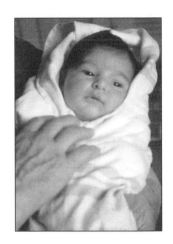

That baby was the
beautifulist thing I ever saw....
You look at him, and it seemed
he'd been born a long time.
His head was right up like he
was lookin' at me, looking
right into my heart, so I said to
the midwife, "Can this baby see?"
She said, "No," but I
figured he was seeing. I believe
that to this day.

—Pearl Broaster, from *Mothers Talking, Sharing the Secret* by Frances Wells Burck

I recognize

My first vivid memory is...when first I looked into her face and she looked into mine. That I do remember, and that exchanging look I have carried with me all my life. We recognized each other. I was her child and she was my mother.

—PEARL S. BUCK

Often at the time of birth we are so preoccupied with bodies—the mother's big one, the baby's tiny, breathing one—that we do not stop to consider what is the most outstanding characteristic of the newborn baby. Look at his eyes. Evidently they are seeing next to nothing, and yet seeingness or alertness is what they express most of all. Clearly he knows next to nothing and yet there he is, conscious, aware, alert, above all interested in seeing—not judging, not liking or disliking—just seeing what is so.

This consciousness is his definition. Any mother thinking back to the first moments when she and her baby looked at each other can remember it—the wide-awake looking. This quality of awareness is most memorable because it more than anything else is the truth of the child. As the wave is to water, the baby is to consciousness. He comes of it (conception), is made of it, and to it he returns. Only insofar as he becomes fully conscious does he become fully himself. This recognition on the part of the parent is basic to true parental love.

—Polly Berrien Berends, from *Whole Child/Whole Parent*

...The click! of recognition, that parenthesis of truth around a little thing that completes the puzzle of reality in women's minds—the moment that brings a gleam to our eyes....

—JANE O'REILLY

I thrive

I feel I would be hollow now if I had not been a mother. I have developed patience and tolerance of others. I was not born with this; I developed it. I have learned to enjoy each day as it is given to me. I have learned to control my temper and discipline myself. I have learned to discipline with love, not anger. I have learned to pray about a lot of things and listen to what God tells me. I have grown from a young, selfish child-woman into a wiser, more patient person. I have the ability to love without reservations and to absorb pain, hold up and grow with wisdom. I've learned patience and tolerance and that nothing is ever perfect. I've learned to be content with what I have but never to give up the dream, and that perseverance is surely a virtue.

—from *The Motherhood Report: How Women Feel About Being Mothers*

DOULA: SECOND MOTHER

A birthing companion or *doula* (Greek for an experienced woman who helps other women) first meets with prospective parents during the third trimester of pregnancy to create a birth plan. She later returns when the woman begins her labor. The doula never leaves the mother's side throughout labor and delivery. She holds the laboring mother close when she needs physical reassurance, massages her back, and helps her breathe. The doula's assurance can be incredibly powerful for a pregnant woman. She feels nurtured and empowered, dependent and independent at the same time. The doula becomes a mother figure to her. The birthing mother can thus internalize the doula's nurturing behaviors during labor, a passage in which she is especially sensitive to her environment and open to learning and growth. When she's held close in such a loving way, the new mother becomes more able to give the same care to her child.

According to childbirth experts, women who were aided during childbirth by trained, female labor companions required fewer cesarean births, needed less anesthesia, had more interest in their newborns, and interacted more with their babies than women who delivered without this assistance.

I am the center

In the sheltered simplicity of the first days after a baby is born, one sees again the magical closed circle, the miraculous sense of two people existing only for each other.

—ANNE MORROW LINDBERGH

I wanted, on the occasion of my farewell, to leave you, my dear children, instructions and rules for conduct. As all of you, however, are grown up, I cannot advise you as is usual with minors. I shall therefore limit myself to some general though important instructions.

Above all I admonish you to cherish virtue and fear God: otherwise you can neither achieve full happiness on earth nor find peace and reward in the world to come. Content yourself with your fate and fortune and accommodate your needs to your income; behave peacefully to everybody and among yourselves. Do not allow yourselves to become involved in harmful family conflicts. Live, moreover, in concord and assist one each other with advice and deeds.

You must hold together ever more closely and firmly. You need such closeness, and you will need it more than ever, once the sad event occurs—so much sadder for you than for me—your mother's being torn from you, and thus, as it were, the center disappearing from the circle.

Farewell, and accept the blessing of your always faithful mother, Fani Wolf

—Fran Fani Wolf, from her last will (1849)

✥ The Pueblo Tewa people see every village as a microcosm of the world. Their villages are framed by four sacred mountains, four hills, four shrines, four dance plazas, and, at the center, the most sacred spot: "earth mother earth navel middle place."

I am independent

Each of us must make his own way, and when we do, that way will express the universal way. This is the mystery. When you understand one thing through and through, you understand everything. When you try to understand everything, you will not understand anything. The best way is to understand yourself, and then you will understand everything. So when you try hard to make your own way, you will help others, and you will be helped by others. Before you make your own way you cannot help anyone, and no one can help you. To be independent in this true sense, we have to forget everything which we have in our mind and discover something quite new and different moment after moment. This is how we live in this world.

—Shunryu Suzuki, from *Zen Mind, Beginner's Mind*

A mother is not a person to lean on but a person to make leaning unnecessary.

—DOROTHY CANFIELD FISHER

THE ENCHANTED CHILD

Thomas Traherne, a poet of the Romantic era, vividly expressed a child's gift for introspection. His focus on nature and childhood when "Som thing infinit Behind evry thing appeared" revealed the sensory texture of his enchantment with children.

All mine! And seen so Easily! How Great, how Blest!
How soon am I of all possest!
My Infancie no Sooner Opes its Eys,
But Straight the Spacious Earth
Abounds with Joy Peace Glory Mirth
And being Wise,
The very Skies,
And Stars do mine becom; being all possest
Even in the Way that is the Best.

—Thomas Traherne

I improve

*Train up a child in a way
he should go–and walk there
yourself once in a while.*

—Josh Billings

*Perhaps the greatest gift that
women can give their daughters
is to take precious care of their
own lives–to develop their
natural talents and to honor the
opportunities that come their way.
By so doing, they become vital
models for their children as well
as full women in their own right.*

—Evelyn Bassoff

O Great Spirit,
Whose voice I hear in the winds,
and whose breath gives life to all the world,
hear me! I am small and weak, I need your
strength and wisdom.

Let Me Walk In Beauty, and make my eyes
ever behold the red and purple sunset.

Make My Hands respect the things you have
made and my ears sharp to hear your voice.

Make Me Wise so that I may understand the
things you have taught my people.

Let Me Learn the lessons you have hidden
in every leaf and rock.

I Seek Strength, not to be greater than my
brother, but to fight my greatest enemy myself.

Make Me Always Ready to come to you with
clean hands and straight eyes.

So When Life Fades, as the fading sunset,
my spirit may come to you without shame.

—Native American prayer

❖ In ancient times women wore small keys to
symbolize the key that would keep the door of
the womb securely closed until the time was
right for the baby's birth.

I lead

One afternoon dragon woman pointed out a cloud to the little crane. "Up there. Does that not look like a face?"

Crane woman squinted. A cry burst from her lips.

"That is my mother!"

"Your mother?"

Sure enough, high in the sky was the old woman's head; the eyes were closed and the head was bald, like that of a new-born child.

Little crane strained her head upward. The face stayed with them for only a few moments. The wind made the face wispier and wispier until it dissolved. Tears were running down crane woman's face.

"Ma ma...ma ma..." She searched the sky through her tears but the face was nowhere to be seen. Then, in the west she saw colors—faint shades of lavender, yellow and orange.

"Look, do you see what I see?"

"Yes, a patch of colors."

The two friends looked at each other. What did it mean?...

"Maybe your mother is trying to guide

you," offered Siew Lung, "telling you to follow the direction of the colors."

"Why does she not come to me? Why are her eyes shut? Ma ma I miss you so. Why did she leave me, why?"

"Your mother is with you. She's above us, in the sky.... She is watching over you like a star and showing you the way."

"But I miss her."

Dragon woman held her and stroked her feathers.

"Let us rest now. The way ahead has been shown. Sleep, dear one."

— Kitty Tsui, from *Why the Sea Is Salty*

❖ West Africans believe that "any woman who has given birth knows enough to be a midwife, and even some of the very young ones are very competent due to grandmother's prescriptions."

I am honey

Our mother's body is the earth,
her aura the air, her spirit
is in the middle, round like an egg,
and she contains all good things in herself,
like a honeycomb....

— MARY McANALLY

I have sat this summer in my garden watching bees and yellow jackets flitting through our raspberry canes. The raspberries have been good this year, and now the canes stand dry, stick-looking, with limp leaves and tangled branches. We have eaten all the goodness from them. But the bees still come humming over us where we sit, circling the late yellow-flowering broccoli gone to seed. We are reading; my son sitting snug between my thighs, smooth bulwarks against any stings, while splashy sounds of other siblings reach us now and then above the hums. Niobe-like, languid and proud, I hold him at the end of summer, his golden skin challenging any radiance sent down from the sky. Smooth rounded-browness, now squirming to be off; white soles flashing as he races through the meadow to join the others, crushing wild strawberries and clover with his heels.

—Anna Maria Murdoch, from *Motherhood and Mythology*

Physical closeness between mothers and babies provides immense benefits for both. When a mother breast feeds her baby, an intimate bond is created and health and well-being are enhanced. In addition, the baby receives individual attention and emotional security along with antibodies from the mother to ward off infections. The mother's body physically responds to her baby's cry by producing breastmilk—nature's perfect food. Breast feeding after delivery speeds expulsion of the placenta and protects the mother from hemorrhaging. Simply holding her baby close helps a new mother regulate her own body temperature, heart and metabolic rate, hormone and enzyme levels, and breathing. Conversely, the baby's look and touch stimulate powerful nurturing feelings and instincts in the mother necessary for successful caretaking.

I illustrate

My daughter's birth is inextricably woven into the women's movement in my psyche. I remember pushing and pushing, face all red, body straining, doctors and nurses and husband about me, like a cheering section: "One more time: Push! Now look!" I saw her wet head emerging out of me in the large, delivery-room mirror. She hardly cried. Instead, with a cool, intelligent gaze, she looked around the delivery room. I thought: "My goodness! A daughter who is going to be looking at me!" I knew then I would have to become true to myself, so I would not be ashamed of what she saw in me.

—Naomi Ruth Lowinsky, from *Stories from the Motherline*

To dream in the falling snow, to clothe the ground and leaf out trees, to turn the pages of my brilliant trove of flower pictures and gaze into my heart where I can feel and not see, almost touch, a boy or girl whose coloring or features I imagine as watercolors brushed into the edges of a form.

—LOUISE ERDRICH

I am a jewel

What I'd like to wear, my baby, is a hundred-breasted, thousand-jeweled garment of sapphire; a great coat of many colors; disposable downs flecked with fake precious metals. Large, exotic clothes, to loudly and gorgeously proclaim your passage into being. Where can I buy such clothes? Where can I wear such clothes? —PHYLLIS CHESLER

With the birth of her only child, a daughter, my mother pulled jewels out of thin air, giving me a name that translates as "the Brilliance of Diamonds."

"I wanted to give you prosperity," she explained, "something that my family couldn't give to me.... I thought a long time about your name," she told me. "A name can determine your life, who you will be. Each letter has a certain power, each person a special name, told in the stars. If you can find the secret of your name, you can unlock the universe."

In truth, though, I know my mother waited not because she was trying to decide on the best possible name, but because she couldn't get anyone to name me. In Korea, as she explained to me, the paternal grandfather is supposed to name his sons' babies. Since my mother didn't know the family of my absent father, and since her own father was dead, she had hoped a substitute grandfather, one of the *ajushis*, from the village would volunteer. No one did; naming, I suppose, is such a big responsibility.

She waited and hoped, however, long enough for several of the village gossips to start calling me Moo Myung: "Baby No Name." When my mother caught herself calling me that, she decided to read the stars and count letters herself, hoping to find—if not the right name—at least a name that wouldn't hurt me. Finally, she settled on Myung Ja, playing on the words for "name" and "sparking."

—Nora Okja Keller, from "The Brilliance of Diamonds," *Making More Waves*

I am light

Mother, do you know, almost all people love their mothers, but I have never met anybody in my life, I think, who loved his mother as much as I love you. I don't believe there ever was anybody who did, quite so much, and in quite so many wonderful ways. I was telling somebody yesterday that the reason I am a poet is entirely because you wanted me to be and intended I should be, even from the very first. You brought me up in the tradition of poetry, and everything I did you encouraged. I cannot remember once in life when you were not interested in what I was working on, or even suggested that I should put it aside for something else....

—Edna St. Vincent Millay, from a letter dated June 15, 1921

The stars about the lovely moon hide their shining forms when it lights up the earth at its fullest. —SAPPHO, FRAGMENT 4

❖ The moon became the prime symbol of the mother goddess in ancient times because of its apparent connection to women's cycles of "lunar blood," presumed to give life to every human being in the womb.

May the blessing of light be on you,
light without and light within.
May the blessed sunshine shine on you
and warm your heart
till it glows like a great peat fire,
so that the stranger may come
and warm himself at it,
and also a friend.

I impel

BIRTH STORY

I saw a videotape once of a baby giraffe being born. The mother giraffe delivered standing up—while walking even. (Giraffes can't afford to lay down and do it—they would be too vulnerable to lions.) So the baby giraffe fell out of its mother six or seven feet to the ground. Its landing caused a small dust cloud. The baby breathed right away—(no wonder) and immediately began struggling to its feet with the help of mother. It figured out how to walk in the next minute or two, and mother and baby caught up again with the rest of the herd. Nature does not always arrange that birth be gentle. In the case of the giraffe, the chances for survival of the species seem to indicate that a rough landing on the planet is the best way.

—Ina May Gaskin, from *Spiritual Midwifery*

My mother sang with me in her stomach. I sang with Bobbi Kris in my stomach. I believe the child starts to develop within, and whatever is put inside of you—whatever you read, whatever you think, whatever you do—affects the child.

—WHITNEY HOUSTON

I am leading you to the crossroad.
See, this is your road to the market!
This is your road when going for firewood!
This is your road to the water place!
This is your road to your farm!
This is your road to your hometown!
May you grow up!
And walk on it to the market,
And walk on it for firewood,
And walk on it to the water place,
And walk on it to the farm,
And walk on it to your hometown!
May the child stand fast on the ground!
May it grow strong!

—From the Krobo of Ghana "Greeting to the Newborn"

I am safe

I do not believe there is any greater moment than holding your baby for the first time and looking into her eyes. There is such a feeling of wonderment and magic—a moment when everything mysterious and sacred in the universe can be seen in one body.

On March 2, 1978, I experienced something I had never felt before and have not felt since. After a long and difficult labor and delivery, the nurse brought my daughter to me for her first feeding at two o'clock in the morning. (My husband, nervously present at the birth, had gone home to recover and to make long-distance phone calls to herald her arrival.) The room was illuminated by a single soft light over the hospital bed.

As I held my daughter for the first time, I felt a strong presence of warmth surrounding us. This presence—unseen, but definitely felt—in the room was that of safe and loving beings—perhaps her ancestors come to welcome her…. I know I was not afraid. There we were, Michaela and I, alone in the world for the first time. I held this little, fragile being as though we were the only gift I would receive in this lifetime.

—Marsha R. Leslie, from "The Gifts of Children and Angels," from *The Single Mother's Companion*

Relax completely, body and mind. Imagine yourself on a beautiful natural beach, warm and comfortable. Imagine the deep blue or emerald green water. Watch the waves for a few minutes, surging and ebbing, surging and ebbing. Now imagine that you are out on the water. You are floating securely on the water's surface, perfectly safe. Each time a  wave surges, feel it lifting you, gently supporting the weight of your entire body, carrying you along. As the waves surge higher, let your breathing become a little deeper, let your body become a little more relaxed. If thoughts or fears come into your mind, imagine they are pieces of driftwood carried away by the waves. Feel the waves surging strong, rising, rising, reaching a crest and ebbing, ebbing, ebbing away. Imagine that these powerful waves are massaging the baby, preparing him or her for the first breath. The waves are preparing you to welcome your child. Now allow the waves to bring you to shore. Imagine that you and your baby are together on the shore, warm, relaxed. Look at your child. Let thoughts and feelings come as they will.

—Carl Jones, *Visualizations for an Easier Childbirth*

I yearn

[When] I consider my marriage, no matter where I am, I enter a different place, a kind of shelter, a white room.

My wife and I are the conduit through which other souls pass. These souls are in this room with us. From her side and all the sides that made her, come the precisions of Switzerland, the passions of Sicily, the close voices of her father and mother and the distant sadness of her grandparents, immigrants in time who worked in kitchens and in factories and called to one another or did not call at all. And from my side comes the sharp fatalism of Truman's country, the shadows of prairie schooners, and some madness, and the vanity of itinerant artists, and, long before that, the veined hands of silk farmers. And through both of us come the pain and the hope of Cro Magnon and perhaps Neanderthal, and round-eyed lemurs watching. Before that, there was only wind, and desire.

All of this and more comes with us to this room, and out of our marriage it will move on, and we will move with it through our children, into other rooms. Our voices and longings will join those of future Swedes or Africans or Venetian colonists, and their stories will become ours, and ours theirs.

When I look carefully at my wife, I see her true beauty, both frightening and comforting. She has come to me, and I to her, to give the past a future and the future a past, to live for a while in this room.

—Richard Louv, from *The Web of Life*

POLYNESIAN BIRTH POEM

Slowly the babe expands life's course,
fills the gateway of life.
She slips downward,
becomes visible,
Now the living child,
long cherished by a mother's heart,
bursts forth into the light of day,
as the waters of childbirth flow away.

—ADAPTATION, ORIGINALLY TRANSLATED
BY WILLARD TRASK

I acclaim

Amalia [Nathalson Freud, mother of Sigmund Freud] was a very happy mother. She fed her first-born at the breast and watched his growth not only with immense pleasure but also with great pride. The fact that he was born in a caul seemed, according to an ancient tradition, to insure him happiness and fame. But, in addition, she firmly believed in a prophecy of an old peasant woman who, when Amalia met her one day by chance in a shop, assured the young mother that she had brought a great man into the world. She never tired of repeating this inspiring prediction again and again. Later, when Sigmund was a boy of eleven or twelve and lived in Vienna, his mother was even to fortify the early legend by interweaving it with another forecast, this time of an improvisator who, one evening at a restaurant in the Prater, created a few

My mother's love for me was so great that I have worked hard to justify it.

—MARC CHAGALL

rhymes about the young Sigmund and told him and his parents that if he could trust his inspiration the boy would probably one day become a "minister" [statesman]. "Perhaps," Freud's oldest sister, Anna Freud-Bernays, said many years afterwards, "my mother's trust in Sigmund's future destiny played a definite part in the trend given his whole life."

—Franz Kobler, from *Her Children Call Her Blessed*

❖ In folklore, the caul or "veil" is part of the amnion which, sometimes, remains attached to the child when it is born. This has been considered a good luck omen since at least the time of the Romans. The caul, when preserved as a talisman, is also a protection against drowning. (It is widely believed to be a protection against demons, particularly storm demons. Hence, the caul is, among sailors, a valuable charm). The possessor of a caul is believed to obtain from it several magical and medicinal virtues. She can see ghosts and talk to them; even if deaf, she can hear the spirits talk. An early American Negro belief, adopted from the English, was that the person born with a caul could tell fortunes.

embrace

Hands, come to me,
speak to me. Tell.
Your gestures, at first light
are silent but then,
alive like a sunburst or poet's surprise,
these hands reveal the heartbeat of life.

I sit on my bench by the sea and I watch
hands passing by me, caressing red plums,
hands holding fire, their passionate lock
slowly hands creviced, thrumming aged love
hands in dark pockets, alone for the stroll
solemn hands praying to luminous skies
tiny hands swaying like oats in the wind
insistent, reaching for mother's embrace.

Hands,
come to me, gather me.
SHOUT.
Meander my belly
transcendent with child.
Joining two worlds in waves lapping shore,
these hands awaken your fingers
FOR LIFE.

ANDREA ALBAN GOSLINE

I embrace

I thought of how
I would hold the baby,
the new soft skin
against my breast.
My nipples would be
the center of the baby's
life, and my arms
folding around the
infant would fold
around myself, holding
the two of us together.

—ANNE ROIPHE

I spent a summer baking bread for fifty children on a farm outside Willits…Children swarmed me, tugged at my apron, took little balls of dough, and rolled them lightly between their teeth. The bread rose and came out of the oven, broke into tender crumbs, tasted good. I watched the children and gave them small lumps of dough to press. I touched their miniature shoulders and smiled…Today I look at my hands. I remember the bodies I touched, the lives that came through them. I look at my hands sometimes and trace the edges of my fingers, like children do in kindergarten on newsprint with green tempera paint. Hands become what they have held; our hands shape themselves around what they hold most dear.

—Brenda Miller, from "A Thousand Buddhas"

During normal childbirth your baby does not feel pain…. The baby's sensation is one of healthy stimulation—stress but not distress. Your baby is massaged by your uterine contractions, and you may think of your contractions as hugging your baby, as he or she moves through labor…. Think of it as a child learning to swim, first crouching with feet on the wall of the pool, then pushing forcefully toward the center of the pool. In this way you and your baby work together during labor.

Your baby's head molds easily, fitting through the cervix as it opens. You might imagine how pleasant it can feel to have hands cupped around your head, as often happens during a massage….And so it is for your baby….

Like many women, you may feel protective of your baby during labor. It can be comforting to visualize the normal labor process as a stimulating massage for your baby.

—Gayle Peterson, from *An Easier Childbirth: A Mother's Workbook for Health and Emotional Well-Being During Pregnancy and Delivery*

I journey

In anticipation of becoming parents, my husband and I, in a candlelit ceremony, extended this offer to a spirit somewhere in the cosmos that would choose to become a member of our family:

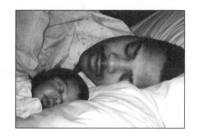

We invite a child to enter our lives this year. It is the right time. We are emerging from our self-centered twenties and have figured out some of life's mysteries. We want to invite a child to share in the loving relationship we have, to help create a family, and to share our company as we grow older. We want to complete the cycle of life. Just as the child learns from the parents, so too the parents learn to see the world through the eyes of a child. We invite a child to join in our life's adventure.

We feel an attachment to you already. We will try not to have any expectations of the person you will become. We will try not to make you something you are not. We hope you will receive and emulate the best attributes of both of your parents.

Your father offers you originality, independence of thought, a sense of wonder and fair play, self-confidence, insightfulness, love of music, and balance.

Your mother offers you warmth of personality, positivity, the beauty of words, openness, creativity, and *joie de vivre.*

With you we hope to share selfless and unconditional love, to renew our childlike sense of wonder, to recapture the missing years of our childhoods, to build a functioning family free of secrets and unspoken anger, and to share our journeys, our triumphs, and our disappointments.

Accept this invitation and enter a life of love and discovery.

Maya McKenzie responded to our invitation and arrived on February 9, 1995.

—Michelle Zundel

It is good to have an end to journey toward; but it is the journey that matters in the end.

—Ursula K. LeGuin

RITUAL

Massage your belly and bring the healing power of touch to your unborn child. Start by circling your belly button. Then use broad strokes over your belly, waist, and breasts. Massage with or without oil. Tell your baby what you're doing and invite him into this pleasurable journey.

Pregnancy is a journey. At the end, a woman gives birth not only to a baby, but also to her own identity as a mother.

—Gayle Peterson

I am the nest

*I read somewhere
that pregnant women like
to watch swimming turtles.
Then I realized the
connection between them
and the child living
inside of us who is
also encased and slowly
drifting in its own
sea world,
and I felt affirmed.*

— AMY SHELDON

The nesting urge has a significance other than preparing a clean house for your baby. For your husband perhaps it's a way to be involved other than just standing by. For you, as labor approaches, bringing on a subtle restlessness, and your energy starts to peak, being active is a way of letting off steam that keeps you from feeling anxious.

I also think the nesting urge has a spiritual dimension to it. While some folks insist that there's nothing redeeming about washing dishes or scrubbing the bathtub, I don't agree. We've all heard spiritual teachers tell us of the joy and meaning in doing simple, everyday tasks—tasks that keep your family going. The Buddhists talk about the satisfaction of chopping wood and carrying water. What better way to express your gratefulness for your family than keeping one's home in order. Take a moment as you dust the furniture to acknowledge how blessed you are to have a piece of furniture to dust. As you put a load of laundry in the dryer, imagine your loved one's face and, as you prepare the evening meal, pour your love into it. Do your chores with a grateful heart. When no one seems to notice how much effort you are extending, remember that when your children are grown and have a home of their own, they'll look back with fondness at the loving energy you gave to transform their house into a home.

The nesting urge has a purpose to it, and when it hits you can't sit still. There's excitement in the air as if something special is about to happen—and it is.

— Judy Ford, from *Blessed Expectations*

I prepare

I got up and started cleaning the house again,
feeling compelled to put everything in its place....
The house had to be straightened up or else the
baby could not come out! I knew when our
dog was about to go into labor because
she scratched and clawed at the rags
and newpapers in her box and
turned round and round trying to
make herself comfortable there. I was
doing the same thing. —JANET ISAACS ASHFORD

THE NESTING HOUSE

When the time of birth was near, early North
American women departed alone to a secluded
place near a brook or stream and prepared a
shelter with mats and covering, called a nesting
house. With ample food and provisions, they
awaited their delivery without the company or
help of any person. These birth huts were used
in North America and in some parts of South
America and Asia. Universally, they were built
by the pregnant woman herself, or by her female
relatives. (In fact, women in tribal societies were
often the builders and architects of all the tribe's
dwellings.) Birth huts were frequently con-
structed near a body of water, both for disposal
of waste and for washing up after the birth.

Wherever you live
is your temple if you
treat it like one.

—JACK KORNFIELD

❖ **In the Middle Ages, new-**
born babies were passed to
the midwife, who rubbed the
infant's gums and mouth
with honey and salt, or myr-
tle oil and roses, before the
child was tightly swaddled.

I am insightful

During a nature walk in the Maine woods…I had fallen back a bit and was hurrying to catch up when, through the trees, I saw a glade. It had a lush fir tree at the far side and a knoll in the center covered in bright, almost luminous green moss…. The little roof of visible sky was perfect-

ly blue…I went to the edge and then, softly, as though into a magical or holy place, to the center, where I sat, then lay down with my cheek against the freshness of the moss. It is here, I thought, and I felt the anxiety that colored my life fall away…. Everything was in its place…. In autumn, it would be right; in winter under the snow, it would be perfect in its wintriness. Spring would come again and miracle within miracle would unfold, each at its spe-

cial pace, some things having died off, some sprouting in their first spring, but all of equal and utter rightness.

I felt I had discovered the missing center of things, the key to right-ness itself, and must hold on to this knowledge which was so clear in that place. I was tempted for a moment to take a scrap of moss away with me, to keep as a reminder; but a rather grown-up thought pre-vented me. I suddenly feared that in treasuring an amulet of moss, I might lose the real prize: the insight I had had.

—Jean Liedloff, from *The Glade*

✣ A standard piece of equipment for a midwife in medieval Europe was a specially designed birthing chair. The chairs were horse-shoe shaped with short legs and a hole in the middle.

To my mother I tell the truth.
I have no thought, no feeling that I cannot
share with my mother, and she is like a
second conscience to me, her eyes like a mirror
reflecting my own image.

—WILLIAM GERHARDI

I am the circle

I often feel spiritual communion with all the other mothers who are feeding their babies in the still of the night. Having a baby makes me feel a general closeness with humanity.

—SIMONE BLOOM

············ RITUAL ············

Choose a night once a week to sit together as a family. Place large pillows in a circle on the floor. Light a scented candle and put it in the middle. Let each family member speak for ten minutes, uninterrupted, about the joys and challenges of the past week. Draw your baby into this family circle right from birth.

My mother is a poem I'll never be able to write
though everything I write is a poem to my mother...
I don't know why she is hard to find.
She has given me all the stories.
She is the story line of this poem. My mother, my
        optimist...

My mother is a poem I'll never write.
In her as John Muir says
one may think the clouds themselves
are plants...

O, wild girl of the river I named my son for. Mother,
Father. Brother. Sister, Daughter, Country.
She summons them out of the flowers and stones,
on the road disappearing around the hill,
down the tracks of the one who was lost.
She hunts them to where the sea begins.
She rides a runaway horse through this poem,
a strange opium through my blood.
She tells me the stories, a search
for the living, a hidden road
out from
all the known places.

This is a poem that cannot end

—Sharon Doubiago, from "Mother," from *Hard Country*

I sense

*We say "I love you"
to our children, but it's not
enough. Maybe that's why
mothers hug and hold and
rock and kiss and pat.*

—Joan McIntosh

*In touch there are
no language barriers;
anything that can walk,
fly, creep, crawl, or
swim already has it.*

—Ina May Gaskin

When I look at my oldest daughter, now twenty-five, I feel the oddest metaphysical start or shock to realize that this adult person is the same burrowing, suckling creature I nursed so many years ago. This gives me a special tenderness toward all adults, as I can psychically unpeel the layers of maturity and see the needy and vulnerable infant that all of the adult unfolding builds from and covers over. Perhaps women, through caring for infants and especially through the very concrete act of nursing, have a sense of the primordial seed in each person and of the mystery of human development which is often harder for men to come by.

—Stephanie Demetrakopoulos, from *Listening to Our Bodies*

❖ In 1975, French obstetrician Frederick Leboyer took the controversial stand that newborn babies are in possession of all their senses at birth and thus, their cries of pain are authentic. He called for the end of cold, chaotic delivery rooms. His suggestions for improving the environment into which babies are born included turning down the lights, laying the baby directly on the mother's warm stomach, keeping noise to a minimum, and handling the newborn very gently.

I slow

September 3

We are in a tranquil sea together, passing from pregnancy through birth, to life apart. You are quiet and still, wriggling occasionally and in the evenings pushing down.

Yesterday morning as I awoke I felt the first contraction, a girdle of tightness around my lower back and belly. You are in no hurry to be born, and I'm enjoying this time of quiet anticipation. I spend my days resting, reading, making your birth announcement and thinking about a welcoming ceremony for you....Summer is unraveling into fall, the days less hot, the nights cooler: a good time to be born. We will be able to go on long walks together and feel the season change.

—Willow Rain, from "A Journal for Baby Kate," from *Hearts Open Wide*

WOMAN: ✧ I am a strong, capable woman.... ✧ My pelvis will release and open as have those of countless women before me. ✧ I accept my labor and believe that it is the right labor for me, and for my baby. ✧ I feel the love that others have for me during the birth. ✧ I treat my mate lovingly during the birthing.... ✧ I have a beautiful body. My body is my friend. ✧ Contractions are an effortless way to assist my baby into the world. ✧ I can see my birth as a learning experience from which I will grow and change. ✧ I embrace the concept of healthy pain.... ✧ I can be strong, confident, assured, and assertive and still be feminine. ✧ My baby knew how to "get in" and it knows how to "get out." ✧ I help my baby feel safe so that it can get born.

MAN: ✧ I take care of myself during this pregnancy. ✧ I see my wife as a strong and capable woman.... ✧ I support her during her labor.... ✧ I express my love to my wife easily and frequently. ✧ I accept the labor that is meant for us. ✧ I accept feelings of helplessness. ✧ I am sensitive, tender, open, and trusting.... ✧ I feel the love that others have for me when I need support.

—Nancy Wainer Cohen, from *Artemis Speaks* by Nan Koehler

RITUAL *During the last month of your pregnancy, go out of your way to take the long way home. Travel leisurely, slow your pace, take in your surroundings, and discover new sights and sounds along your usual path. This will help you get in synch with the innocent and wondrous vantage point of the newborn.*

I belong

My baby has changed my life. I no longer have to ask myself who I am or how I fit in. I am a mother. This has allowed me to step into my full self: protector, nurturer, teacher, provider and student.

I love how my body makes nourishment. I love giving my baby a bath, watching him sleep, and playing with him. I am in awe of his growth and transformation from a newborn to a little person.

I'm most in my power when I let my capacity for loving reach beyond the boundaries.

—Felicia Soth, from *My Spirit Flies: Portraits and Prose of Women in Their Power*

✦ Instead of cigars, Nigerian fathers give out calabashes of kolanuts upon the birth of their children.

A CHILD'S DWELLING PLACE

In his ship Scuppers had a little room. In his room Scuppers had a hook for his hat and a hook for his rope and a hook for his spyglass and a place for his shoes and a bunk for his bed to put himself in.

At night Scuppers threw the anchor into the sea and he went down to his little room.

He put his hat on the hook for his hat, and his rope on the hook for his rope, and his spyglass on the hook for his spyglass, and he put his shoes under the bed, and got into his bed, which was a bunk, and went to sleep.

—Margaret Wise Brown, from *The Sailor Dog*

As soon as I was visibly and clearly pregnant, I felt, for the first time in my adolescent and adult life, not guilty. The atmosphere of approval in which I was bathed—even by strangers on the street, it seemed—was like an aura I carried with me, in which doubts, fears, misgivings, met with absolute denial. This is what women have always done.

—ADRIENNE RICH, FROM *THE FIFTIES*

I am home

As mothers, we are bound by depths of pain and waves of joy that those who have not raised children will never know. In each of our children we see a miracle of life—even as we realize, with sudden insight, that the world is full of just such miracles. I called my own mother at three A.M.—as the obstetrician sat on a stool between my legs, stitching my episiotomy with long black thread—and told her she was a grandmother. An hour and a half later, she slipped into my room, having driven alone in the dark, without directions, to a city hospital she had never seen before. She talked her way past the security guards and the night nurses, and she came to me. I was not altogether surprised to see her, though; it was just beginning to dawn on me what it means to be a mother....

Overnight the world had changed. I felt like a traveler who sets foot on foreign soil only to realize that she has journeyed to the right place after all, that she has found home. Settling into this new home meant coming to know myself as a mother, discovering my child, and, with my husband, enlarging our marriage to include and embrace a third....When I joined the tribe of mothers, the experiences of mothers everywhere became, in some measure, my own.

—Katrina Kenison, from *Mothers: Twenty Stories of Contemporary Motherhood*

The house holds childhood maternally "in its arms."

—VANGIE BERGUM

SPIRIT OF THE NURSERY

Your baby's nursery is where her spiritual life will be fostered. This is "her home" in which peace, protection, and love will reign. As you decorate the space, consider how you can imbue it with special meaning for your child: ❖ Think of the floor as the foundation for groundedness. Cover it with a colorful rug, on which your child may enjoy many hours of play and contemplation. ❖ Walls evoke protection and privacy. Paint them a warm color and hang whimsical artwork. Keep the window treatment simple to encourage your child's delight in the view. ❖ Your baby's bed is a place of serenity. Choose a sturdy mattress and decorate the ceiling with glow-in-the-dark, celestial shapes. Then bedtime will reveal a magical "night sky."

I surrender

What I know now about parenting is to "surrender." I've learned how childbirth brings with it self-discovery, self-healing, and adaptation to the new selves we become every single day of our lives. No one ever told me that, as an adult, I would keep on changing. I would have to move and flow with changes in myself, as well as all around me, for the rest of my life. No one ever explained that this process never ends, that it is infinite. Learning to surrender means learning to go with change. And change requires surrender.

From the first days of pregnancy, when the beautiful creature inside your body begins to puff out your belly and breasts, makes you nauseated and tired, makes you have emotional depths and heights, radically affects your relationship with everyone around you, you are asked by this tiny new life to adapt to all these changes. If you resist you will suffer. You must give in. You do let go. You shed your old self. Perhaps pregnancy, more than any other

period in a woman's life, enables her to understand the complexity of this requirement in life—to change and to adapt.

Pregnancy enables us to open a multitude of doorways—into ourselves, into our ancestral past, and into our future. Sometimes walking through these doorways can give us insights that can shift old patterns on this planet. The gift of childbirth challenges us to take nothing for granted, and to flow and to move like a great ocean, around any rocky obstacle.

—Chris Pritchard, from "Surrender Into Mothering"

Whoever is soft and yielding
is a disciple of life.
The hard and stiff will be broken.
The soft and supple will prevail.

—TAO TE CHING

RITUAL

Surrender! So, you're late. Things are changing! Stop and breathe. Slow it down. Go outside with the kids and lie down on the ground. Or sit in the grass or near anything green. Feel the Earth below you. Breathe in and breathe out. Look at your child. Surround your child like the great ocean and surrender to this moment. Laugh out loud. Cry out loud. Love yourself and your child. This is the only moment that matters: right now. Savor this green moment, this earth moment, this love moment. This moment of sweet surrender. –Chris Pritchard

I am simplicity

I came to give birth as a complicated person, with nine months of pregnancy literally under my belt. They were nine months of introspection and rumination. Conjecture, sometimes rhapsodic, sometimes anguished. And now I am catapulted into a ritual ring where introspection, rhapsody and anguish are irrelevant. I am face to face with an enormous simplicity. The immediacy of my body's functioning envelopes me and I give in to the embrace. I follow the inexorable commands. I obey the demands of now. A second ago is ancient, a second from now does not exist. I am the process, numbed and ennobled.

—Melisa Cassell, from *Written by Parents, 9 months, 1 day, 1 year*

To keep life simple, for each task ask:
- *Does it have to be done?*
- *Does it have to be done now?*
- *Can I delegate it?*
- *Does it have to be perfect?*
- *Is there a simpler way to do it?*

—LA LECHE LEAGUE

Manifest plainness,
Embrace simplicity,
Reduce selfishness,
Have few desires.

—THE WAY OF LAO-TZU,
TRANSLATED BY
WING-TSIT CHAN

WINNOWING

In parts of Asia, a ritual called winnowing is performed for a newborn baby to bond him or her to the family and home. The baby is placed upon a special tray along with items representing characteristics, skills, and hopes for his or her future, such as a book to signify knowledge and learning or a sewing needle to symbolize embroidery skills. Once all the objects are placed, the parents must appoint a trusted and respected person to raise the child up and simultaneously catch the tray as it falls. Making this choice is very important since the selected person also symbolizes characteristics hoped to be passed on to the baby. After lifting the baby and securing the tray, pieces of sacred thread are gently tied around the infant's wrists and ankles to welcome him or her into the world as a traditional blessing is recited.

I am happiness

❖ **In China a pregnant woman is said to have "happiness in her body."**
❖ **"She who hatches" is the Fulani phrase for a woman giving birth.**

May I give birth to Pollen Girl, may I give birth to Cornbeetle Girl, may I give birth to Long-Life Girl, may I give birth to Happiness Girl.

    With long-life happiness surrounding me, may I in blessing give birth. May I quickly give birth.

    In blessing may I arise again, in blessing may I recover. As one who is long-life-happiness may I live on.

    —Mother's Prayer for a girl (Navajo)

From Pure Joy springs all creation. By Joy it is sustained, toward Joy it proceeds and to Joy it returns. —Sanskrit saying

MOTHER NATURE'S COMFORT

❖ Cheyenne Indians dusted babies' legs and navels with powder from the prairie puffball fungus.
❖ The Rappahannocks used scorched cornmeal as an anti-chafing remedy.
❖ Micmac mothers used a powder of dry, rotted wood under the baby's bottom in their cradleboards.
❖ Navajo Indians made an ointment of red ochre, mutton tallow, and pitch that they rubbed on the baby's skin as a sunscreen, moisturizer, and protection against wetness.
❖ The Negrito of the Philippines kept their children shaded and applied ashes to their skin to protect from sun exposure.
❖ The Gros Ventre covered babies' faces with red paint after their baths to block the sun.
❖ In South Africa, the Kafir cover the baby with grease and red clay to soothe the skin and block out sun and windburn.

Blessed are we who can laugh at ourselves for we shall never cease to be amused.

—ANONYMOUS

I am the moment

There are just these blissful moments…the most intimate connection with another person, just watching [my daughter] respond to the world. We'd have these days that were just gorgeous, and we'd be able to be outside and enjoy it, which most of us as adults don't get to do.…So there I was being able to be outside, and enjoy life and enjoy the world and share it with her.…And I have these memories of walking in the park with her when she was fourteen months old, and being outside with her on this gorgeous fall day, and her handing me leaves.… You are also being given this privilege of seeing the world again through a child's eyes, sort of getting to start over again yourself. It's a real renewal when you have those moments, when you really share your child's vision.

—Robin, from *Mothering the New Mother: Your Postpartum Resource Companion*

ACTIVITY

Wrap your favorite flower petals, shells, feathers, scents, or any special found objects in a beautiful piece of cloth and tie it with ribbon. Before the birth of your baby, state your wishes for his life. Once he arrives, keep the charm in his room.

POEM TO EASE BIRTH

in the house with the tortoise chair
she will give birth to the pearl
to the beautiful feather

in the house of the goddess who sits on a tortoise
she will give birth to the necklace of pearls
to the beautiful feathers we are

there she sits on the tortoise
swelling to give us birth

on your way on your way
child be on your way to me here
you whom I made new

come here child come be pearl be beautiful feather

—ANONYMOUS (NAHUATL AZTEC), FROM *A BOOK OF WOMEN POETS, A BOOK OF PUZZLEMENTS: FROM ANTIQUITY TO NOW*

I am a friend

1 November 1751
[My Dear Child]
That part of [my life] which we passed together you have reason to remember with gratitude, though I think you misplace it; you are no more obliged to me for bringing you into the world, than I am to you for coming into it, and I never made use of that commonplace (and like most commonplaces, false) argument, as exacting any return of affection.... In the case of your infancy, there was so great a mixture of instinct, I can scarce even put that in the number of the proofs I have given you [of] my love; but I confess I think it a great one, if you compare my after-conduct towards you with that of other mothers, who generally look on their children as devoted to their pleasures, and bound by duty to have no sentiments but what they please to give them.... I have always thought of you in a different manner. Your happiness was my first wish, and the pursuit of all my actions, divested of all self-interest. So far I think you ought, and believe you do, remember me as your real friend.

—Lady Mary Wortley Montagu, a letter to her daughter Mary Bute

What is a friend?
A single soul dwelling
in two bodies.

—ARISTOTLE

I want to be your friend
For ever and ever without break or decay.
When the hills are all flat
And the rivers are all dry,
When it lightens and thunders in winter,
When it rains and snows in summer,
When Heaven and Earth mingle
Not till then will I part from you.

—FIRST-CENTURY CHINESE OATH OF FRIENDSHIP

I encompass

I see the hospital room. It seems later, perhaps a day later. It stands out that this is the first time I knew the difference between anyone who held me. This time, when she [mother] held me, I could tell that she was a different person—someone special. Somehow I just knew that I was safe with her, that I had nothing to worry about with this person.

She repeated my name several times proudly, as if to say, "This is my son." She was just repeating my name for her own satisfaction. When she spoke to me or about me, it made me feel good. When she held me or spoke to me, there was just something different. I could tell she cared for me in a way the others didn't. The others were concerned but she was totally concerned. With the others I was just a part of the job. With her I was her only thought—that's the feeling I got.

She is holding me now. I see her holding a bottle. This person is concerned about me. This person has nothing but me on her mind.

—Jeffrey, remembering his birth under hypnosis, from *Babies Remember Birth*

KOREAN CHILDBIRTH CUSTOMS

Since it was customary for married Korean women to live in their husband's community, a mother-to-be was assisted by her mother-in-law. After the baby was born, the mother did not receive any visitors—not even her own mother—for twenty-one days. During this three-week period, the new mother slept, ate, and nursed the baby. A rice stalk was erected in front of the house and if the baby was a boy, a dried red pepper was placed on it; a piece of wooden charcoal announced a girl. Aside from sharing the happy news, this custom also let the neighbors know that a newborn was in the house and it was not an appropriate time to visit. When the baby was 100 days old, the family held a big party. Plates of food were passed to family and neighbors. They in turn placed pieces of long white cotton thread on them to symbolize long life for the infant.

God could not be everywhere, therefore he made mothers.

—OLD JEWISH SAYING

I revel

And she was happy with her little girl, if not, as she'd anticipated, ecstatic; except of course in bursts of feeling; wayward, unexpected, dazzling, and brief. These are the moments for which we live, she thought. —JOYCE CAROL OATES

I always fantasized that on my fortieth birthday I'd be doing something exotically wonderful, like sitting on a beach in St. Thomas. I can't believe that I got up to change a diaper instead. Who would have thought? Look at me—I was twenty-five when I had my first child. Now, thirteen years later, I'm a new mother again. What a blessing—baby Taylor is another little miracle. She's brought us so much joy. I didn't plan to get pregnant, it just happened. When you're pregnant you just have this feeling. Somehow you just know. I had just dropped my husband off at a job site when the familiar sensation came over me. I thought to myself, "No way!" But I stopped at a shopping mall, bought a pregnancy test, and went into the rest room. Sure enough, it was positive!...

CONTEMPLATION

Childbirth, like lovemaking, is a natural process. Birth is a social event—the beginning of a family— and as such is an occasion for revelry.

My eldest daughter, Heather, is thrilled to have a little sister. She wrote me a note when I was in the hospital giving birth that said, "This is the best Christmas present you ever gave me."

—Noreen West, from *The Right Side of Forty: Celebrating Timeless Wisdom*

✥ In Greek mythology, fingers were named after the Dactyls, spirits born from the fingerprints of the Goddess Rhea while she gave birth to Zeus.

I touch

When I visit Mama, I always look first at her hands and feet to reassure myself. The skin of her hands is transparent—large-veined, wrinkled and bruised—while her feet are soft with the lotions I rubbed into them every other night of my childhood. That was a special thing between my mother and me, the way she'd give herself the care of my hands, lying across the daybed, telling me stories of what she'd served down at the truckstop, who had complained and who tipped specially well, and most important, who had said what and what she'd said back. I would sit at her feet, laughing and nodding and stroking away the tightness in her muscles, watching the way her mouth would pull taut while under her pale eyelids the pulse of her eyes moved like kittens behind a blanket. Sometimes my love for her would choke me, and I would ache to have her open her eyes and see me there, to see how much I loved her.

—Dorothy Allison, from "Mama," from *Trash*

Breathing in, I am so happy to hug my child.
Breathing out, I know she is real and alive in my arms.

Suppose a lovely child comes and presents herself to us. If we are not really there—if we are thinking of the past, worrying about the future, or possessed by anger or fear—the child, although present, will not exist for us. She is like a ghost, and we are like a ghost also. If we want to meet the child, we have to go back to the present moment in order to meet her. If we want to hug her, it is in the present moment that we can hug her.

So we breathe consciously, uniting body and mind, making ourselves into a real person again. When we become a real person, the child becomes real also. She is a wondrous presence and the encounter with life is possible at that moment. If we hold her in our arms and  continue to breathe, life is. This *gatha* can help us remember the preciousness of our loved one as we hold him or her in our arms.

—Thich Nhat Hanh, from *Present Moment Wonderful Moment: Mindfulness Verses for Daily Living*

I am destiny

*We are not trying to send
[children] into the world
as finished products—
we send them forward as
persons well begun.*

—Angelo Boyo

❖ For centuries, babies' bottoms were clothed with a variety of materials, most commonly hemp or linen cloths. Native American Indians used sphagnum moss collected from cranberry bogs which they stretched and pulled to soften. Able to absorb as much as twenty-two times its weight in water, the moss functioned quite well in this capacity. It also possessed antibiotic properties and disinfectant substances that helped prevent diaper rash.

My mother never worked outside the home, but she had the sophistication to know her parenting would have to be unique if it was to guide us through the new and changing world ahead. She was one of the healthiest people—mentally, spiritually and emotionally—I have ever known. She was a dedicated mother and homemaker. She and my father were both fluent in their native language, and she accepted her role, as a woman's responsibility, to pass on our traditional teachings…She was happy, giving and patient and, by just observing her, I learned how to relate to people and to move away from fear. She taught me to take risks.

One of the great lessons she gave to her children was the respect for all life: not just people, but also plants, birds, animals, everything around us. We lived on a big ranch and there was a large spring on our property surrounded by trees. We often walked there, and she would have us listen to birds singing as we went. She told us we should walk often among birds and animals and experience the connection among us all.

I didn't realize until I left the reservation how different our culture was from the one I was about to enter. The whole idea of healing, practiced in our ceremonies, was so clear. My mother and father, as their parents before them, had a strong sense of enlightenment and destiny.

—Wynn Dubray, from "Lakota Ways," from *Catch the Whisper of the Wind* by Cheewa James

I pause

I live in suspended time, as you are suspended within me—floating, buoyant. It is spring and I have been raking autumn's old leaves for days…. Pregnant and raking, eternally.

I am slow with your weight. I attempt vigorous strokes, but you tighten into a knotted ball of rock. "Slow down…" you are calling. "We have time…."

By heeding your call, I find that raking is an end in itself—not the clean lawn, the carefully piled hills, or the smoke of burnt leaves spiraling skyward—but rather, the stroke upon stroke, the swoosh and wisk of bamboo tines on nature's crisp paper. This, and the pauses in between—to inspect progress, to catch breath, to listen to the eerie wooing sounds of swans flying overhead. As I feel you relax and my own muscles ease, I pick up my rake and begin again.

—Mary Knight, from *Love Letters Before Birth and Beyond*

INFANT BLESSINGS

Ho! Sun, Moon, and Stars,
All you that move
In the Sky,
Listen to me!
Into your midst
New Life has come.
Make its path smooth.

—OMAHA

Woman must be still as the axis of a wheel in the midst of her activities;…she must be the pioneer in acheiving this stillness, not only for her own salvation, but for the salvation of family life, of society, perhaps even of our civilization.

—ANNE MORROW LINDBERGH

I am community

The room was crowded with other women who had come to give their encouragement and support. Some popped in and out between household duties and all took turns to physically support Miryam in whatever position she felt most

comfortable. She was never at a loss of a shoulder to grip, a chest to lean against, or a strong hand to steady an ankle or knee. If one woman tired or had to return to her children another would quickly take her place.

The atmosphere was cheerful and relaxed, with good-natured bantering between the women…. As she tensed up for another contraction, the desultory chatter stopped and the women would again focus their attention on the labouring woman, getting themselves ready to support

her in any way she wished. Sometimes she knelt or lay on her side and at other times stood with her arms around a friend's neck.

During a contraction she would utter a long, loud but controlled call to God—"Y'Allah!"—followed by pleas to God for help and protection. Her attendants would join in and echo her prayers, sometimes so earnestly that it was almost as if they themselves were enduring the contraction.

—a British midwife, describing the birth of a baby in a Yemeni village

MOTHERING THE MOTHERS

After giving birth to a child, a woman of the Baganda tribe of Uganda is attended by friends and relatives (for an entire month) who help her in almost every aspect of her postpartum life. Her body is massaged and kneaded with a concoction of boiled banana fibers, and her stomach is tied and braced with a wide piece of cloth to help it revert to its pre-pregnancy shape. The relatives prepare meals for the family, bathe the newborn, wash the laundry, and prepare special soups for the mother to stimulate breastmilk production. The family sets a relaxed tone with no time schedules or agendas. At this time it is also customary for every person in the village to pay a visit to the new mother and baby and give the baby a gift of money to ensure a prosperous future.

I am the elements

The earthwoman by her oven
tends her cakes of good grain.
The waterwoman's children
are spindle thin.
The earthwoman
has oaktree arms. Her children
full of blood and milk
      stamp through the woods shouting.
        The waterwoman
sings gay songs in a sad voice
        with her moonshine children.
When the earthwoman
has had her fill of the good day
      she curls to sleep in her warm hut
        a dark fruitcake sleep
but the waterwoman
        goes dancing in the misty lit-up town
in dragonfly dresses and blue shoes.

—Denise Levertov, from "The Earthwoman and the
Waterwoman," from *Collected Earlier Poems*

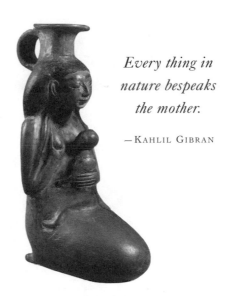

*Every thing in
nature bespeaks
the mother.*

—KAHLIL GIBRAN

❖❖❖ **GODDESSES** ❖❖❖

*The Chinese regard the birth of their babies as life's greatest
blessing, and invoke a legion of goddesses to protect them:*
❖ *Hsieh Jên Hsing Chun, the star-goddess of childbirth, for
protection and ease during pregnancy and birth* ❖ *Sung Tzu,
goddess of a child's blessings, for grace* ❖ *Ch'uang P'o, goddess
of the bed, for sound sleep and peace within the family* ❖ *Nai
Mu, goddess of wet nurses, for nourishment.*

✦ The lotus symbolizes all four of the classical elements—earth, water, air, and fire—representing the unity of these elements in the cosmic womb prior to creation. Earth is the mud in which the flower is rooted. Water surrounds and supports the stalk. The lotus blossom is believed to breathe the essence of air and releases its perfume into the breeze. The flower's fertility is drawn from the fire of the sun.

I awaken

PAWNEE PRAYER

Earth, ourselves,
breathe and awaken,
leaves are stirring,
all things moving,
new day coming,
life renewing.

My daughter Lily Camille was born under a full summer moon, one week after I finished compiling this book. On her eighteenth day of life, we welcomed her into our family with a *simchat bat* (joy of the daughter) ceremony. I wrote the ceremony to reflect the blessed sense of responsibility my husband and I feel as parents. The following ritual, adapted from *The Jewish Baby Book*, was the highlight of the evening, bringing the focus of our appreciation to the miracle of our baby's senses.

Jasmine sweet, Perfect rose
Violet feet, Sundrop nose
Lily small, Beneath our sight
Blossom tall, Dazzling white

—VIVIAN DUDRO

❖ **Mother:** I awaken Lily's sense of sight with the light of this candle. (Light one white candle.) Women have kindled the spiritual flame for family since ancient times. With each new day, may Lily remember the spark of life and share her enlightenment with everyone she meets.

❖ **Father:** I awaken Lily's sense of taste with this drop of sweet nectar. (Place a drop of fruit juice in baby's mouth.) Nature provides the fruit which nourishes our body and spirit. May Lily take what nature provides and make it sacred.

❖ **Grandmother:** I awaken Lily's sense of sound with this song (Sing or hum a song that has special meaning to your family.) May the sound of blessing caress Lily's ears and fill her heart.

❖ **Aunt:** I awaken Lily's sense of smell with these flowers. (Pass aromatic flowers beneath baby's nose.) May the fragrance of beauty and peace surround Lily as she remembers the wisdom of her soul.

❖ **Sibling(s):** We awaken Lily's sense of touch. (Wash baby's hands with water.) With this purifying water, we wash, awaken and welcome you. May Lily return often to the pure spring of life and immerse herself in truth, hope, and happiness.

—Andrea Alban Gosline

I hold

I learned to hold a baby simply by holding a baby, starting with the fullness of father love at childbirth. When I held our first daughter after she was born, her skin touching mine, I realized that, advertising pitches notwithstanding, the words baby soft must be reserved for babies alone, rather than any manufactured product.

Family photographs document how rapidly father and child acclimate. In one picture, our two-week-old stretches in my lap while at the piano I play Bach's "Jesu, Joy of Man's Desiring." In another, I sit reading the newspaper with a cat in my lap; the baby sleeps on my shoulder,

I drew him close to me with affection and love; picked him up and held him close to my cheek; I bent down to him, and fed him.

— HOSEA 11:4

snuggled in a turquoise receiving blanket. Her head nestles in the crook of my neck. My hand wraps around her bottom. (Then, in one of those Daddy's-doing-something-Mama-shouldn't-watch-pictures, pingpong paddle in one hand and baby in another, I return service: point and game.)...

"I got a ten-pound sack of sugar, ten-pound sack of beans," I sang as I circled the house with our girls. Tufts of baby hair tickled my neck. I used a baby sling to carry my daughters and strolled them in carriages, too. Day and night, they gave me gifts to redeem lost sleep. They took me to see stars, crescent moons, and nearby mountains at sunrise.

—Berkley Hudson, from "Birth of a Father: Hands-on Dad," *Pregnancy Magazine*

❖ The Navajo of Arizona call the woman who assists a birthing woman "the one who holds." This conveys the helper's responsibility to physically support and massage the new mother.

I am sensual

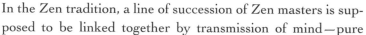

In the Zen tradition, a line of succession of Zen masters is supposed to be linked together by transmission of mind—pure thought transferred from mind to mind with no words.

I think that with midwives there is a similar kind of transmission…that is a transmission of touch.

Touch is the most basic, the most non-conceptual form of communication that we have. In touch there are no language barriers; anything that can walk, fly, creep, crawl, or swim already speaks it.

I first experienced a transmission of this kind, not with another midwife, but with a lady Capuchin monkey.… Her touch was incredibly alive and electric. There was so much concentrated feelingness in her hand that I felt this warm glow travel from her hand to mine.… I had a flash of realization then that my hand wasn't made any different than hers.… I knew that my hand and everyone else's too, was potentially that powerful and sensitive, but that most people think so much and are so unconscious of their whole range of sensory perceptors and receptors that their touch feels blank compared to what it would feel like if their awareness was one hundred percent. I call this "original touch" because it's something that everybody has as a brand-new baby, it's part of the kit.

—Ina May Gaskin, from *Spiritual Midwifery*

I would be happy if I never did another thing
in my whole life but lie on my bed, head propped up
by pillows, hands on my belly, seeing and feeling this baby
move inside me. My baby stretches—slow, sensuous
movements, rolling hills across my vast belly.

—Maren Tonder Hansen, from *Mother Mysteries*

I am ecstatic

Then came the birth—and of all the exciting experiences I ever read or imagined, it was the most exhilarating. They shouted and I shouted—not because it was painful but because something elemental and stupendous was happening and I was in on it. And then she was there and I saw her, rosy and perfect. I felt as if I could move mountains. It was early on a Sunday morning; the sun was just rising, birds were singing, and bells ringing for Mass. Words cannot recreate this moment. It was one of ecstasy.

—Richard Wertz, from *Lying-In: A History of Childbirth in America*

Happily may I walk.
May it be beautiful before me.
May it be beautiful behind me.
May it be beautiful below me.
May it be beautiful above me.
May it be beautiful all around me.
In beauty it is finished.

—NAVAJO EVENING CHANT

THE CUDDLE CHEMICAL

Oxytocin, a hormone that encourages labor and the contractions during childbirth, seems to play an important role in mother love. The sound of a crying baby makes its mother's body secrete more oxytocin, which in turn erects her nipples and helps the milk to flow. As the baby nurses, even more oxytocin is released, making the mother want to nuzzle and hug it. It's been called the cuddle chemical by zoologists and has many functions, some of them beneficial for the mother. The baby feels warm and safe as it nurses, and its digestive and respiratory systems run smoothly. The baby's nursing, which also coaxes the oxytocin level to rise in the mother, results, too, in contractions of the uterus that stops bleeding and detaches the placenta. So mother and baby find themselves swept away in a chemical dance of love, interdependency, and survival.

—Diane Ackerman, from *A Natural History of Love*

I heal

There is symbolic as well as actual beauty in the migration of the birds, the ebb and flow of the tides, the folded bud ready for spring. There is something infinitely healing in the repeated refrains of nature—the assurance that dawn comes after night, and spring after the winter. —RACHEL CARSON

My daughters, children of my grandfathers' and grandmothers' dreams. You were a reality long before my passion and your father's seed conceived you on those winter and spring nights. Visions preceded flesh from my womb. And my generations shall be as one. Spirits healing my mother's madness, my father's sadness. As the daughters of my grandfather's and grandmother's dreams touch hands with wind and water, light and love....

I gave birth because I was born a woman. The seeds of the future generations were carried in my womb. I remember conception because the female side of life is always fertile first. I gave birth three times as naturally as possible, given the situation, because as a woman my body and heart knew what to do. I nursed because my breasts filled with milk. I remember their names because that is how they will be recognized by their grandfathers and grandmothers who have gone on before. I am a mother because I was given three daughters to love. I am a midwife because women will continue to give birth. That is my story.

—Marcie Rendon (Eagle Clan, Ojibwe), from *Birthstories: The Experience Remembered*

✦ "The womb enters its cradle" is a Thai expression for a woman's postpartum recovery.

I am spellbound

Suddenly, there was our baby, lying silently on my hand, caught at her hips halfway out. I saw a bubble at her mouth and knew everything was fine. As the baby lay on my hand, I suctioned her mouth and watched her breathe on her own. She never cried, but she opened her eyes, focused on me, and sighed. Then she closed her eyes and seemed to sleep.

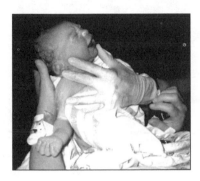

As I watched, the deep red color of her own blood circulating moved outward from her heart, chasing away the bluish tint from her chest, then her face. It was like seeing the passage of a rainbow, or more like the rising of a sun, bringing warmth and indescribable joy. There were no dry eyes or unsmiling faces as she came alive in such a magical way.

—Bill London, Idaho, 1978, from *Birthstories: The Experience Remembered*

CLAN MOTHER WISDOM

In the tradition of my two Kiowa Grandmother teachers, each moon has a Clan Mother who is the keeper of the rites of passage that mark human growth cycles. These Clan Mothers offer wisdom and practical daily rituals that allow us to remain in balance during the best and worst of times. These are the thirteen daily guidelines that I would like to share:

❖ Focus on positive, happy thoughts.
❖ Be kind and merciful with yourself and all living things.
❖ Be good to your body.
❖ Follow your heart and honor your inner-knowing
❖ Quiet your mind.
❖ Cherish every act in life as an expression of your creativity
❖ Let go of stress and tension.
❖ Drop all judgements.
❖ Be grateful.
❖ Breathe deeply.
❖ Connect with the Earth.
❖ Allow, allow, allow.
❖ Savor the art of being.

—Jamie Sams, from "Messages for Women of the Millenium" from *The Fabric of the Future: Women Visionaries Illuminate the Path to Tomorrow*

I appreciate

AMISH BIRTH STORY

At least an hour before, Amos had crawled up on the bed next to [Naomi], and since then, with his massive farmer's fingers dusted with baby powder, he'd been rubbing her back. Her whole body loosened up from the heat of labor and from his massaging....

Since Naomi had so little extra weight on her, you could almost see the bones of her pelvis giving way to the force of her pushing. They spread slowly, grindingly and firmly, the way plates of the earth would move during a quake; they allowed the baby's head to pass downward, the shoulders to turn along the spiraling route to the outside world. Naomi waited, breathed deeply, took Amos' hand, and threw all her strength into her abdomen again, and as if burying a heavy rock there, she gave another push. I could see the top of the baby's head.... The head made a quarter turn and Naomi—pausing only a moment—pushed out her new baby girl. I cut the cord, wrapped the baby quickly, and Amos grabbed it, cooing, chuckling, and hopping from side to side like a father bird. Later, when I took the baby out to the kitchen for a bath...I told her about how a long shaft of morning light was reaching across the kitchen countertop and making the faucet handles glow; how the windmill was creaking to life, pulling water from the well. I showed her, once I had the towel fluffed about her head, how the lawn, through the panes at the sink window, was iridescent, and I watched while the long branches of the protective yard oak stretched and lazily flapped. The morning was lavender and frost.

—Penny Armstrong, from *A Midwife's Story*

Through an Amishman's eyes, the days look like handcrafted gifts from God.

—PENNY ARMSTRONG

RITUAL

Hold your new baby against your bare chest or abdomen immediately after he is born. Skin-to-skin contact contributes to the bonding process. Encourage your partner to do the same while you acquaint yourselves with this miraculous child. Your shared experience in the first hours and days after birth establishes a very special beginning; you are making history; you are making family. Enjoy this time and remember it for the future. This will become part of your family's folklore. One day, your child will love to hear the story of his birth, his first meeting with you, and those first momentous weeks at home.

I give birth

Then on the next contraction I started to push, and was suddenly swept away with primitive strength. Everything went blank and lightening-like streaks flashed, it seemed. It was ecstatic, wonderful, thrilling! I heard myself moaning—in triumph, not in pain! There was no pain whatsoever, only a primitive and sexual elation. From my grimace, the nurse thought I was in pain and started to put the mask over my face. How annoying! In the middle of a push, I gasped, "Go away! It doesn't hurt...." I felt as if I had enough strength to pull the world apart—everything was bright, illuminated. In between contractions, I shouted deliriously, "This is wonderful! My husband only wants two babies, but I want a thousand."

—from *Natural Childbirth in the Christian Family*

The birth of every child is important.... We, too, are sons and daughters of God and the children of our parents. We have to take special care of each birth.

—THICH NHAT HANH

Spiritual growth is like childbirth. You dilate, then you contract. You dilate, then you contract again. As painful as it all feels, it's the necessary rhythm for reaching the ultimate goal of total openness. The pain of childbirth is more bearable as we realize where it's leading. Giving birth to our selves, our new selves, our real selves, whether we are men or women, is a lot like giving birth to a child. It's an idea that is conceived, then incubates. Childbirth is dif-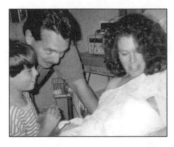ficult, but holding the child makes the pain worthwhile. And so it is when we finally have a glimpse of our own completion as human beings—regardless of our husband or lack of one, our boyfriend or lack of one, our job or lack of one, our money or lack of it, our children or lack of any, or whatever else we think we need in order to thrive and be happy. When we have finally touched on a spiritual high that is real and enduring, then we know that the pain of getting there was worth it, and the years ahead will never be as lonely.

—Marianne Williamson, from *A Woman's Worth*

pledge to my children

I will *anticipate* your birth, your childhood, and your life and encourage you to look forward too.

I will watch you *flourish* and discover your home in this magnificent world.

I will *nurture* your innocence and never forget the sacred place it comes from.

I will show you the way of *wonder* and walk along beside you.

I will *stand* for you as a parent and a friend, valuing your dreams just as I value my own.

I will *voice* my feelings honestly and honor the promises I make.

I will *listen* to you thoughtfully and give you the freedom to expand your own mind.

I will *envision* your happy future, always mindful of the precious, present moment.

I will *embrace* you and enjoy you with my heart open wide.

CONTRIBUTORS

Pamela Castle Alba
Cathy Angell
Karen Benke
Jennifer Graham Billings
Molly Chisaakay
Elizabeth Curry
Rhoda Curtis
Vivian Dudro
Ann Fuller
Beppy Gibson
Yvonne Menonca Johns
Margie Beiser Lapanja
Mary Hughes Lee
Barbara Brock Moller
Cindy Angell Keeling
Michele Mason
Stephanie Keenan Moon
Maureen O'Brien
Chris Pritchard
Margaret Steele
Renée Turcott
Elizabeth Von Radics
Michelle Zundel

ART CONTRIBUTORS

Anne Bossi
Collette Crutcher
Carl E. Gosline
D.J. Johns
Richard Morgenstein
Kallan Nishimoto
Wendy Walsh
Elaine Warshaw

about the creators

Andrea Alban Gosline is a poet and author and is the creative director of AmbleDance Studios. *Celebrating Motherhood* was her first book, which she conceived and created while pregnant with her second child. Andrea lives in San Francisco, California, with her husband and two children.

Lisa Burnett Bossi is an illustrator, graphic designer and the art director of AmbleDance Studios. Her enchanting paintings and designs are inspired by nature and the simple pleasures of family life. Lisa lives in Brunswick, Maine, with her husband and daughter. They are expecting their second child.

Ame Mahler Beanland is an art director, graphic designer, and writer. Co-author of the bestselling *It's A Chick Thing,* Ame lives in Pleasanton, California with her husband and daughter.

TOOLS FOR YOUR JOURNEY

AUDIO AND VIDEO

Heartsongs (audio, 60 minutes) by Leon Thurman and Anna Peter Langness
5000 Bloomington Avenue So. Minneapolis, MN 55417
14 songs based on traditional folk songs with verses for expectant and new parents.

Love Chords (audio, 40 minutes) by Thomas Verby, M.D. And Sandra Collier, B.A.
Birth and Life Bookstore
7001 Alonzo Avenue
P.O. Box 70625 Seattle, WA 98107-0625
Music by Baroque composers. Includes pregnancy guide and baby growth chart.

It's a Parent: Songs for the Lighter Side of Pregnancy (CD or cassette) by Randy Bobish and
Rebecca Kupka
A hilarious musical journey through pregnancy, childbirth, and new parenthood.
888-YOU-BABY

World Sings Goodnight (CD) Silver Wave Records
An eclectic collection of lullabies from around the world. Songs from Vietnam, Ireland,
Hawaii, Lebanon, and Brazil are featured, all sung in native languages. For babies of all ages.
Available at music stores.

Relax & Enjoy Your Baby: A Complete Program of Relaxation for New and Expectant Parents
(two cassettes, five, ten, and fifteen minute segments)
by Sylvia Klein Oklin, M.S. The Relaxation Co. Inc.
Helps mom and dad relax during pregnancy and early parenthood. Music includes works by
Bach, Vivaldi, and Mozart, coupled with sounds of water and birds.
800-788-6670 or 516-621-2727

A Gift for the Unborn Child (video, 26 minutes) by Laura Uplinger
Bradley Boatman Productions
P.O. Box 4141 Malibu, CA 90265
Prenatal psychology, interviews, visual imagery and music.

Denise Austin's Pregnancy Plus (video, 62 minutes)
An easy, low-impact pregnancy program and a more intense mixed-impact
post-pregnancy routine. Emphasizes simple dance steps, lower-body toning
and relaxation breathing. 800-433-6769

Prenatal Yoga (video, 70 minutes) by Colette Crawford, RN
Custom yoga routine for pregnant women for a safe, gentle, and energizing
prenatal practice. 206-547-9882 Fax: 206-547-9978

The First Years Last Forever (video, 28 minutes) Hosted by Rob Reiner
The new brain research and your child's healthy development.
888-447-3400 E-mail: yourchild.yahoo.com

PREGNANCY AND PARENTING WEB SITES

Mother's list
A "round robin" created especially for women expecting babies in a given month. This
internet list allows women from around the world to support each other. Subscribers can
send a message to one address and it will be forwarded to all the pregnant subscribers due
in the same month. listserv(at)csi.net

   To subscribe send an e-mail message with the words "subscribe MONTH" (the month
should be the month you're due) to the above address.

Amble Dance Books
www.ambledance.com
For information on the *Mother's Nature Collection* and a free inspirational newsletter for the
pregnancy year.

Stork Net
www.storknet.org
A pregnancy and parenting web station with information links for pregnancy and childbirth.

ParentTime
www.parenttime.com
For on-line information and chats with physicians, ranging from fertility to postpartum self-
care and parenting tips.

Parents Place
www.parentsplace.com
A dynamic community of individuals that care for and love children. Sign up for a cus-
tomized pregnancy newsletter you'll receive each week with info about your baby's development and the changes you're experiencing.

BREASTFEEDING SUPPORT

La Leche League International
Hot Line: 847-519-7730
Web site: www.lalecheleague.org

Patti Neely, R.N., Certified Lactation Consultant
23 South Newport Napa, CA 94559
Phone: 707-256-3081
Offers single and twin-birth newborn education and breast-feeding education.
Available internationally for consultation.

Lactation Consultant at Parentsplace
Web site: www.parentsplace.com

Breastfeeding Advocacy Page
Web site: www.clark.net/pub/activist/bfpage/bfpage.html

CHILD-FRIENDLY ORGANIZATIONS

Child-Friendly Initiative (CFI)
Michele Mason, Founder
CFI was founded to raise consciousness about children and to help businesses and
institutions become child-friendly. For more information or to become a member or sponsor,
call: 800-500-5234
E-mail: mikim@best.com

I Am Your Child
The Reiner Foundation
www.yourchild.org
Focuses on promoting early childhood development, giving children the right emotional
supports during their first three years of life to positively change their lives forever.

SELECTED BIBLIOGRAPHY

Angell, Cathy M. *My Spirit Flies: Portraits and Prose of Women in Their Power.* Bellingham, WA: Bay City Press, 1997.

Baker, Jeannine Parvati. *Conscious Conception.* Berkeley, CA: North Atlantic Books, and Sevier, UT: Freestone Publishing, 1986.

Berends, Berrien Polly. *Whole Child/Whole Parent.* New York: Harper & Row, 1983.

Caldwell Sorel, Nancy. *Ever Since Eve: Personal Reflections on Childbirth.* Oxford University Press, 1984.

Carson, Anne. *Spiritual Parenting in the New Age.* Freedom, CA: The Crossing Press, 1999.

Costa, Shu Shu. *Lotus Seeds and Lucky Stars: Asian Myths and Traditions About Pregnancy and Birthing.* New York: Simon and Schuster,1998.

Ford, Judy. *Expecting Baby.* Berkeley, CA: Conari Press, 1997.

_____. *Wonderful Ways to Love a Child,* Berkeley, CA: Conari Press, 1992.

Frymer-Kensky, Tikva. *Motherprayer: The pregnant woman's spiritual companion.* New York: Riverhead Books, 1995.

Goldsmith, Judith. *Childbirth Wisdom.* New York: Congdon & Weed, Inc., 1984.

Hanh, Thich Nhat, *Being Peace.* Berkeley, CA: Parallax Press, 1987.

_____. *Living Buddha, Living Christ.* New York: Putnam Berkeley. 1995

_____. *Present Moment, Wonderful Moment: Mindfulness Verses for Daily Living.* Berkeley, CA: Parallax Press, 1990.

Israeloff, Roberta, *Coming to Terms.* New York: Alfred A. Knopf, Inc, 1984.

Jean Marzollo, Jean ed. *Written by parents, 9 months, 1 day, 1 year.* New York: Harper & Row, Publishers, Inc., 1975.

Jones, Carl. *Visualizations for an Easier Childbirth*. Deephaven, MN: Meadowbrook Press, 1988.

Kabat-Zinn, Myla and Jon. *Everyday Blessings: The Innerwork of Mindful Parenting*. NY: Hyperion, 1997.

Kenison, Katrina. *Mothers: Twenty Stories of Contemporary Motherhood*. New York: North Point Press, 1996.

Kitzinger, Sheila. *Giving Birth: The Parents' Emotions in Childbirth.*, New York: Schocken Books, 1977.

_____. *Ourselves as Mothers, the Universal Experience of Motherhood*. Reading, MA: Addison Wesley Publishing Company, 1992.

Leboyer, Frederick. *Birth Without Violence*. Rochester, VT: Inner Traditions International, Ltd., 1995.

Logan, Onnie Lee, and Katharine Clark. *Motherwit: An Alabama Midwife's Story*. New York: E.P. Dutton, 1989.

Louden, Jennifer. *The Pregnant Woman's Comfort Book*. San Francisco: HarperSanFrancisco, 1995.

Louv, Richard. *The Web of Life: Weaving the Values that Sustain Us*. Berkeley, CA: Conari Press, 1992.

Lowinsky Ph.D., Naomi Ruth. *Stories from the Motherline: Reclaiming the Mother-Daughter Bond, Finding our Feminine Souls*. New York: St. Martin's Press, 1992.

Lysne, Robin Heerens. *Dancing Up the Moon: A Woman's Guide to Creating Traditions that Bring Sacredness to Daily Life*. Berkeley, CA: Conari Press, 1995.

Meltzer, David. ed. *Birth: An Anthology of Ancient Texts, Songs, Prayers, and Stories*. San Francisco: North Point Press, 1981.

Mines, Stephanie. *Two Births*. Berkeley, CA: The Bookworks and New York: Random House Inc. 1972.

Murdoch, Anna Maria. *Motherhood and Mythology.* Commonweal Publishing Co. Inc., 1979

Payne, Karen ed. *Between Ourselves: Letters, Between Mothers & Daughters.* Boston: Houghton Mifflin Company, 1983.

Placksin, Sally. *Mothering the New Mother: Your Postpartum Resource Companion.* New York: New Market Press, 1994.

Reddy, Maureen T.; Roth, Martha; Sheldon, Amy; eds. *Mother Journeys: Feminists Write About Mothering.* MN: Spinsters Ink, 1994.

Rich, Adrienne. *Of Woman Born: Motherhood as Experience and Institution.* New York: Norton, 1976.

Ryan, M.J., ed. *A Grateful Heart: 365 Blessings from Buddha to the Beatles.* Berkeley, CA: Conari Press, 1994.

Schwartz, Leni. *Bonding Before Birth.* Boston: Sigo Press.

_____, *The World of the Unborn.* New York: Richard Merek Publisher, 1980.

Smith, Liz. *The Mother Book: A Compendium of Trivia & Grandeur Concerning Mothers, Motherhood & Maternity.* New York: Doubleday & Company, 1978.

Sorel, Nancy Caldwell. *Ever Since Eve: Personal Reflections on Childbirth.* New York: Oxford University Press, 1984.

Star, Rima Beth. *The Healing Power of Birth.* Austin, TX: Star Pub. 1986.

Stern, M.D., Daniel. *Diary of a Baby.* New York: Basic Books, Harper Collins, 1990.

Stoddard, Alexandra. *Mothers: A Celebration.* New York: Avon Books 1996.

Verny, M.D., Thomas and Weintraub, Pamela. *Nurturing Your Unborn Child.* New York: Delacorte Press 1991.

Wagner, Laurie. *Expectations.* San Francisco: Chronicle Books, 1997.

Weston, Carol. *From Here to Maternity.* Boston: Little Brown & Co., 1991

THANK YOU

We are deeply grateful to many people who helped in nurturing the spirit of this book and sustained us throughout its creation. A special thank you to everyone at Conari Press for embracing *Celebrating Motherhood* and believing in its potential. Publishers Mary Jane Ryan and Will Glennon made us feel cared for and supported throughout the entire process. We are especially grateful to our editor, Claudia Schaab, who graciously and expertly helped us weave the book into its final shape. To Brenda Knight, Sharon Donovan, Nancy Margolis, Nina Lesowitz, and Robin Demers we thank you for your unflagging enthusiasm for *Celebrating Motherhood*. —A.A.G., L.B.B., A.M.B.

I sincerely appreciate my family of friends who continually inspire my muse and made the creation of *Celebrating Motherhood* possible: Vicki Morgan and Karen Bouris, who opened tall doors for my literary dreams. Mrs. McKinnon, Miss Aitken, Nancy Clark, Hal McLean, and Ann Nolan Maisel, my "teachers," who illuminated this work I am so passionate about. Alison Levy and James Koehneke of Phoenix Books, San Francisco, who allowed free access to hundreds of hard-to-find research books. Noe Valley Public Library and Incline Village Library, where I spent hours at a big wooden table, reading and collecting. Kathy Stannard-Friel, who listened, then reflected back my own mothering wisdom. Ame Beanland, whose collaboration blessed the editorial and artistic process. My sister Laura, who taught me how to get along. My parents, Donna and Jan Alban and my "second parents," Lily and Bernie Gross, who enthusiastically offered their gifts: of life, love, family, hope, time, guidance, and opportunity. My husband, Carl, who lives boldly, and adores, supports, calms, and cheers me through our milestones. My precious children, Jacob and Lily, who, though new and small, have succeeded in teaching me the grandest life lessons. And Lisa, my dear friend and book partner, who dreams with me and who so exquisitely translates my words into a lush palette. —Andrea Alban Gosline

Thank you Andrea, for dreaming such dreams. Thank you Carl, for patient generosity. Thank you Adrian, for clear, childlike sensibility. Thank you Lila, for choosing me as your mother. Thank you God, for such a beautiful life. —Lisa Burnett Bossi

Thank you Andrea and Lisa for the invitation to partner with you on this beautiful and inspired book. Being involved in its creation has been a sacred journey of the spirit and a life-affirming adventure. I am blessed by an amazing group of friends and family whose support and enthusiasm sustain me and for whom I am always grateful. Thank you to my mother who embodies the power and love of *Celebrating Motherhood* so beautifully. And in memory of my father whose loving presence I always feel. To my soulmate Peter, the love of my life, thank you for holding my hand through it all. —Ame Mahler Beanland

CONARI PRESS, publishes books on topics ranging from spirituality, personal growth, and relationships to women's issues, parenting, and social issues. Our mission is to publish quality books that will make a difference in people's lives—how we feel about ourselves and how we relate to one another. We value integrity, compassion, and receptivity, both in the books we publish and in the way we do business.

As a member of the community, we donate our damaged books to nonprofit organizations, dedicate a portion of our proceeds from certain books to charitable causes, and continually look for new ways to use natural resources as wisely as possible.

Our readers are our most important resource, and we value your input, suggestions, and ideas about what you would like to see published. Please feel free to contact us, to request our latest book catalog, or to be added to our mailing list.

CONARI PRESS

2550 Ninth Street, Suite 101
Berkeley, California 94710-2551
800-685-9595 • 510-649-7175
fax: 510-649-7190 • e-mail: conari@conari.com
www.conari.com